Understanding risk in criminal justice

CRIME AND JUSTICE
Series editor: Mike Maguire
University College of Wales, College of Cardiff

Crime and Justice is a series of short introductory texts on central topics in criminology. The books in this series are written for students by internationally renowned authors. Each book tackles a key area within criminology, providing a concise and up-to-date overview of the principal concepts, theories, methods and findings relating to the area. Taken as a whole, the *Crime and Justice* series will cover all the core components of an undergraduate criminology course.

Understanding risk in criminal justice

Hazel Kemshall

Open University Press

Open University Press
McGraw-Hill Education
McGraw-Hill House
Shoppenhangers Road
Maidenhead
Berkshire
England
SL6 2QL

email: enquiries@openup.co.uk
world wide web: www.openup.co.uk

and

325 Chestnut Street
Philadelphia, PA 19106, USA

First published 2003

A catalogue record of this book is available from the British Library

ISBN 0 335 20653 0 (pb)   0 335 20654 9 (hb)

Library of Congress Cataloging-in-Publication Data
CIP data applied for

Typeset by RefineCatch Limited, Bungay, Suffolk
Printed in Great Britain by Bell and Bain Ltd, Glasgow

Contents

Series editor's foreword

Understanding Risk and Crime is the ninth book in Open University Press' successful *Crime and Justice* series. The series is now established as a key resource in universities teaching criminology or criminal justice, especially in the UK but increasingly also overseas. The aim from the outset has been to give undergraduates and graduates both a solid grounding in the relevant area and a taste to explore it further. Although aimed primarily at students new to the field, and written as far as possible in plain language, the books are not oversimplified. On the contrary, the authors set out to 'stretch' readers and to encourage them to approach criminological knowledge and theory in a critical and questioning frame of mind.

Professor Kemshall is the leading UK expert on the concept of risk as applied to issues in crime and criminal justice. She has written outstanding books and articles on the topic, particularly in relation to probation work and to the risk assessment and management of sexual and violent offenders. Her writing displays the unusual combination of depth of theoretical analysis, detailed knowledge of policy and practice, and ability to present complex ideas in a straightforward and readily comprehensible manner. In this book, her main focus is upon key arguments and evidence relating to the growth of new forms of penal thinking and practice centered around the organizing principle of risk: what is now widely referred to as the emergence of forms of 'actuarial justice' or a 'risk penalty'. She frames the discussion within the broader debates on risk inspired by major social theorists such as Beck and Giddens, including its integral significance to life in late modern societies, but grounds her account firmly in research evidence about particular processes of risk assessment and risk management, as well as practical and policy developments in individual criminal justice institutions. Thus, in addition to chapters on the 'rise of risk' and its new cultural meanings, and on its role in criminal justice generally, there are chapters on the tools used to assess levels of risk, on the practices of multi-agency public protection panels, and on the short and long term implications of risk focused thinking in probation, policing and the crime prevention field. In doing so, she raises major concerns associated with exaggerated attention to risk, including the erosion of individual rights and civil liberties, the widening of nets of social control, the growth of privatized 'fortress' cities, and the rise of authoritarianism.

Other books previously published in the *Crime and Justice* series – all of whose titles begin with the word 'Understanding' – have covered criminological theory (Sandra Walklate), penal theory (Barbara Hudson), crime data and statistics (Clive Coleman and Jenny Moynihan), youth and crime (Sheila Brown), crime prevention (Gordon Hughes), violent crime (Stephen Jones), community penalties (Peter Raynor and Maurice Vanstone) and white collar crime (Hazel Croall). Two are already in second editions and other second editions are planned. Other new books in the pipeline include texts on prisons, policing, social control, criminological research methods, sentencing and criminal justice, drugs and crime, race and crime, psychology and crime, and crime and social exclusion. All are major topics in university degree courses on crime and criminal justice, and each book should make an ideal foundation text for a relevant module. As an aid to understanding, clear summaries are provided at regular intervals, and a glossary of key terms and concepts is a feature of every book. In addition, to help students expand their knowledge, recommendations for further reading are given at the end of each chapter.

Mike Maguire
2003

Acknowledgements

I have experienced extensive support during the years I have researched risk in criminal justice and probation work. Thanks are extended to all those who have contributed so generously to my work over this time, and indeed continue to do so.

Particular thanks to Chris Neville for friendship and kindness, and to my colleagues at DeMontfort University, who continue to support my work with unstinting generosity. Warm thanks to Mike Maguire, series editor, who provided coaching and sound advice in the early stages of writing this book. My initial project on risk was sponsored by the Economic and Social Research Council's 'Risk and Human Behaviour' programme grant number L211252018.

Introduction

Risk assessment and its appropriate management is 'big business' (Adams 1995), fuelled by a growing precautionary principle in which risk is to be avoided at all costs. Crime risks have been no exception. The identification, assessment, prevention and management of risk have become big business in crime policy, practice and research. The extent of this preoccupation has led some commentators to claim that we have entered a new era of justice, 'actuarial justice', that is the management of crime opportunities and risk distribution rather than the management of individual offenders and behaviours (Feeley and Simon 1992, 1994). Reichman (1986: 153) has characterized this as 'an insurance concept of crime control' in which hazard reduction strategies such as zero tolerance, hard targeting, surveillance, selective incapacitation and exclusion are key features (Kemshall and Maguire 2001). In policing for example this has led to a shift from the 'reactive investigation of individual crimes' to a 'strategic, future-oriented and targeted approach to crime control' (Maguire 2000: 316). In probation practice the traditional rehabilitative focus has been replaced by a risk management and public protection agenda (Kemshall 1998).

The emergence of risk in crime policy has been linked to the demise of the modernist penal agenda, the perceived failure of the rehabilitative and individual corrective aims of modern penality (Garland 1995). The 'grand narrative' and traditional disciplinary techniques of modern penality are in decline, superseded by what Pratt (1995) has called an 'informative system' in which the production and exchange of risk knowledge is a central feature. The extent to which actuarial justice has displaced traditional penal practice is a matter of considerable debate (Garland 1995; Pratt 2000a, 2000b), but the inexorable rise of the 'logic of risk' (Ericson and Haggerty 1997) is manifest in many areas of contemporary criminal justice policy and practice. This book explores the role of risk in contemporary British criminal justice, and in particular the role of risk in framing current penal policy within the **risk society**. By drawing on key areas of criminal justice practice such as policing, probation and situational crime risk management, the case for a new risk-based penology will be explored.

The book is divided into seven chapters. Chapter 1 examines the rise of risk and the emergence of a risk-based *discourse* in contemporary society. Chapter 2 goes on to examine broad risk trends in criminal justice and the recent case made for 'actuarial justice'. In Chapter 3 risk assessment and the emergence of key tools are reviewed. Chapters 4–6 provide exemplars of risk in contemporary criminal justice policy and practice in the areas of probation, community policing and crime prevention.

The final chapter concludes by pulling the threads together and briefly revisits the case made for risk-based criminal justice.

chapter one

The rise of risk

Introducing risk

Risk has been described as the 'world's largest industry' (Adams 1995: 31). It is ubiquitous, pervasive, diverse and global. As one headline put it: 'Warning: You're Risking Death by Being Alive' (Alice Thomson, *Daily Telegraph*, 27 October 2000: 21). A plethora of risks for the twenty-first century were noted, from risks to newborn babies from their mothers' kisses, to vaccines, cot death, food risks and paedophile abductions enroute to school. As the writer put it: 'Being a mother in the 21st century is a fraught business. Everyday there is another reason to worry'.

Myriad risks confront us, from voluntary risks we choose to run (such as smoking, alcohol use, bungee jumping) to involuntary risks imposed upon us (such as environmental pollution), from personal risks (such as choices on lifestyle) to public risks (such as crime). Risks also come in different sizes, with differing levels of probability, impact and consequence. Ranging from low probability/high consequence risks such as nuclear discharge to high probability/low consequence risks often associated with small-scale gambling (for example many of us regularly spend £1.00 on a lottery ticket for the chance of winning millions but consider the high risk of loss as 'worth it'). Some risks are localized, associated with living in 'high crime' areas for example, and some are global with their origins far from the final site of impact, such as acid rain or the risk of flooding from climatic change. The word risk can carry different meanings, positive and negative connotations, and different levels of tolerance and acceptability. Subsistence farmers may choose to live on flood plains for the added benefit of irrigation and soil fertility (Wildavsky 1985), and view the risk of flooding as a natural, seasonal hazard that has to be accepted. Involuntary risks are generally more resented than voluntary risks (Slovic et al. 1980), hence public 'NIMBY' (not in my back yard) reactions to the location of hostels for offenders or the release of paedophiles into the community.

Risk then is a complex phenomenon, not simply about calculating the odds of 'mischance', 'hazard' or 'danger'. While often presented as a 'commonsense' value-neutral term (Adams 1995), risk is increasingly recognized as highly politicized and value-laden (Douglas 1992), with views over probability, impact and consequence hotly contended. As Lupton (1999a: 59) puts it: 'Debates and conflicts over risk have begun to dominate public, political and private arenas'.

What is risk?

The *Oxford English Dictionary* (1989: 987) defines risk as: 'Hazard, danger; exposure to mischance and peril'. The contemporary interrelationship of hazard, danger and peril, and the negative connotations of risk, has a long history. Ayto (1990: 446) notes the derivation of the English word 'risk' from both the seventeenth-century French term *risqué* and the Italian word *risio*, both meaning to 'run into danger'. By the seventeenth century English usage had clearly associated risk with 'peril, jeopardy, danger, hazard' (*Oxford English Dictionary* 1989: 987), later reflected in Dr Johnson's dictionary in 1755 (Alaszewski 1998). This usage was paralleled by the use of risk to mean 'taking a chance' epitomized by the Latin *risicum*, and the association of risk with gambling (for example the Roman soldiers dicing for Christ's clothes at the foot of the cross). The association with gambling inevitably rooted risk in the world of probability, literally 'calculating the odds', particularly from the seventeenth century onwards as formalized mathematical models of probability and statistical models were developed (Hacking 1987, 1990). The increasing linkage of risk to danger and negative consequences was also significant, particularly in areas such as marine insurance where calculating safe return to port with precious cargoes and insuring appropriately against loss was important. The debt owed to Shylock in Shakespeare's *Merchant of Venice* was incurred through a shipping loss. The spread of the slave trade and the growth of shipping fuelled the emerging insurance industry (for example Lloyd's of London), and the use of statistics, particularly on death rates, enabled the rise of 'prudential insurance' based upon actuarial tables (Hacking 1987). In 1762 Equitable Life set up the first life assurance actuaries, calculating life assurance policies based upon statistical tables of death rates among the population as a whole. (This company was sold to avoid bankruptcy in 2001, a situation that arose through its miscalculation of future financial risks and subsequent over-exposure on policies sold.)

By the nineteenth century risk was in common usage, not only as part of the lexicon to describe actions, events or games of chance, but also as part of an industry concerned with the prediction of, and insurance against, future risks. The development of mathematical models and the application of statistics moved insurance from the realm of personal calculation of misfortune to a formalized probability calculation of risk (Daston 1987). Probability and the possibility of prediction were linked and risk calculations were seen as the way to 'tame chance' (Hacking 1987, 1990). The vagaries of nature could be subject to probability models of calculation. However, understanding of risk was not entirely negative or risk averse. During the eighteenth and nineteenth centuries risk had a key role in the development of capitalism, with risk-taking acknowledged as a key feature of entrepreneurship and venture capital (Higgs 1931), a feature of capitalism that continues to the present day.

Actuarial risk, or the calculation of risk probabilities derived from statistical models based on aggregate populations, was extended to numerous areas of social and commercial life throughout the twentieth century (Rowe 1977). Insurance spread from the merchant and corporate spheres into the personal realm with the extension of personal and life insurance to other sections of the population. Workers began to self-insure against the possibility of accidents through friendly societies such as the Cooperative Society, and mutual societies were formed as insurance against the possibility of unemployment and illness. Working-men's clubs and societies often gave the security of insurance as well as social and leisure opportunities, based upon the pooling of collective resources against the possibility of individual risk. After the Second World War and the Beveridge Act 1948, the welfare state adopted such a notion of collective insurance through systems such as National Insurance and the National Health Service.

The twentieth century also saw the rise of high consequence/low probability risks such as nuclear discharge arising from new technologies and the process of industrialization (Douglas 1986). The need to accurately assess, manage and contain these 'manufactured risks' (Beck 1992a, 1992b; see also Giddens 1990, 1991) located risk in the scientific and engineering arenas for much of the century (Ansell and Wharton 1992). This resulted in an 'artefact' approach to risk, in which risk was viewed as a material object amenable to objective calculation and measurement (Horlick-Jones 1998). The 1983 Royal Society Report framed risk in entirely these terms, locating concerns with risk firmly in the arena of science and engineering. The society's main concerns were with the accurate and objective identification of risks and their appropriate management, and in correcting 'exaggerated' public perceptions of risk or public failures to act appropriately upon risk information (for example to increase the efficacy of public health campaigns). In addition to its artefact approach this view of risk also assumed a *homo prudens* view of risk actors, the prudential (hu)man who will make the correct and rational choice if only given the right information by experts. Risk information is presumed to be the preserve of experts, and the relationship between experts and lay public is a didactic one. Accidents for example are seen as caused by human fallibility and error (Reason 1990) that can be learnt from and eradicated from future at-risk situations. 'Zero-risk' human is the aim, held up by large corporations such as Shell as the ultimate risk-aware worker (Visser 1991).

The notion of *homo prudens* is usually accompanied by inquiries and hindsight bias in which both blame allocation and learning are key features. While the imperative is that 'this must never happen again', it often does (Sheppard 1996). Adams (1995: 16) contends that this is because 'Zero-risk man is a figment of the imagination of the safety profession'. We are risk-takers as well as risk-averse, *homo aleatorius* or gambling (hu)man exists, and in many walks of life is positively lauded and rewarded. As Adams (1995) points out, the oil industry owes its existence to the early risk-taking entrepreneurs and 'wild-cats'. Risk then is often double-edged, balancing the benefits of positive risk-taking against our risk aversion to the costs that may follow.

In the early twenty-first century the 'myth of calculability' has been challenged (Reddy 1996), not only by a fin-de-siècle preoccupation with risk and safety (Furedi 1997) but also by the changing nature of risk. This change has been linked to the transformation from **modernity** to **late modernity** or **postmodernity**, concepts that are integral to debates about the contemporary nature of risk. Sociological debates about the extent and nature of this transformation abound (Kellner 1999), along with disputes about the relative usefulness of the terms modernity, late modernity and postmodernity. For those like Giddens (1990, 1998a, 1998b, 1999) who see the transformation as a gradual one, the term late modernity is preferred; for those who see a more radical departure (Leonard 1997) the term postmodernity is used. In brief (a further discussion is provided in the 'Risk and crime' section), the modern age or modernity has been largely characterized as the historical period stretching from the late eighteenth-century Age of Enlightenment to around the 1970s. The age is characterized by faith in reason, scientific knowledge, progress, capitalist development (particularly in the west), and an evolving social order (Leonard 1997).

Contemporary social theorists such as Giddens (1990, 1998a, 1998b, 1999) and Beck (1992a, 1992b, 1999) have argued that since the severe challenges to capitalism in the 1970s the relationship between labour and capital, and between citizen and state has been radically transformed. This is most readily epitomized by the global market, the spread of information technology and technological advances that have radically redistributed both markets and sites of production. This has been paralleled by cultural and social transformations (Leonard 1997) in which claims to universal truths are increasingly doubted and science and reason are subject to challenge and dispute.

Postmodernity describes the period from the late 1970s onwards and the social transformations emerging at the start of the twenty-first century. Postmodernity is characterized by global risks, indeterminate and contingent knowledge about the probability of such risks, and uncertainty over future outcomes and impacts. Postmodernity has been characterized as 'the end of certainty' and the 'politics of difference' (Leonard 1997: 12), a period of late capitalism in which flexibility of labour and capital supply, mass global production and ever-shifting markets are the key features.

Criminologists have also adopted these terms in contemporary analyses of risk and crime, with attention focused on the relationship between risk, postmodernity and new penal forms (Feeley and Simon 1992, 1994), and the centrality of risk to emerging forms of social control (Rose 1996a, 1996b, 2000) (this is discussed in more detail in the section 'Risk and crime').

What Giddens (1990, 1991) and other commentators have dubbed the modern age was characterized by known and calculable risks, predictable and hence controllable. 'Artefact' risk was rooted in objective, scientific knowledge, part of a world in which both the social and the natural 'may be measured, calculated and therefore predicted' (Lupton 1999a: 6). Risk was known through statistical models and the language of probability (Bernstein 1996), based upon knowledge of patterns and frequencies that 'happen regularly enough and often enough in a whole population of people to be broadly predictable, and so insurable' (Giddens 1998a: 27). In essence, aggregated knowledge of past events assisted future prediction (for example death rates to predict life expectancy, previous convictions to predict future offending). However, Beck (1992a, 1992b) and Giddens (1990, 1991, 1998a) have argued that risks in *late* or *postmodernity* are characterized by their global nature, uncertainty, indeterminacy and our contingent knowledge of them. The risks facing us constantly outstrip the tools and technologies used to assess and 'tame' them, producing what Giddens in his 1999 Reith lectures referred to as the 'runaway world' (Giddens 1999). The industrialization and technological developments of late modernity produce risks, or 'manufactured uncertainties' and unintended consequences, often knowable only with hindsight. As Giddens expresses it: 'We just cannot know beforehand when we are actually "scaremongering" and when we are not' (Giddens 1998a: 30). We cannot know the consequences of future risks until we get there.

Late modernity has transformed risk from a probabilistic, calculable artefact to risk as uncertainty, plagued by indeterminate knowledge and subject to a number of 'it depends'. Calculating risk and choosing subsequent courses of action is itself infused with risk as customary patterns of responding to the world are challenged (Giddens 1998a).

The individual's life course is no longer mapped out with any certainty. Choices and the subsequent risks arising from such choices must be individually navigated. However, little help is given 'as to which options should be selected' (Giddens 1991: 80), leaving the individual in a constant state of **reflexivity**, constantly processing and adapting to risk information and myriad risk choices. This personal navigation increases both personal responsibility for risk decisions, and personal anxiety about getting such decisions right. Self-monitoring and anxiety are key features of individual experiences of risk in late or postmodernity.

Summary

Myriad risks confront us and risk has diverse meanings. While often presented as a value-neutral term, risk is actually a highly politicized and contentious concept, and has changed both in terms of meaning and usage through history. The modern view of risk was risk as artefact, measurable, knowable, calculable and predictable. Risks in late or postmodernity, as it has been dubbed, are characterized by uncertainty, indeterminacy, contingency and their global impact. Contemporary risks also require personal choice and navigation, resulting in increased uncertainty, anxiety and reflexivity.

Late modernity and the risk society: new risks or new ways of looking at risk?

The late twentieth century saw a major paradigm shift in social theory with a growing emphasis upon the consequences of postmodernity, in particular the consequences of industrialization and globalization and the rise of what Beck (1992a) has labelled the 'risk society'. The multiplication of risk and its increased spread and impact within the compressed social space of globalization have become key issues for contemporary theorists (Turner 2001). The risks of traditional society have been characterized as fatalistic, framed by a pre-Renaissance discourse of fate in which risks were seen as the product of destiny and the 'will of the Gods' (Green 1997). The Black Death was seen in exactly these terms, unseen and spreading at the whim of the Gods. With the hindsight of the twenty-first century we see the Black Death rather differently: as a powerful disease carried by fleas on the back of rats, transported across the world from the Middle East as shipping and trade routes expanded. However, for the villagers of Eyam in Derbyshire, all but wiped out by the Black Death, this must have seemed like the terrible hand of fate.

The risks of modernization have been characterized as increasingly calculable, knowable and controllable through mathematical models and the advances of science. The risks of nature could be tamed, and the 'will of the Gods' need not be accepted. Advances in medical science in the nineteenth century for example began to tame the threat of numerous 'natural' risks such as cholera, typhoid, smallpox and bubonic plague as disease was subjugated to the discipline of science (Adams 1995). However, Beck argues that this very industrialization of society itself produces risk: 'new technologies', 'atomic fallout', 'ecological disaster', all arising from the very processes of science and technology associated with a relentless modernization, industrialization and globalization (Beck 1992a). For Beck, these risks are different: global in nature, high impact, unseen and 'open to social definition and construction'. No longer is nature the source of risk, it is nature itself which is threatened by risk. The risk society is also peculiarly defensive, characterized by fear and anxiety: 'the commonality of anxiety takes the place of the commonality of need' (Beck 1992a: 49). While the 'class society' of modernity had been concerned with the equitable distribution of goods (everyone getting a fair share of the pie), the risk society is concerned with the equitable distribution of risks, and in particular the avoidance of risks: 'one is concerned not with attaining something good, but with preventing the worst' (Beck 1992a: 49). The risk society's central feature is the 'precautionary principle', better safe than sorry, underpinned by a critique of the Enlightenment's promise of progress (Leonard 1997) and lack of trust in experts (Freudenberg 1988, 1993). The risk society is also characterized by the increased democratization of risks. While Beck does acknowledge that disadvantaged groups are likely to experience the highest degrees of risk and have the least resources to successfully manage them, we are all exposed to some degree. Acid rain is no respecter of social class.

However, some commentators argue that Beck's notion of the risk society is overstated (Steuer 1998; Turner 2001). Critiques of the risk society tend to cluster around the following themes:

- The contention that the distinction between traditional and late modern risks is overstated.
- The thesis that risks are under-regulated and weakened social control of technology has contributed to risk proliferation is incorrect.
- The claim that the end of traditional bonds exacerbates risk is overstated.
- The multiplication of risk is overemphasized.

The contention that the distinction between traditional and late modern risks is overstated

Beck characterizes late modern risks as unseen and global. However, as Adams (1995) and Turner (2001) point out, these characteristics are not new. Disease, particularly the high impact and large spread diseases like the bubonic plague and smallpox have exactly these characteristics. Deadly disease has always existed; all that has changed is our ability to discover such risks through medical science. As Turner points out, the Black Death in the fourteenth century killed about one-third of the population travelling from as far as the Middle East to Greenland (McNeill 1977), and had its origins in the Mongol armies that attacked the Crimea in 1346. Not only does this challenge Beck's dichotomy of risk between traditional 'dangers' and 'manufactured risks', but also the neat periodization of history implied by his thesis is confronted. Rigakos and Hadden (2001) for example dispute the view that 'risk society' is a late modern phenomenon, and link it to the seventeenth-century development of capitalism rather than the nineteenth-century rise of probabilistic science. They see risk and its attendant calculative attitude to matters of public policy and regulation as rooted in early capitalist society's accounting systems and aligned to entrepreneurial calculations of profit and loss. Such seventeenth-century probabilistic calculation was the precursor of nineteenth-century probabilistic science and the deployment of actuarial practices to areas of public policy and population regulation. Risk and surveillance also have a long history in the management of civil disorder, paralleling the use of a politicized arithmetic in the disciplining and regulation of populations (Lynch 1996).

More recently, the late modern AIDS pandemic has much in common with the Black Death of the Middle Ages; and while not the actions of an 'angry God' in return for humankind's wickedness, the floods of contemporary society are increasingly a consequence of human behaviour (Smith 1992). It is therefore difficult to totally accept Beck's position that contemporary risks are entirely new. This position is exacerbated by Beck's focus on high consequence–low probability risks such as Chernobyl. As Turner (2001) argues, these are perhaps more accurately known as 'environmental hazards'. However, not all risks can be categorized as environmental hazard (Douglas 1986): the risk of a road accident is not the same as the risk of nuclear discharge, and the risk of ill-health run by smokers is not the same as the risk to health emanating from radiation leaks. There is a crucial difference between voluntary and involuntary risks, and those embedded in technological advance and breaches of regulation, and those arising from the complexity of social life.

The thesis that risks are under-regulated and weakened social control of technology has contributed to risk proliferation is incorrect

Giddens has described late modern society as a 'runaway world', a world that is beyond our control (Giddens 1999: 2), with future risks unknown until we get there (Giddens 1998b). For Giddens (1993: 3), 'we face risk situations that no one in previous history has had to confront', such as environmental hazards like global warming. The key contention is that globalization has spread both the possibility and impact of risks. Rather than providing control and risk reduction, science and technology themselves produce risks (for example acid rain, or nuclear discharge: Wildavsky 1988). Such risks can be transnational, with impacts far from their origins, and precipitated by global social and economic changes. These risks are also embedded within capitalist society's future-oriented and calculative attitude. Risk is integral to speculation, entrepreneurship, profit and loss. For Giddens, this is what distinguishes contemporary risk from traditional hazard: 'Risk refers to hazards that are actively assessed in relation to future possibilities' (Giddens 1999: 22). The active and reflexive calculation of future risk possibilities is the hallmark of late modernity.

The diversity and globalization of risk requires diverse systems of regulation in addition to that provided by state government, including corporate regulation, self-regulation and regulation by non-governmental bodies in addition to that provided by supranational bodies like the European Union. This necessarily raises issues about the integrity of such systems, and the attribution of political responsibility when such regulation fails. The Phillips report showed that the British government's response to the BSE (bovine spongiform encephalopathy) crisis was both inadequate and secretive (bordering on the dishonest: Phillips 2000). It may not be a simple matter of technological complexity producing risk, but rather the extent to which such risks are involuntary, exported and under-regulated. Is it the 'fault' of technology or the failure of governments to ensure appropriate regulation? There is an important distinction then to be made between:

> voluntary risk where governments accept the presence of risk as an unavoidable aspect of social change (such as car accidents) and involuntary risks where a risk is imported without the knowledge or consent of a government (e.g. acid rain or global warming).
>
> (Turner 2001: 13)

The effective control of such risks is increasingly located in systems of audit

(Power 1999), that is, formalized rules, regulations and procedures that are regularly audited and gate-kept. Systems replace judgement, and formalized tools of risk assessment and risk management procedures supersede professional autonomy (Kemshall et al. 1997). In essence, audit replaces trust, particularly in professionals and experts. Competing information and competing advice has resulted in a weakened trust in experts resulting in an increased scepticism in the role of science to regulate risk (Beck 1992a, 1992b). This has led commentators such as Hood (1996) to argue that the issue is not necessarily one of under-regulation but rather a question of the type of regulation and public trust in the risk management systems that are used.

In arenas where risks are contested and differently understood, trust is a key issue, especially in risk acceptability (Douglas 1986). Trust is a critical factor in building bridges between groups with different views of risk, for example criminal justice professionals and members of the public over paedophile risks. Children are more likely to be sexually abused or murdered by parents than by strangers, yet 'stranger-danger' has dominated both public reaction and public policy responses (Wyre 1997; Kitzinger 1999a, 1999b). In a society defensive about risk, concerned with risk avoidance and the prevention of harms, the regulation of risk necessarily attracts public scrutiny and concern.

Increased scrutiny carries with it the spectre of blame, or what Mary Douglas (1992: 27) has called the 'forensic functions of risk'. She expresses the contemporary preoccupation with risk thus:

> the [system] we are in now is almost ready to treat every death as chargeable to someone's account, every accident as caused by someone's criminal negligence, every sickness a threatened prosecution. Whose fault? is the first question.
>
> (Douglas 1992: 15–16)

As Green (1997) puts it: accidents happen but risks are caused. All risks are subject to 'hindsight scrutiny' (Carson 1996), and with the luxury of hindsight, a key test for risk decisions is their defensibility (Kemshall 1998), in terms of both media scrutiny and litigation. This has resulted in the strange paradox that as risks have become increasingly unpredictable, unknowable and contingent, formalized systems for assessing and managing risks have grown (Kemshall et al. 1997). The increased 'McDonaldization' of risk has been a key response to uncertainty (Kemshall 1998), and most particularly in the arena of social risks (welfare, health, social policy, social care and criminal justice). The contemporary response to the uncertainty of risk and the spectre of blame that accompanies it is the imposition of regulation through the use of increasingly prescriptive rules. However, the inability of rules to 'capture' risk is well documented, not least the inability of rules to foster creative and dynamic responses to changing risk (Hood and Jones

1996), the response of practitioners to such 'McDonaldization' (Kemshall 1998, 2000), and the inability of rules to adequately capture the local context of risk decision-making or the contingent nature of many risks (Wynne 1992).

The claim that the end of traditional bonds exacerbates risk is overstated

Giddens has argued that one major impact of globalization is the emergence of a 'global cosmopolitan society' in which 'tradition has ended' (Giddens 1999: 43). The natural world has been superseded by a manipulated world, a world not free from human agency. Within this world the given truths and actions of tradition are challenged. Living without tradition also creates challenges for our self-identity; our sense of self is constantly challenged by the differing views of others, and by the fluidity of our social world.

Similarly, Beck (1998: 12) has contended that 'risk begins where tradition ends'. The weakening of traditional bonds and social factors such as class position mean that a person's life course can no longer be predicted with any degree of certainty. While risks are likely to remain distributed along existing lines of inequality in the short term (Beck 1992a: 35), different choices can be made about 'life-styles, subcultures, social ties and identities' (Beck 1992a: 131). A process of what Beck calls 'individualization' is characterized by the loss of traditional certainties and ties, increased emphasis upon individual control and responsibility for the life course, and transformation of the citizen into an active consumer (Beck 1992a, 1992b). In this world, class position is less important than one's risk position, that is exposure to, and ability, to negotiate risk. However, Engel and Strasser (1998) dispute the contention that postmodern societies are being transformed from 'class societies' to 'risk societies'. While postmodern society does raise significant challenges to traditional forms of social integration, it cannot be assumed that traditional forms of social inequality will be eradicated by risk. On the contrary, they may well be exacerbated by risk, leaving such inequalities to be negotiated and resolved at the micro level of the individual.

From substantial research into the lives of young people, Furlong and Cartmel (1997) have explored the impact of risk upon structural inequalities. Life chances and choices for Furlong and Cartmel's young people remain severely restricted, and their exposure to and ability to negotiate risk is constrained by their class position. The significant difference in the risk society is that such risks are individually framed and are subject to individual negotiation. Risks are a matter of personal assessment, adequate reflection and choice, rather than a matter of social position or structural inequalities. Failure to adequately negotiate a risk is rewritten as an individual failure rather than understood as a result of social processes outside of the individual's control. The consequence of such individualization is that social inequalities remain hidden and collective responses are delegitimized. 'Public issues' are literally transformed into 'private troubles' (Wright Mills 1970). In addition, global economic transformations and technological advances in the workplace have challenged the relative stability and certainty of the middle-class life course. For the first time in living memory the relative security of the professional middle class has been significantly eroded, resulting in increased unease and a greater preoccupation with risk.

The multiplication of risk is overemphasized

Is the risk society a more risky and dangerous place? Are risks proliferating? Or is it that late modern risks are different in their nature and extent? Beck himself eloquently poses the question:

> Aren't all risks at least as old as industrial society, possibly even as old as the human race itself? Isn't all life subject to the risk of death? Aren't and weren't all societies in all epochs 'risk societies'?
>
> (Beck 1992b: 97)

Certainly risks existed in the past, but for Beck, contemporary risks are different, not only that there is a multiplicity of competing risks, but also that such risks are global in nature and almost entirely attributable to human agency. These risks result from human decisions, not from acts of God. The location of risks in the social, economic and political processes of modernization increases the individual's exposure to risk. As a consequence we literally see risk everywhere. Non-fatalistic risks are also avoidable. If caused by organizational failure and human agency then surely such risks are predictable and preventable? Increased regulation and blame attribution are the usual responses to contemporary risk. Risks are resisted rather than accepted, and regulatory systems are increasingly held to account for their failure to protect us. In this sense, the risk society can be distinguished from traditional societies. In late or postmodernity risk is increasingly framed as uncertainty within a discourse of contingency and competing values. This is particularly exemplified by the rejection of the Enlightenment's progressive agenda and the role of science in providing both certainty and risk protection (Leonard 1997). Experts are no longer trusted, and views of risk (including scientific ones) are seen as driven by vested interest and as therefore inherently trustworthy (Freudenberg 1988, 1993). Contemporary risks are therefore contested, an arena in which different world views and values are played out.

Summary

Is the risk society about new risks, or merely a new way of looking at risk? Certainly risks have always existed, including low probability/high consequence risks (such as fatal diseases), and some (such as epidemics) have been global in nature. However, such risks can be increasingly characterized by their knowability, we literally have the scientific ability to discover them (their origins, nature and potential extent), and we can increasingly attribute them to human agency rather than the will of the Gods. Fatalistic risk discourse has been replaced by a growing discourse of risk as uncertainty and dispute, with blame attribution and a questioning stance towards regulatory systems as key features. Uncertainty, particularly in terms of life course, and the transfer of risk decisions from the social to the individual sphere, has heightened both personal responsibility and anxiety for risk, although it cannot be assumed that the impact of such uncertainty will be uniform across the population. While risks are far from uniform, and the distinction between environmental hazards and those arising from uncertainties and changes of social life is a useful one, contemporary risks are characterized by conflict, blame attribution and personal negotiation. While it is certainly the case that some risks are new, for example the risk of nuclear discharge or the risk of toxic waste, the risk society is perhaps best characterized by its particular framing of and preoccupation with risk rather than with the proliferation (or otherwise) of risks.

Risk and crime

The implications of the risk society and of postmodernity for criminal justice, social control and crime management have been much discussed (Pratt 2000a; Rose 2000; Sparks 2000). In particular, the modernist disciplinary agenda based upon penal-welfare techniques has been challenged, not least by the failure of such techniques to achieve crime control through the rehabilitation and treatment of offenders (Garland 1995, 1996). Garland identifies the modern penal period from about 1895 onward, and as characterized by a 'shift from the private, ad hoc and charitable to a more systematically organised, publicly funded, national agency' (Garland 1985: 22). He characterizes modern penality by its concern to assess and classify offenders for normalizing techniques. While classification in penality was not new (houses of correction usually classified their prisoners), modern penality acknowledged a diverse range of offenders when 'measured' against the 'normal citizen'. This prompted the notion of assessment, necessary to answer the question 'Who are you?', so essential to the classification of offenders for individual sanctions. Garland sums the transition up thus:

> There has been a move from a calibrated, hierarchical structure (of fines, prison, death), into which offenders were inserted according to the severity of their offence, to an extended grid of non-equivalent and

diverse dispositions, into which the offender is inscribed according to the diagnosis of his or her condition and the treatment appropriate to it.

(Garland 1985: 28)

For Garland the significant shift is from individualism to individualization. Central to this shift is the use of the 'psy' disciplines to assess and individuate (Foucault 1977) and the consequent expansion of such techniques to the realm of welfare and 'softer' areas of social control like social work (Donzelot 1980). Repression was replaced by **normalization**, carried out through reforming techniques (such as probation), and treatment, in essence the replacement of 'prohibition and penalty' with corrective treatments towards pre-specified normative requirements. Modern penality presumed that the 'normal' individual could be trusted to undertake this 'state-induced self-control' carried through the various institutions of the social realm (for example education and welfare agencies). Within the criminal justice sphere the Probation Service occupied a key position in this normalizing process, providing both individualized assessments and classifications of offenders, and personal supervision aimed at preventing law breaking and inculcating acceptable norms, attitudes and behaviours.

The demise of the modernist agenda

The close of the twentieth century saw increasing disquiet with the modernist penal agenda. Modern penal practices were seen as inadequate for the containment of crime (Pratt 2000a), and their spread into the practices of welfare were seen as increasingly oppressive (Leonard 1997). Disillusionment with the 'grand narrative' of 'reform, progress and humanitarianism' (Pratt 2000a) combined with a lack of trust in both science and experts to deliver the promised reformation of offenders challenged the dominance of modern penality. In particular the construction of crime as a social problem amenable to social engineering through individualized interventions was challenged by the New Right political era in anglophone countries such as Britain, Australia and the USA. The 'causes of crime', particularly those linked to notions of social deprivation were dismissed, and the notion of the 'criminal act' as symptomatic of other social ills was rejected. Reformation, particularly through treatment was seen as a failure, epitomized by Martinson's (1974) famous claim that 'nothing works', and prison was seen as a natural and effective alternative. The Thatcher years in Britain (1979–90) saw a commonsense view of crime prevail, crime as individual wickedness and moral decline that had to be countered by tough sentencing, heralding an era of 'prison works' and tougher community penalties. As Flynn (1978) notes, the post-1970s era both in the USA and Britain saw a shift from a 'greater selectivity and sophistication in the use of crime control and correctional methods' (Flynn 1978: 131) towards a harsher punitive climate in which greater state executive control over the judiciary and the extended use of custody were key features.

Economic and social changes were also significant, in particular the 'hollowing out of the state' (Jessop 1993) and a withdrawal to a residual welfare state position, and the transition to **post-Fordist** modes of production. Far from eradicating social problems, the welfare state was seen to perversely encourage them through dependency and 'moral hazard' (that is encouraging decisions that are immoral and illegal) (Parker 1982; Giddens 1998b). The burgeoning cost of welfare was not seen as delivering 'value for money', and was posed as a severe hindrance to the productivity of the private sector (Langan 1998). Increased marketization and privatization were seen as the solution to the highly inefficient and bureaucratized public sector, paralleled by the introduction of audit and private sector management techniques to bring the public sector into line (Clarke and Newman 1997). The result was a residual welfare state in which eligibility was severely restricted and the emphasis was placed upon the 'positive welfare' of return to work, rather than the 'negative welfare' of 'moral hazard' (Giddens 1998b; Kemshall 2002a).

The globalized marketplace also requires greater flexibility in the labour force, with workers prepared to retrain, reskill, accept non-standard conditions and flexible work patterns. The safety net of the welfare state must therefore encourage such adaptive behaviours rather than counter them through dependency and moral hazard. Jessop (1993) has argued that global markets pose a severe challenge to national markets, and traditional capitalist economies must adapt to constant innovation, flexible labour supply and flexible production if they are to compete. This has resulted in a significant restructuring of the relationship 'between the citizen and the state' (Clarke and Newman 1997), not least that the citizen now has reduced entitlement to state protection. The state's commitment to social engineering through the welfare state has also been significantly reduced (Jordan 1998).

Leonard (1997) has argued that the modernist agenda has also been challenged by a growing recognition that the pursuit of normalization and inclusivity has often been accompanied by oppression and social exclusion. The oppressive social control functions of welfare as 'discipline' have received much attention since Foucault's (1965, 1973) initial work, and sentencing to welfare with its perpetuation of an 'underclass' has been much critiqued (Murray 1990). Those most set to benefit from modernity's welfare agenda, such as women, the young and elderly people remain the most marginalized. As Leonard (1997) expresses it, social inclusion is promoted at the expense of the excluded 'Other', the 'bad mother', 'the work-shy' and the 'spongers'. The 'Oneness' of universal provision is quick to collapse under the 'brute reality of economic recession' and the 'ever-deepening dichotomies of rich/poor, employed/unemployed, male/female, white/black' (Leonard 1997: 25). 'Criminals' are of course one such group, simultaneously promised inclusion through reform, rehabilitation and treatment and excluded through those very 'rescuing' discourses and penal practices of exclusion such as prison.

Postmodernity and the rise of risk

The 'grand theorizing' of risk society and postmodernity has gained currency within criminology. This can be discerned in the following areas:

- the importation of contemporary social theory into criminological theorizing and analyses (Sparks 1997; Garland and Sparks 2000; Loader and Sparks 2002)
- the application of risk theorization to issues of social control and social regulation (Rose 1996a, 1996b, 2000)
- the contention that disciplinary practices have radically altered with the rise of a 'new penality' based upon risk and actuarial justice (Feeley and Simon 1992, 1994)

The debate over postmodernity has been described as a 'firestorm of controversy' (Kellner 1999: 639), with some commentators such as Giddens (1990) seeing the characteristics of postmodernity as merely accentuated aspects of modernity: a *late modernity*. Others such as Leonard (1997) identify radical and transformative change within which established structures and categories are challenged, and the future looms uncertainly before us. The debate over nomenclature is to some extent unhelpful, as Bauman (1997: 79) puts it: 'Perhaps we live in a post-modern age, perhaps we do not'. Within the debate some areas of consensus can be discerned:

- Traditional cultural and social forms are increasingly undermined and displaced by globalization. The certainty of the Enlightenment project of progress is no longer uncritically accepted and claims to universal truth and knowledge no longer hold (Leonard 1997). The extent of this transformation and its impact are disputed, with late modern theorists such as Giddens arguing for a more gradual transformation. Those such as Leonard argue that the contemporary period of late capitalism presents a much more radical and fundamental 'rupture' with modernity. For Leonard (1997: 22), we literally are living in 'New Times'.
- Uncertainty, and the constant reflexivity that this necessitates, are also seen as endemic to life in postmodernity and manifested as a pervasive risk discourse and 'risk climate' (Giddens 1990, 1998b).

Within criminology these two theoretical features can be seen in debates about the extent or otherwise of the 'new penality' and the extent to which penal practices have been transformed by conditions of postmodernity (Garland 1996; Pratt 2000a, 2000b, 2000c). These theoretical influences can also be discerned in attention to the increasingly politicized approach to crime (Garland and Sparks 2000) and the attendant controversies of penal politics as a manifestation of risk debates (Sparks 2000, 2001a, 2001b). In addition, the ontological insecurity of risk society has been linked to a growing penal populism in which all citizens are 'crime-conscious', 'attuned to the crime problem, and many exhibit high levels of fear and crime' (Garland and Sparks 2000: 200).

Risk theorization has also been applied to issues of social control and social regulation, with Rose (1996a, 1996b, 2000) in particular analysing its significance for **governance** and control strategies. Rose has argued that one of the central features of **advanced liberal** societies is the technique of governing at a distance through subtle and dispersed disciplinary techniques. While direct state coercion is thus reduced, and individual freedom is espoused, micro systems of power are exercised through the mesh of daily life: employment, family, locale and the responsibilities of citizenship. In essence, Rose argues that this is rule at the 'molecular level', a system of governance (that is regulating conduct) in which the active citizen is required to self-regulate and self-manage as a 'responsible citizen', or government through **responsibilization** (see also Loader and Sparks 2002). The 'soft policing' of welfare agencies and their normalization techniques (Donzelot 1980; Rodger 2000), seen by Foucault (1973, 1977, 1978) as integral to the identification, classification and regulation of deviant groups, is replaced by individualized risk management towards the pre-set prudential aims of advanced liberal societies. The state's role becomes that of facilitator of **prudentialism** through education, training, health campaigns and moral revitalization. The well-informed citizen will make the prudential choice, and self-regulate in line with advanced liberal expectations. Such prudentialism requires citizens to adopt a calculating attitude toward all of their decisions, whether this be the risks of the labour market or the risks of becoming a crime victim. Thus the individual becomes the primary site of risk management, not society, and the 'good' citizen is recast as the prudential one. Citizens who do not make the desired choice are recast as imprudent and reckless, blameworthy and responsible for their own misfortune. Disadvantage and exclusion are reframed as matters of choice and not of structural processes, crime itself becomes a matter of irrational and imprudent choices. Citizens who fall into the imprudent category are seen as ripe for remoralization and 'ethical reconstruction as active citizens' through 'training, counselling, empowerment, and community action', what Rose has dubbed 'ethopolitics' (Rose 1996a: 60; 2000; see also Cruikshank 1996). Offenders are of course a key group for such a remoralization and responsibilization agenda, for example through the new probation programmes aimed at correcting both cognitions and behaviours and facilitating 'straight thinking' and 'rational choice'.

While prudence is not a new concept (the Victorian age stressed prudence as the cornerstone distinction between the 'deserving' and 'undeserving' poor), what is new in the contemporary use of prudentialism is the 'construction of active citizenship in an active society' as the basis of governance regardless of political spectrum or ideology (Rose 1996a, 1996b, 2000). While the 'professions of welfare' and penality exercised 'disciplinary power' in modernity (Leonard 1997: 55), within the post-modernity of advanced liberalism self-surveillance is pursued as a more 'efficient and cost-effective form of social control' (Foucault 1991; Leonard 1997: 56). The regulatory professions take on an enhanced role, their expertise deployed to ensure self-surveillance and self-regulation, a discourse of expertise through which the prudent individual is encouraged to pursue rational choice.

Paralleling Rose's analysis of the governance of advanced liberal societies has been the contention that the disciplinary practices of modernity have been replaced by a new penality based upon risk and actuarial justice (Feeley and Simon 1992, 1994). Feeley and Simon in particular have argued that this strategic and risk-based approach to penality has the following attributes:

- 'Clinical diagnosis and retributive judgement' are replaced by risk calculations and risk probability assessments, hence the term 'actuarialism'.
- A systemic approach to justice matters, with an increased emphasis upon managing offenders in place rather than securing rehabilitation. Crime control per se replaces attention to individual responsibility or culpability.
- The pursuit of new crime control techniques such as targeting of offenders, managing offenders as an aggregate group, situational crime risk management, crime prevention techniques, increased surveillance of at-risk groups such as sex offenders.
- Management replaces change as the key objective of criminal justice.
  (Feeley and Simon 1992: 450; 1994)

For Feeley and Simon this represents a significant paradigm shift from an 'old' penology concerned with individuals, guilt, responsibility, obligation, and the diagnosis and treatment of individual offenders to a 'new' penology based upon actuarial justice and acceptance of 'deviance as normal' (Feeley and Simon 1994: 173). In a rather pessimistic view of crime control they see the role of penology as transformed from a mechanism of guilt attribution and reformation, to a merely administrative function of risk categorization and the regulation and management of 'dangerous people'. With the death of the liberal reformative ideal, regulation and containment of the 'dangerous classes' has come to the fore (for a full discussion of actuarial justice and the 'New Penology' see Chapter 2).

Feeley and Simon argue that three current penal practices exemplify this transition: incapacitation, preventive detention and profiling. Incapacitation as a strategy of crime management aims not to reform individual offenders but to redistribute the risks away from society to prison, a policy recently intensified by the use of selective incapacitation aimed at high-risk offenders and targeting the small number of persistent offenders responsible for the majority of crime (Halliday 2001). Preventive sentencing, including the preventive use of custody, has paralleled selective incapacitation, with sentencing driven by risk factors rather than seriousness of the offence, and 'future risk of harm' playing a significant role in the sentencing of sexual and violent offenders (Wasik and Taylor 1991). Criminal profiling has also expanded (Canter 1989; Hopton 1998), using risk factors to profile likely offenders and likely criminal situations, resulting in 'high-crime areas' targeted for intensive policing, profiles of paedophiles and violent offenders, and profiling likely drug-traffickers in order to effectively target and use surveillance resources.

However, the extent of actuarial justice in the practice of criminal justice has been doubted (Garland 1996; Lynch 1998, 2000; Kemshall and Maguire 2001). These doubts have been expressed on two grounds: first, that the case is somewhat overstated and that penal policy and practice has not radically transformed (Garland 1996), and second, that actuarial justice is largely rhetorical with actual frontline practice little transformed by risk calculations (Kemshall and Maguire 2001).

The distinction between a risk-based penalty and a retributive one has also been disputed, and the 'periodic' approach to both risk and penalty is increasingly contested (O'Malley 2001a). While some theorists argue for a clear delineation between risk and retribution (Shearing 2001), with retributive justice concerned with 'healing the past', punishment, deterrence and symbolic punishment (Shearing 2001: 206) and actuarial justice concerned with future avoidance of harms and risk reduction strategies, others see the relationship as more symbiotic (O'Malley 1992, 1999a). Garland (1997a, 1997b) for example expresses this as the relationship between economic and expressive rationalities of penality. Essentially an economic rationality of crime control can be understood as 'situational engineering' and the economical management of dangers and risks in which 'risk, rationality, choice, the supply of criminal opportunities, market share, customers' are emphasized (Garland 1997a: 4), 'a language that translates "economic forms of reasoning" and calculations into the criminological field' (Garland 1997b: 185). However, he points out that this economic discourse of crime control can quickly be replaced by an expressive one, and rationalistic approaches to the control of penal expenditure can be displaced in the interests of populism and symbolic punishment (see for example Bottoms 1995; Sparks 2000). Recent media and legislative responses to sex offenders and paedophiles are a case in point, with penal policy driven as much by media campaigning and public opinion as by risk (Sparks 2000, 2001a, 2001b).

Pratt (2000b) has also argued that while administrative penality may have occupied a key role post-1970s, 'emotive and ostentatious' punishment has increasingly come to the fore. He points to two key trends as an expression of this: Braithwaite's (1989) reintegrative shaming, and the involvement of the public in the denunciation, shaming and community risk management of sex offenders (for example the *News of the World* campaign in 2000, and the subsequent demands for a 'Sarah's Law'). While the former may be aimed at reintegration, the latter is clearly constituted to exclude and demonize. For Pratt (2000b) such trends coexist alongside the late modern penal trend towards rationalization, bureaucracy and managerialism, and are indicative of a dual and contradictory approach to penality (see also Hudson 2002). He roots his argument in Norbert Elias' (1978, 1982) notion of the civilizing process to examine this duality, arguing that penal power reflects both 'civilizing and decivilizing influences and thereby pulling the possibilities of punishment in competing and contradictory directions' (Pratt 2000b: 431). Globalization, technological advance and mass communication are seen as contributors to the civilizing process, literally creating a 'global village' and a pluralistic society in which personal relationships and interdependencies are strengthened. However, globalization also challenges national sovereignty and state power, erodes traditional bonds and established forms of authority. Pluralism weakens rather than strengthens tolerance, and citizens see themselves as exposed to increased risks against which the state cannot protect them (Giddens 1990).

The social world comes to be seen as inherently risky and unstable, an arena in which safety and security are mere commodities to be purchased. This purchasing need not necessarily be from the state, and the effective control of risks is not seen as solely a matter of national sovereignty. For Pratt (2000b), ostentatious displays of punishment can be understood in part as a compensation for state ineffectiveness in other areas of risk management, a tactic of reassurance to a risk-fearful public. 'Populist punitiveness' (Bottoms 1995) is seen as one expression of this wider decivilizing process in which 'the "demonization" of particular forms of criminal behaviour leading to responses that actually merge the opposing penal trends' (Pratt 2000b: 432).

The result is that both punishment and penality are highly contested areas, with the emotive punishments of expressive penality existing side by side with the cold calculations of actuarial justice. The 'inexorable logic of risk' (Simon 1987) is not necessarily borne out by the empirical evidence of penal practices. There is no Darwinian predisposition towards unilinear progression (Simon 1988; O'Malley 1992). O'Malley (1992: 257) for example argues that there is no overarching 'logic of power', rather technologies of power cannot be divorced from the 'substantive political programs' which deploy them:

> The history of the prison or of actuarial techniques in crime prevention . . . is not to be understood as the gradual encroachment of a more efficient technology of power, but the uneven and negotiated . . . implementation of a political program and the consequent . . . installation of appropriate techniques.
>
> (O'Malley 1992: 258)

This 'unevenness' is manifested in varying responses and institutional practices on risk, begging the question whether risk logic shapes institutional practices or is shaped and mediated by existing institutional forms and day-to-day operations. O'Malley for example, points out how even in the era of early probability marine insurance mariners 'rejected actuarial models in favour of the accumulation of information about each individual case' (O'Malley 2001a: 88). Similar findings can be found in the response of probation officers to the growing actuarialism of probation practice (Kemshall 1998). Kemshall and Maguire (2001) for example, following an extensive review of Multi-Agency Public Protection Panels, ask:

> whether this very diverse set of developments can convincingly be portrayed as part of one definite movement in a particular direction, or whether current developments are better seen as forming an unclear and messy picture, exhibiting a number of trends in different directions.
>
> (Kemshall and Maguire 2001: 246)

Garland argues that transformations in penality should be evident in its 'material forms' as well as in its 'objectives and orientations' (1995: 200). The detailed study of local practice in public protection panels illustrates that systems supposedly led by the new penology of risk do not necessarily exhibit all its key features. In brief, panel members resembled O'Malley's (2001a) mariners, as much informed by 'professional judgement', 'instinct' and anecdote as by formal risk assessment tools. Actuarial tools do not neatly replace professional judgement, and risk assessments tend towards a hybrid of the two with assessors mediating actuarial scores with overriding clinical judgements. Such judgements are themselves embedded in particular agency cultures and objectives, with key value disputes between risk, rehabilitation, community protection and individual rights. There is also considerable dissonance between stated policy and management objectives and practitioner views on risk, with managers and policy-makers valuing actuarially based knowledge for its consistency and accountability, and practitioners valuing professional, individualized judgement for its flexibility and responsiveness to individual factors (Kemshall 2000). The acceptance and implementation of the risk agenda also varies, with frontline staff more resistant to the new penal agenda than managers (Kemshall 1998; Lynch 1998; Kemshall and Maguire 2001). This is not merely a case of 'poor' or inconsistent implementation, but reflects that penal programmes and policies are not 'univocal', but are 'multivocal, internally contested and . . . often internally contradictory' (O'Malley et al. 1997: 513).

The evidence for a new risk-based penology is by no means clear cut, and risk is perhaps more readily characterized by discontinuity, resistance and mediation than by continuity and any 'inexorable logic' (O'Malley 2001a), and that while many of its key features have subsequently become embedded in penal practice, we can agree with O'Malley that the case is somewhat overstated and that other significant developments have been under-examined (O'Malley 2001b).

Summary

Crime and risk have increasingly forged a partnership in the risk society, although the extent to which this is a totally new and transformative partnership is contested. Preoccupations with the 'dangerous classes' and the threat of the masses to social order are long standing, and notions of risk have been integral to social control and regulation for some time (Rigakos and Hadden 2001). Similarly, risk has played a significant role in penal policy, ranging from the rudimentary risk classifications of houses of correction, to the present sophistication of formalized risk assessment tools. While debates about the genealogy of risk may have a limited value (O'Malley 2001a, 2001b), the recognition that risk, albeit in various framings and within different discourses, had been used to identify, classify, assess, punish and treat offenders well before the risk society is important. The significance however is in the type of framing and mode of use, rather than in any inexorable logic of risk. Risk, and its co-option to varying institutional practices and organizational forms, is often a process of contestation, meditation and resistance. The gap between 'material form' and 'stated objectives and orientations' can be wide. The chapters that follow will examine the role and use of risk in a range of criminal justice settings, policies and practices. The areas chosen reflect their topicality in current debates about risk in criminal justice, for example risk in work with sex offender registration, public protection panels, hard targeting and zero tolerance; risk and probation practice including current risk policies and work with dangerous offenders; and the role of risk in situational crime risk management. Although they are necessarily selective and other areas could have been chosen, the areas selected are key exemplars of the current place of risk in contemporary debates about criminal justice and penal policy. However, before exploring these areas, the next chapter will review the role of risk in contemporary penal policy.

Further reading

Beck, U. (1992) *Risk Society: Towards a New Modernity*. London: Sage.

Feeley, M. and Simon, J. (1994) Actuarial justice: the emerging new criminal law, in D. Nelken (ed.) *The Futures of Criminology*. London: Sage.

Garland, D. (1995) Penal modernism and postmodernism, in T. Blomberg and S. Cohen (eds) *Punishment and Social Control: Essays in Honor of Sheldon Messinger*. New York: Aldine de Gruyter.

Rose, N. (2000) Government and control, *British Journal of Criminology*, 40: 321–39.

chapter two

The role of risk in criminal justice and penal policy

Introducing the new penality

The role of risk in contemporary penal policy and criminal justice is well documented (Feeley and Simon 1992, 1994; Hudson 1998, 2002; Brown and Pratt 2000; O'Malley 2000), although the extent of its role and the framing of justice as entirely actuarial is contested (O'Malley 2000; Hudson 2002; Loader and Sparks 2002). The prevalence of risk concerns and the impact of actuarialism on the organization and delivery of criminal justice has however been offered as evidence of a 'new penality' (Feeley and Simon 1992, 1994). Whilst key examples of risk-based policy and practice can be identified, for example the increased centrality of risk to probation practice (Kemshall 1998), or in 'targeted' policing (Maguire 2000), a number of broader trends have been identified in the new penality:

- The emphasis upon dangerousness and social regulation and social exclusion of the 'dangerous Other'.
- Preventive sentencing on the grounds of 'serious risk' (for example the Criminal Justice Act 1991, section 2(2)(b).
- The replacement of clinical and 'professional' judgement with formalized, actuarial risk tools.
- The extension of risk management techniques into non-criminalized areas, for example Anti-Social Behaviour Orders (Maguire 1998), and the increased use of informal regulatory systems.
- A move towards technological systems of monitoring, surveillance and control, coupled with a de-prioritization of the rights of individuals.
- A growth in 'populist punitiveness' (Bottoms 1995) coupled with a demise in the trust in, and influence of, penal experts. The 'economic rationality' of actuarial justice is often paralleled and superseded by an 'expressive' and symbolic rationality of punishment.
- Increasing use of partnerships and co-option of the non-state sector to crime control, and the use of multi-agency approaches in the delivery of criminal justice policy. This is often associated with new, dispersed forms of accountability (Kemshall 1998).
- A rise in 'managerialism' and the use of audit, performance indicators, and the economic language of 'value for money'. This is often reflected in narrow concerns with inputs and outputs, efficiency and fiscal monitoring, with less emphasis upon effectiveness and outcomes (Simon 1993).

(adapted from Kemshall and Maguire 2001: 245)

Feeley and Simon (1992, 1994) in particular have argued that the actuarial justice of the new penology represents a key shift not just in crime management, but in the constitution of the individual. Modern penality constituted the individual as the site of intervention and the object of assessment through the knowledge base of social science (Garland 1985, 1996). Importantly, individuals were constituted as moral agents, capable of culpability, remorse and change, with transformation delivered through the welfare agencies of social care and probation (Garland 1985, 1996). The well-documented demise of the modernist penal agenda (Garland 1985, 1996, 1999; Pratt 2000a, 2000b) has resulted in a penological transition from 'normalization', described by Simon (1988) as 'closing the gap between distribution and norm' to 'accommodation', that is, 'responding to variations in distributions', especially distributions of risk. As Simon goes on to state, accommodation is the cheaper and more efficient option 'because changing people is difficult and expensive . . . In our present social circumstances, it is cheaper to know and plan around people's failings than to normalize them' (Simon 1988: 773–4).

As Feeley and Simon (1992) put it:

> The new penology is . . . less concerned with responsibility, fault, moral sensibility, diagnosis, or intervention and treatment of the individual offender. Rather, it is concerned with techniques to identify, classify, and manage groupings sorted by dangerousness. The task is managerial, not transformative . . . It seeks to *regulate* levels of deviance, not intervene or respond to individual deviants or social malformations.
> (Feeley and Simon 1992: 452; emphasis as original)

Individual diagnosis is replaced by aggregated indicators of risk and statistical tables of probability. Categorization and classification are therefore essential to this enterprise of managing and regulating people, hence the centrality of risk to late or postmodern penology.

The rise of risk and actuarial justice

Simon (1987) in an important article reviewing the rise and impact of actuarial practices and insurance approaches to risk management argues that such practices have a tendency to objectify and aggregate individuals. The rise of commercial insurance and the extension of such practices to all aspects of social life (Rowe 1977), including the institutions of the welfare state, are based upon actuarial tools for aggregating individuals and responding to their risk factors. Actuarial risk tools have their roots in statistical mathematics and formal calculations of probability (Hacking 1975), dating from at least the eighteenth century. (Some like Rigakos and Hadden (2001) would argue for origins in the seventeenth century and early capitalism and mercantile enterprises.) Statistical techniques are then used to generate reliable risk factors from aggregated data, used subsequently to predict and profile offenders. Within criminal justice, one of the earliest examples of this technique is Burgess' (1928, 1929, 1936) parole predictor, in which data on factors associated with success or failure on parole were collected and aggregated, applied retrospectively to a sample for validation and subsequently turned into a predictor of parole violation probabilities. However, as Feeley and Simon (1992) argue, while statistical and risk based, Burgess' work was still located within the broader normalization agenda of sociological criminology, concerned to identify the key individual and social factors associated with parole violation ('alcoholism, unemployment'). In contrast, 'actuarial criminology' generates 'the subject itself', for example the career criminal, the high-risk offender (Feeley and Simon 1992: 466).

Thus while individual information is collected, in this case about individual success or failure on parole, the statistical aggregation transforms this individual data into a classificatory schema (Rigakos and Hadden

2001). Thus, risk serves a dual function: to both individualize through responsibilization of the individual and fragmentation from traditional social bonds, and also to group and objectify individuals through aggregation and classification. Risk both individuates and objectifies, a combination that has reduced the individual to little more than a collection of risk factors, a risk inventory to be managed. For Simon (1987, 1988) this has radically altered the relationship between the citizen and the state. The citizen can no longer necessarily rely on the state for a range of traditional protections, and the contract between citizen and state is no longer underpinned by moral concerns, but rather by economic ones, in essence the cost–benefit equation of risk.

Mapping the rise of actuarially based justice has been contentious (O'Malley 2001a) with some commentators such as Feeley and Simon (1994) and Simon (1987, 1988) seeing the roots of actuarial justice in the rapid twentieth-century extension of insurance-based risk calculations across all aspects of social life, coupled with a demise in the modernist penal-welfare agenda (Garland 1985). Others see the preoccupation with risk calculations and the regulation of the dangerous classes as predating the twentieth century, with key drivers for actuarial risk management lying in seventeenth-century systems of record keeping, prudentialism and the 'econometric constructions' of 'populations' under capitalism (Rigakos and Hadden 2001: 64). While disputes about historical roots and periodization continue to rage (see for example O'Malley 2001a; Rigakos and Hadden 2001), there is some consensus about the main precursors and key themes of actuarial justice:

- the rise and extension of capitalism, and in particular the development of techniques to regulate and discipline the labour force
- the use of actuarial risk practices to ensure civil stability and social order
- concerns with the management of the 'dangerous classes' and the risk distribution of 'bads'
- the role of risk in 'social utility' thinking, in particular the influence of modernist reason and rational thought in the development of economic and legal approaches to social and penal policy
- economic pressures on crime management and concerns to effectively and efficiently manage criminal justice systems
- the retreat from liberal crime management and penal policy under conditions of advanced liberalism.

Theoretical approaches: class versus governmentality

In tracing the origins or 'genealogy' of risk society and risk penality two main theoretical approaches can be discerned: a broadly Marxist approach that foregrounds notions of capital and class, and bases its analysis upon the restructuring of class structures under conditions of advanced capitalism; and a governance approach based upon Foucauldian theories of knowledge and power in which issues of governance, that is how mechanisms of governing are deployed, are central to the analysis (Foucault 1991). The debate between Rigakos and Hadden (2001) and O'Malley (2001a) on the origins of risk is a debate between these two theoretical approaches and the subsequent analyses of risk society and criminal justice produced. The essential differences can be expressed as differences of epistemology and ontology as well of substantive analysis. Class-based analysis is more often associated with a realist epistemology, concerned with real empirical events, and most usually expressed in 'totalizing' and causal 'theoretical scenarios' (O'Malley 2001a). The governmentality literature (with some exceptions, for example O'Malley et al. 1997) locates and examines the practices of governing at the level of the individual subject and local micro settings rather than at the level of the totalizing state, what Rose (1996a) has called 'ethopolitics'. This does not mean that the rule of the state is ignored. On the contrary, governmentality focuses on how government is carried out through specific programmes and the 'mentality of rule' exemplified by the actual practices of governing. For O'Malley et al. (1997) this has resulted in an important connection between analyses of the micro, everyday practices of individuals and abstract, macro techniques of government. For example the responsibilization of individuals to manage their own health risks in the health promotion campaigns of advanced liberal societies (Petersen 1997), epitomized by the 'duty to be well' (Greco 1993). Dean (1999) has described this as the 'conduct of conduct' (see also Foucault 1982, 1991; Gordon 1991), with conduct referring to 'our behaviour, our actions, even our comportment', a concern with self-direction and self-guidance. A pre-set normative standard is presumed and set as an: 'ideal towards which individuals and groups should strive' (Dean 1999: 10). Thus 'personal goals and desires' are linked to 'social order and stability' (Cruikshank 1993: 327). This is underpinned by a notion that conduct can be controlled and regulated towards such norms through control agents such as 'teachers' or other agents and agencies involved in the shaping of conduct. Government is essentially through those agencies who regulate every aspect of our conduct (Dean 1999).

This contrasts with the macro theories that foreground notions of class and state, and examine government in the context of class divisions, capitalist modes of production, and a state apparatus 'which conserves the inequalities of . . . social order' (Garland 1990: 126). Rigakos and Hadden (2001: 61) for example link the emergence of risk concerns with the 'techniques, aims and interests of seventeenth century English capitalists' and the social relations arising out of early mercantile capitalism. For them, actuarial thought and the penal practices that result from it are rooted in seventeenth-century economic thinking and the 'bourgeois logics of . . .

an emerging rational state' (Rigakos and Hadden 2001: 79). In terms of penality, class-based explanations emphasize the role of the criminal justice system in regulating and alleviating the worst effects of neoliberal market reforms and globalization (Stenson 2000a), forming a 'prison net' in the absence of a social security net (Feeley and Simon 1992). However, Garland (1990) has warned against framing the relationship between modes of production and penal forms as a simple, causal deterministic one. Rather, penal forms 'are negotiated within the limits which these broader structures lay down' (Garland 1990: 128). For Garland, the major contribution of class-based analyses of penality is in the following five areas:

- The role of penality in the governance and regulation of one class by another.
- The role of penality in supporting the 'political objectives and ideological commitments of the ruling bloc'.
- The role of penality in reinforcing and legitimizing state power and force through the rule of law.
- Penality is interrelated with social policies for the management of the poor (for example the traditional welfare state).
- Penality plays a key role in 'policing and social policy measures which together regulate the poor and seek to manage problem populations'.

(from Garland 1990: 129–31)

These substantive and conceptual concerns are by no means unique to class-based analyses, and have played a significant role in more recent governmentality analyses of penality (see for example Garland 1990; Stenson 2000a; O'Malley 2001a).

Governmentalists are concerned with the 'power–knowledge' nexus within which risk is constituted and deployed. Unlike Beck, governmentalists do not see risks as mere ideological forms or social constructs, amplified and socially filtered 'unreal risks', products of an unknowable future (Beck 1992a: 33–4). Rather they are concerned to map and analyse 'governmental mentalities and techniques of risk' (O'Malley 2001a). In addition, while class-based analyses may focus on tracing the single trajectory of risk to the risk society, governmentalists perceive such a genealogy of risk as more complex and subject to various discontinuities. However, many of the key concerns of each approach overlap (Stenson 2000a) and these will now be explored.

Risk and capitalism

The link between actuarial practices on risk and the rise of capitalism has been examined in some detail (Rigakos and Hadden 2001), and in particular the development of techniques to regulate and discipline the labour force. The rise of capitalism has been paralleled not only by the expansion of an industrialized labour force but also by growing preoccupations with 'dangerous classes', largely located in an underclass 'permanently excluded from social mobility and economic integration' (Feeley and Simon 1992: 467). This preoccupation is by no means new, and reflects a tension between the creation of a large pool of reserve labour and the potential danger and unruliness represented by a large group of marginalized and excluded citizens.

The concern with regulation is epitomized by the rise of the Benthamite panopticon as both a mechanism of punishment and discipline. In Foucault's (1977) seminal examination of such developments it is expressed as the transition from sovereign executions to the regulatory discipline of the panopticon, the notion of total surveillance both within and without the prison. Rigakos and Hadden (2001; see also Rigakos 1999) have described this as the 'panoptic impulse', exemplified in the seventeenth-century schemes to govern all aspects of social life through statistical information, and the increased politicized use of mathematics to classify and manipulate individuals. Indeed this approach began to transform individuals into 'populations' and resulted in a panoptic surveillance of problematic populations in the interests of 'civil stability' and economic prosperity. Petty's seventeenth-century politicized arithmetic for example was aimed at 'persuading individuals to discipline their own behaviour, and accept social controls freely of their own volition' (Greengrass 1996: 17; Rigakos and Hadden 2001: 69). The twin concerns of crime and economy are meshed around the key themes of risk and social order, predicated on the binary social constructs of 'insider' and 'outsider', still prevalent today (Leonard 1997). The result is what Gordon (1991) has called a modern system of economic sovereignty and a preoccupation with managing threats to civil stability and social order.

Risk and social order

The meshing of risk with concerns about civil stability and social order has a long history. Rigakos and Hadden (2001) trace it back to seventeenth-century concerns with panoptical surveillance and regulation of citizens, especially within the emerging capitalist cities such as London (Mykannen 1994). This meshing represents an early precursor of the risk society deploying techniques of discipline through 'knowing' and 'aggregating' populations, and controlling dangers through calculative techniques of assessment and profiling individuals for increased surveillance and where necessary segregation especially through prison and asylums (Bartlett 1997). However, the distinction between the modernist panoptical agenda and the late or postmodern is important. The former was concerned with the normalization of deviance through the panoptical systems of welfarism and social engineering (Donzelot 1980) and had reintegration and rehabilitation as key aims. The latter has a rather more gloomy agenda, and accepts the existence of a permanent underclass and permanent offender population. In this scenario, risk is not reduced, it is warehoused in prisons (or contained through intensive risk management and surveillance strategies in the community) and essentially distributed away from the rest of the population (Feeley and Simon 1992). Risk is thus managed away, and risk itself becomes a self-justificatory logic for increased extension of the surveillance network into every aspect of social life. Risk, especially the prevention of risk, replaces individual rights as a key principle of judicial judgements, and as a central element in the relationship between citizen and state (Rose 2000). The price of protection from risk is literally greater intrusion and a weakening of individual rights (Pratt 2000c).

Risk avoidance and the 'management of bads'

While risk-taking is at the heart of entrepreneurial capitalism and mercantile activities, preoccupation with risk avoidance and the distribution of risks has been integral to the development of actuarial risk practices. The prime 'bad' has been the perennial threat of the 'dangerous classes', documented as a key social policy concern in the seventeenth century (Rigakos and Hadden 2001), and a significant issue in the nineteenth and twentieth centuries (Pratt 2000c). In part, this reflected the fragile nature of modern society and significant threats to civil stability and social order from key groups such as 'trade unions, urban masses, political agitators, dispossessed agricultural workers, criminals, and returning ticket of leave men' all of whom constituted the 'dangerous classes' of the time (Pratt 2000c). Pratt argues that as these threats were ameliorated in the latter part of the nineteenth century by social reform, the notion of 'dangerousness' began to crystallize around criminals. Interestingly this encompassed persistent criminals as well as the notorious and the serious, some 40,000 in England and Wales in 1887 (Solly 1887 in Pratt 2000c; Crackanthorpe 1902). This preoccupation was paralleled by developments in record keeping (for example police indexing and finger printing) and data collection techniques to make such risks both knowable and calculable (Pratt 2000c). Such techniques transformed the uncertainty and unpredictability of the dangerous classes into the knowable, calculable and controllable. Indeed the 'knowability' of its citizens and hence the knowability of risk is the hallmark of the modern state. Knowability and calculability are essential to risk avoidance and control of risk distribution.

In his history of dangerousness Pratt (1997) argues that the nineteenth and twentieth centuries saw a dual approach to dangerousness: increased categorization, surveillance and segregation of the dangerous, and an extension of the state's remit to protect endangered citizens from such criminals. This high point of modernity saw the transformation of risk protection from individuals to the state (Foucault 1979), but as Pratt (1997) states, the price was greater intervention and regulation over our lives.

Risk and the role of modern thought

The importance of modernist thought has also been noted, for example the rise of law and economics in deploying what Feeley and Simon (1994: 186) call 'social utility analysis or actuarial thinking' to policy considerations. Leonard (1997) has noted the significant influence of 'reason' as a concept in the development of modern thought and the application of the Enlightenment project to scientific and social progress. Central to the notion of reason is the concept of rationality, based upon universal truth claims, knowledge of the present, and the operation of agreed norms and laws rooted in proven (by the canons of science) knowledge. Hence the importance of both mathematics and science to the Enlightenment project, and as underpinning disciplines for the development of actuarial risk practices (Hacking 1975).

Rose (1993) has examined the role of expertise, particularly in economics, auditing, management and business, in the regulatory mechanisms of the liberal state. Such expertise provides a locus of independent and objective authority for social planning, engineering and regulation of populations towards pre-specified norms, epitomized by social policy trends in the twentieth century (Kemshall 2002a). Rose has expressed this as 'governing through society', shaping the activities of individuals towards pre-specified norms through complex networks like the welfare state and the activities of various experts and professionals – in effect, government at arm's length. The state does not explicitly outline the expected norms or directly hold citizens to account for meeting them, rather they are mediated by various professionals (for example welfare workers) and the 'soft' social controllers of the welfare state. In such a climate the truth and knowledge claims of experts are sacrosanct, and legitimize extensive intrusion and 'treatment' of those deemed to be 'in need' of adjustment, resocialization and normalization. For Rose, this use of expertise is the hallmark of the modern state and its resolution of the 'problematics of order' (Rose 1993, 1996a, 1996b, 2000).

O'Malley (1992, 2001b) has charted the transformation of the social disciplines of welfare expertise into the positivist, quantitatively evaluated 'psy' disciplines of the neoliberal state. The latter are subject to extensive cost–benefit evaluations (such as 'what works'), deployed in professional calculations and predictions of behaviour (for example actuarial risk assessment tools for offenders) and extensively used to 'make up' citizens as active, responsibilized individuals responsible for their own crime. The Probation Service for example has seen a sea-change from a rehabilitative agenda rooted in social causation theories of crime and welfarism to an 'effective practice' agenda rooted in cognitive-behavioural psychology and individual theories of crime causation (Robinson 2001; Kemshall 2002b). The 'human sciences' have not so much been replaced as transformed within the advanced liberal agenda of responsibilization and 'ethopolitics'.

Economic crime management and actuarial risk practices

The link between economic crime management and actuarial risk practices has also been explored (Flynn 1978; Posner 1985; Feeley and Simon 1994), although the extent to which this has been a recent or perennial issue is not clear (Stenson and Sullivan 2001). Indeed how to economically punish and contain offenders preoccupied those charged with the early houses of correction in the 1800s (Cotswold District Council 1994), and the costs of managing an ever-burgeoning 'dangerous class' has taxed penal commentators for some time (Solly 1887; Pratt 1997). The post-1970s economic pressure, particularly on anglophone systems of welfare and justice, has been recognized as a key driver for developments in the efficient management of criminal justice (Flynn 1978). Within this, two main themes can be discerned: a systems approach to justice, and techniques to rationalize the allocation of resources according to levels of risk. The systems approach is exemplified by attention to joining up the agencies of the criminal justice system, applying systems theory and processes to crime management, identifying blockages in the system and fast-tracking, gatekeeping and diversion tactics, and emphasis upon targets, economy and efficiency (Heydebrand and Seron 1990; Davies et al. 1995). In Britain this was epitomized by the 1980s systemic approach to juvenile and young offenders (Thorpe et al. 1980; Morris and Giller 1987), the introduction of national objectives for key criminal justice agencies such as the Probation Service (Home Office 1984a; Faulkner 1989) and more recently concerted efforts to join the system up (for example the Joint Prisons and Probation Review: Home Office 1998). Similar developments took place in the USA, particularly as a response to 'rising demand and declining resources' (Heydebrand and Seron 1990: 81) and increasing concerns with the rationalization and administration of justice rather than its judicial functions. This was paralleled by an emphasis upon the diversion of low-risk offenders and fast-tracking and selective incapacitation of the most dangerous following the 1982 RAND Corporation report on sentencing (Greenwood and Abrahamse 1982; Blackmore and Welsh 1983).

The notion of 'selective incapacitation' reflected concerns not only with the management of dangerousness, but also with the burgeoning cost of custody. Flynn for example in 1978 talked about the 'American criminal justice system' being 'buffeted by strong winds of discontent and is in great turmoil concerning its purposes, objectives and methods' (Flynn 1978: 131). She noted the calls for a 'hard-line', increased effectiveness, the imposition of mandatory sentencing, and increased use of custody. Flynn was writing at a time of discontent and disillusion with the rehabilitative ideal, and the reformative agenda of the criminal justice system was under attack. Recidivism rates were seen as unacceptably high and coercive correction was seen as a failure. Similar trends also occurred in Britain (Stenson 2001). However, Flynn (1978) also noted that the swing from rehabilitation to 'just deserts' punishment was also doomed to failure, not least because deterrence cannot be guaranteed and long-term recidivism may not be affected, and because there is a need 'to reassess the use of prisons . . . to find ways to reduce their burgeoning populations in ways consistent with public safety' (Flynn 1978: 133). The role of 'just deserts' sentencing in producing large prison populations in Britain and the USA throughout the 1980s is well documented (Young 1999). As predicted by Flynn, prison populations are bound to outstrip prison capacity and building programmes, and in such circumstances techniques to determine those who require incarceration and those who can be diverted to community penalties or released from custody early will be actively sought.

New right crime policies, advanced liberalism and risk

Commentators have also linked the rise of actuarial justice to New Right politics and the advanced-liberal agenda on crime control (Christie 1994; O'Malley 1996; Stenson 2001; Sullivan 2001). The period since the late 1970s has seen extensive global, political, economic and cultural change during which crime and its effective management has become a core issue for those liberal societies confronted with significant issues in the management of pluralism and diversity (Rodger 2000; Stenson 2001). This period has seen an increased politicization of crime control in western European and anglophone countries coupled with the growth of a 'populist punitiveness' fuelled by media attention and blame allocation (Sparks 2000, 2001a). As Stenson points out, this has applied even in the most liberal of countries, the Netherlands, which has seen a fivefold increase in its prison capacity since 1975 (Van Swaaningen 2000; Stenson 2001).

   Stenson has described this as a retreat from traditional liberalism, a trend that has continued into the twenty-first century on both sides of the Atlantic regardless of political orientation of individual governments, and in particular a retreat from the liberal welfarism of the Beveridge welfare state. Liberal welfarism provided a particular contract between citizen and state centred around safety-net supports and minimum protection against the vagaries of the market. Rooted in the modern promise of social progression and social justice, welfarism is characterized by the pursuit of inclusivity, equality, full and secure employment, and social solidarity (Jordan 1998), and a social care and penal complex seen as rightly located in the realm of professional experts and largely hidden from either public or political scrutiny (Stenson 2000a, 2000b). Rose (1993, 1996a, 1996b) has argued that this strategy of rule has fundamentally changed since the early 1950s, arising in large part from the acknowledged cost of welfare and the failures of the welfare state to meet its stated intentions. Paradoxically the success of the welfare state in mediating state rule, expressing norms and deploying expertise has in part facilitated this change. What Rose (1996a: 41) terms 'advanced liberal' rule 'depends upon expertise in a different way'. Expertise is no longer solely meshed in the networks of welfare and understood as universal and uncontested. Rather it is located in the sphere of the market and the consumer, linked to choice, but an informed and prudential choice in which expertise has a key role in framing the regulated and prudent choices of the individual. This is what Rose (1996b) has called the 'death of the social'. The 'self' as a 'subject of government' is reconstituted as the risk-alert, calculative, prudential individual, an 'active agent in his or her government' (Rose 1993: 296). 'Expertise' no longer merely implants norms into citizens, rather the active, prudent citizen *demands* advice, counselling and expertise to enable them to make the prudent, rational risk choice. Thus the bureaucracy of expertise (epitomized by the welfare state) is replaced by a plural market of expertise in which the consumer rather than the welfare recipient is key. Indeed the market itself extends to the commodification of welfare expertise through internal markets and purchaser–provider arrangements.

Rose's 'post-social' world is characterized by the self-regulation and responsibilization of individuals in which personal capacity to predict and manage one's own risks is central (Rose 1996b). In this world the role of experts is reconstituted away from reformation, transformation, treatment and change, to risk assessors and risk managers (Castel 1991). Experts are now responsible for the calculation and reduction of risk, both risks arising from their own professional conduct, and the risks presented by their clientele, including risks to the 'general public' (Rose 1996b: 349). The deployment of this expertise is integral to what Rose has called 'governing the margins', those who fail to exercise the prudential risk choice either through incapacity, incompetence or intransigence. The underclass is of course a key example, a class qualitatively distinguished from the poor by their 'anti-social behaviour', moral degeneracy, and personal incapacity to function as full and economically productive citizens (Murray 1990). While the binary concepts of included and excluded have long posed tensions for social order (Leonard 1997), recent social and penal policy commentators contend that this position has been exacerbated by the creation of a permanent underclass during the post-1970s transition to post-Fordist economies (see for example Jessop 1993, 1994, 2000; Rodger 2000). In brief, the latter are characterized by the globalization of capital, interdependence of markets, information technology, constant innovation and requirements for a flexible labour supply and multi-skilling. (For a full review see Kemshall 2002a.)

One specific outcome for crime control and penality is the creation of an unemployable underclass of ill-educated and unskilled young males (although not exclusively male), usually located in depressed inner-city neighbourhoods and increasingly characterized as disorderly, violent and threatening (Campbell 1993; Stenson 2000a). The underclass and dangerousness have become intertwined themes in the concerns of the new penology (Feeley and Simon 1992) expressed in the twin objectives of displacing risky populations (usually to prisons), and redistributing risk away from the non-risky through dispersal of 'dangerous populations' and the recolonization of threatened public spaces (Stenson 2000a). This is not merely a redistribution away from 'fortress middle England', but from the 'hardworking working class' (Jordan 1998). The latter in particular are seen to be overly exposed to risk, least able to protect themselves against it (for example they cannot afford security guards and other private measures), and regard themselves as assuming a proportionately high tax burden to support the economically inactive and disorderly in their neighbourhood (Murray 1994; Jordan 1998). In such neighbourhoods techniques of risk displacement like 'zero-tolerance policing' and situational crime prevention techniques such as closed-circuit television (CCTV), Neighbourhood Watch, antisocial behaviour orders and 'gated communities' have gained ready acceptance (Blakely and Snyder 1997; Hughes 1998).

The 'death of the social', the demise of the welfare state and the impact of post-Fordist economies have all played a significant role in the 'criminalisation of social policy' (Crawford 1998). As Feeley and Simon (1992) starkly express it, as the safety net of welfare has shrunk, its place has been taken by the safety net of prison, and issues of crime control have moved centre stage in 'the agendas of the liberal democracies in the last twenty years' (Stenson 2000a: 230). Stenson for example has argued that a significant discursive shift has occurred in the political discourse of the anglophone democracies, exemplified by the delegitimation of the welfare state under New Right regimes and the relocation of social regulation concerns from the welfare state and its instruments of social engineering to the penal realm. For Stenson this is exemplified by Nixon's replacement of the traditional liberal agenda of 'War on Poverty' with the 'War on Crime' in the 1970s, and the subsequent agendas of both Reagan and Clinton.

In the UK similar trends occurred under the New Right agenda of the Thatcher years (1979–90). James and Raine (1998) in an important review of the 'new politics of criminal justice' see the crucial period of change lying between 1979 and 1997, a period 'marked by disjuncture in direction and rapid legislative and policy change' (James and Raine 1998: 3). Rather than seeing this as a period of incoherent penal policy development, they characterize the broader transition in terms of four key dynamics:

- Politicisation of crime and crime control.
- Managerialism and increased accountability.
- Adminstrative processing.
- Public voice and participation, and the rise of populism.

(James and Raine 1998: 4)

They locate the transition within a climate of increased challenge to the effectiveness of criminal justice (Uglow 1995; McLaughlin and Muncie 1996), growing crime rates, increased public concern about crime (particularly violent crime), and growing disenchantment with the 'welfare' paradigm of criminal justice. The latter located both the causes and explanations of crime within the social and 'psy disciplines', with particular emphasis upon sociological analyses and the social causes of crime. The waning influence of such disciplines following Martinson's (1974) famous 'nothing works' article has been well documented (Garland 1990), epitomized by Margaret Thatcher's famous statement that there is 'no such thing as society'. The welfare paradigm was rapidly replaced by the justice paradigm, emphasizing personal responsibility, culpability and blame; a 'just deserts' approach to sentencing in which the punishment should literally fit the crime and not the criminal; punishment prioritized above rehabilitation; and a 'tough on crime' policy that firmly placed custody at its centre. UK penal policy in the 1980s and early 1990s was characterized by 'tough on crime' and 'law and order', and the importation of penal policies and strategies from the USA. A key influence in this importation was the work of Charles Murray (1997) propounding the 'prison works' thesis, seen as validating the prison works philosophy of the Howard era. However, Murray's work had a wider significance, not least for introducing a cost–benefit calculation into penal discourse and in essence a risk calculation to the use of prison as a strategy of crime control. When taken alongside his work on the underclass (Murray 1990, 1994; Lister 1996), Murray effectively meshed concerns with the regulation of the underclass with economic crime control strategies such as prison. In his work *Underclass: The Crisis Deepens*, Murray (1994) predicts the creation of a 'New Rabble', an underclass of unskilled and unemployable persons largely engaged in criminal activities, a class who will increasingly be subject to prison or community custody measures such as curfews and intensive surveillance, and who will increasingly become the site of public hostility and exclusion. While the term 'New Rabble' has been replaced in social policy terms by the less pejorative term 'socially excluded' (Alcock 1996), the effective management of this group has remained largely within the penal realm, and continues to be a perennial problem of liberal democracies. As Harris (1999) expresses it, the key issue for liberal governance is how to reconcile the relationship between the independent and economically active citizenry and those who are dependent and economically inactive. This issue is exacerbated by the pluralism and fragmentation of post-Fordist societies (Rodger 2000).

Crime control under advanced liberal modes of government has reconstituted the contract between citizen and state. For the included and economically active citizen the state has continued to provide protection from crime risks. However, the mechanisms of delivery have become more dispersed to a mixed economy including the private and voluntary sector, and to locales and communities as well as from the centre (Garland 1996; James and Raine 1998; Stenson 2000a; Stenson and Edwards 2001). Individual responsibility for risk management has also been promoted, for example avoiding risky places, ensuring appropriate security measures, and taking adequate precautions against personal and property crime (Rose 1996a, 2000). This combination of pluralism and individuation in crime control produces both uncertainty and fear (James and Raine 1998; Sparks 2001a). Uncertainty and fear for governments and policy makers, and uncertainty and fear for workers and citizens. The increased individual responsibility for crime risk management has heightened individual perceptions of personal risk and vulnerability resulting in an increased fear of crime unconnected to personal experience of victimization (Lupton and Tulloch 1999). As James and Raine (1998: 30) contend, this combination of uncertainty and fear breeds the conditions 'under which both government and the public become eager participants in a tough stance on crime'.

Summary

Actuarial justice and a risk-based penalty are evidenced by a number of broad trends, although the extent to which this constitutes a new penality is contested (Pratt 2000a; Kemshall and Maguire 2001). The origins and rise of actuarial justice are similarly contested, within which two theoretical approaches can be discerned. However, overlapping themes can be identified as significant precursors of a shift to a risk-based penalty. Most notable are concerns with governance, regulation and social order, and the 'problematics of rule' in advanced liberal societies. Central to the issue of rule has been a shift in the relationship between citizen and state in crime control, resulting in greater individuation and individual responsibility for risk and crime management. In this climate, harsh penal responses to the fear and uncertainty arising from the pluralism and fragmentation of post-Fordist societies have become the norm.

Punitive sovereignty and the place of risk

The predicament of crime control in advanced liberal societies has been succinctly expressed by Garland (2000). In brief, how to effectively manage crime in societies where fear of crime is endemic, high crime rates are 'a normal social fact', penal-welfare approaches are seen to have failed, and the citizen sees the state as failing to deliver adequate levels of personal security (Garland 2000: 348; 2001: 140). Garland discerns two major responses: an '*adaptive strategy* stressing prevention and partnership' and a '*sovereign state strategy* stressing enhanced control and expressive punishment' (Garland 2000: 348; emphases as original). As will be seen, risk has a key role in both.

Adaptive strategies

Crime prevention and partnership are the hallmarks of such an adaptive strategy. In essence, the state acknowledges its limited role in the provision of guaranteed security and devolves both responsibility and accountability for its provision to local communities and new hybrid organizations (Garland 2000) concerned with crime prevention (Hughes 1998), community management of high-risk offenders (Kemshall and Maguire 2001), or local crime and disorder management (Stenson 2000a). Such partnerships have a proactive brief, characterized by a risk logic of early identification, assessment and prevention. The central characteristics of such partnerships are:

- Their dispersed accountability and the displacement of risk responsibility from the centre to locales and newly established hybrid organizations (Leiss and Chociolko 1994; Kemshall 1998), and the removal of central government responsibility for crime causation.
- The combination of state and non-state organizations, and the increased role of the private sector in crime control (Garland 2000, 2001).
- The increased use of entrepreneurial capitalism in crime control, for example in reacquiring 'threatened spaces' for the ordinary citizen, (for example inner-city regeneration, dockland developments: Stenson 2000a) coupled with zero-tolerance policing to remove 'undesirables' from problematic locales (Stenson 1999).

These features not only represent changing modes of crime management, but also represent changing modes of risk management. As Hope and Sparks (2000: 3) express it: 'They ... portend new ways of sharing out the provision of security between state agents, commercial organisations and individual consumers.'

It is this change, rather than partnership per se, that is significant. Risks, especially the problematic, endemic and frequent risks associated with economic and social dislocation, are devolved to local communities. Stenson (2000a: 233) has described this as 'community security' in which the emphasis is upon community action and responsibility for local crime management. In essence, communities are 'responsibilized' (although the language of 'empowerment' is more often used), tasked with increasing informal social controls, weeding out undesirables, and removing 'crimino-genic' opportunities through regeneration and social inclusion. However, as O'Malley (1992) notes, social inclusion in this context should not be confused with social justice. Repeat victimization studies indicate that such strategies do not necessarily reduce risk or redistribute it away from those least able to tolerate it (Karmen 1990; Walklate 1997). Crime risks may only be managed in place or at worst displaced to other sites of vulnerability (Barr and Pease 1992; Walklate 1997).

The dispersal of crime risks to communities also reflects the advanced liberal break with the agenda of traditional welfare states and universal strategies for pooling and managing risks (Giddens 1998b). With the 'death of the social' (Rose 1996b) (or at least its transformation), collectivity for risk has been replaced by individuation and community. This agenda has continued under New Labour's 'Third Way', with government policy wrestling with the economic and social implications of post-Fordism and the need to 'foster an inclusive social solidarity at all levels while not losing the support of the fearful, fiscally conservative middle classes' (Stenson and Edwards 2001: 68). Stenson and Edwards describe this tension as the 'meta-dilemma' of third way progressive governance, in essence how to achieve social inclusion of the underclass without alienating the economically active, law-abiding citizen, and more importantly without raising taxation. Social inclusion policies are therefore severely restricted by low public expenditure and low public acceptability of grand interventionist strategies. In this climate, legitimacy for social inclusion policies are achieved through an economic rhetoric that emphasizes inclusion through the labour market and not through the welfare state (Jordan 1998), a social policy of 'tough love' that stresses a 'something for something' contract between citizen and state (Jordan 2000). The welfare safety net is replaced by targeted social investment policies (Downes 1998; Stenson and Edwards 2001), in which those communities seen as presenting a significant challenge to liberal democracy are targeted for intervention or 'regeneration'. The language of regeneration itself is economically framed: 'social investment' replacing traditional terms like community or social work, the promotion of 'social capital' as the preconditions for regeneration, and a meshing of crime and social policy agendas under the broader notion of social inclusion (Hope 1996; Stenson and Watt 1999; Walklate 2000). In essence, social policy is recast as economic policy within which the crime control of the economically inactive is a central feature (Rodger 2000).

Stenson and Edwards (2001) see 'community security' as crystallized in three broad technologies of crime control:

- The reclamation of threatened spaces from disorderly and criminal groups.
- Target hardening, both of criminals and opportunities, rooted in early risk assessment and preventative risk management tactics such as preventative policing.
- The development of local security measures such as private security, 'gated' communities.

(Stenson and Edwards 2001: 72)

However, governing *through* the community is not without difficulty, not least the hybrid and inconsistent nature of the partnerships subsequently formed, the impact of local arrangements and personnel, local political and economic cultures, and the acceptance of regeneration agendas by local people (Stenson and Edwards 2001). Targeting itself necessitates inclusion of some and the exclusion of others, and social investment runs the risk of failing and of falling into disrepute when it is perceived by the 'fearful middle class' to have been a costly mistake. These are the potential seeds of discontent, mistrust and intolerance, between the included and the excluded, and between central government and communities.

Sovereign state strategies

The dual nature of contemporary penal policy has been noted by a number of commentators, but primarily by Garland (1996, 1997b, 2001) who discerns the twin but interlinked approaches of an economic crime rationality, based on prevention and regeneration and cast within a primarily economic discourse of crime control; and an expressive rationality, based on harsher, 'tougher' penalties and cast within an expressive, punitive rationality (Garland 2000: 350; 2001: 140). For Garland, contemporary penal policy is a curious hybrid of the two:

> Typically each measure operates upon two different registers: an expressive, punitive scale that uses the symbols of condemnation and suffering to communicate its message; and an instrumental register, attuned to public protection and risk management. The favoured modes of punitive expression are also, and importantly, modes of penal segregation and marking. The policy concern today is neither purely punitive nor solely oriented towards public protection. *The new penal ideal is that the public be protected and its sentiments be expressed.*
>
> (Garland 2000: 350; emphases as original)

Expressive, punitive penality has been targeted predominantly at two key groups: dangerous violent offenders and sex offenders (particularly paedophiles), and more recently persistent offenders (Halliday 2001). Policy and statute has reflected a growing concern to target, selectively incapacitate, and intensively community manage these groups based upon risk levels. This approach has taken place in the absence of well-established and highly reliable risk prediction tools (Kemshall 1998; Kemshall and Maguire 2001), and in the absence of definitive evidence of the efficacy of such strategies, particularly selective incapacitation, to reduce risk and danger (Young 1997). In contrast to the 'dangerousness debate' of the 1970s the New Right introduction of punitive measures has encountered little resistance beyond the judiciary (Freiberg 2000) and those criminal justice workers required to make extensive ideological adjustments (Millar and Buchanan 1995; Kemshall and Maguire 2001). The most notable changes have been in parole restrictions for violent and sexual offenders in 1983 extended in the Criminal Justice Act 1991 and the introduction of risk-based sentencing for violent and sexual offenders (Wasik and Taylor 1991); the subsequent introduction of mandatory life sentencing for violent and sexual offenders upon second conviction in the Crime Sentence Act 1997; the increased regulation and surveillance of sexual offenders through the Sex Offenders Act 1997; and the introduction of the Sex Offender Order under the Crime and Disorder Act 1998. This has paralleled punitive developments in the USA, most notably the 'three strikes and you're out' legislation, tracking and community outing of sex offenders, longer sentences and intensive parole restrictions. Similar trends have been identified in Australian legislative concerns, although Freiberg (2000) has noted that this has been the site of more significant judicial resistance than in the USA. Nor has this been an exclusively anglophone phenomenon, with discernible trends in the liberal democracies of northern Europe (Van Swaaningen 2000).

Central to this hybrid agenda are the role of populism and the highly politicized agenda of crime control (Bottoms 1995; Sparks 2001a, 2001b; Loader and Sparks 2002) and the foregrounding of the victim (Walklate 1998; Garland 2000). This is not merely a matter of media influence on public perceptions of crime risks, although the influence of the media has been extensively reviewed (Gerbner 1987; Sparks 1992). Garland (2001) for example has argued that the particular social and cultural conditions of late modernity have been important precursors for punitive populism. In late modern societies crime has become a common, everyday experience; even the liberal middle class has been increasingly exposed. The perceived seepage of crime, particularly drug-related crime into traditionally low-crime areas, has been a powerful leveller and a key mechanism in undermining professional middle-class support for welfare approaches to crime management. This, coupled with the demise of professional expertise and the general eradication of the authority and status of most welfare professional groups, has removed a significant buffer between citizen and state in the arena of penal policy. The post-1970s collapse of the welfare state also increased the vulnerability of the middle class: to unemployment, insecurity and the seepage of the 'dangerous classes'. Fear and insecurity have become a daily experience requiring constant self-monitoring, vigilance and reflexivity (Giddens 1991; Garland 2001). In the words of Hope and Sparks (2000), fear of crime and its perpetual insecurity is the new 'private trouble' (Wright Mills 1970).

Populism, and its key features fear and insecurity, have also been exacerbated by the social dislocation of post-Fordism and the social policies of the New Right (Rodger 2000). The impact of globalization on traditional industries has resulted in the transition of many working-class communities into deprived and socially excluded ones, with both criminality and unemployment endemic and with attendant problems of social stability and order (Campbell 1993; Morris 1994; Rodger 2000). The perceived threat to 'decent citizenry' coupled with the prevailing ontological insecurity of risk society (Giddens 1991) have contributed to what Garland has called 'the institutionalisation of crime awareness' (Garland 2000: 367; 2001) in which individuals are constantly aware of, and make constant adaptations to, crime threats. This provides a fertile ground for more emotive and more punitive attitudes to punishment to take root. Crime policies are not merely concerned with the instrumental and effective objectives of criminal justice, they are also reflective of deeper seated emotional and symbolic concerns (Freiberg 2001). As Freiberg puts it, this may mean that 'success' in crime control is about 'capturing the public imagination rather than success in controlling crime' (2001: 273). In these terms punitive penalty has been largely successful, as evidenced by the 'bidding war' between the incumbent Tory Home Secretary Michael Howard and New Labour's Jack Straw on 'tough' law and order policies preceding the 1997 election (Stenson 2001: 17), and the continuing New Labour emphasis on 'tough on crime and tough on the causes of crime'.

However, important caveats should be noted. 'Populist punitiveness' is a complex phenomenon, and not merely the production of a simple inter-action between astute politicians, a cynical media and a gullible public (Young 1999; Freiberg 2001; Sparks 2001a, 2001b). There are varied publics, and the claims of politicians must 'resonate' to be successful (Tonry 1999; Freiberg 2001), and while media campaigns are significant in public perceptions of risk (Kitzinger 1999a) the public should not be treated as a mere 'media dupe' (Young 1999). (See Young 1999 for an important critique of simplistic analyses of fear of crime and public responses. See Sparks 2001a for an extensive analysis of both the term populism and the role of media in public perceptions of risk and fear of crime.) Perceptions of risk and security are embedded in lived experiences, local situations and circumstances, personal investment in local and significant networks and the extent to which these are seen as secure or threatened, and the extent to which they can be defended (Hope and Sparks 2000; Sparks 2001a).

For Sparks, these 'tribulations of place' help to explain the 'fretful concern with the risks of crime that characterize many contemporary societies' and the 'defensive and territorial orientation towards one's "own place" ' (Sparks 2001a: 206; Loader and Sparks 2002). The result is a curious defensive anxiety and 'intolerance of *any* incursion on their cultivated sense of peace and order' (Sparks 2001a: 206; emphasis as original). In addition, Young (1999) has counselled against seeing fear of crime and the demand for harsher measures as a mere metaphor for the ontological insecurity of postmodern society. The issue is not necessarily one of political or public 'irrationality' about real crime rates, real risks, and perceived ones. The issue is rather one of promise and demand:

> In some instances they have risen, in many cases they are exaggerated, but what is important is that the base line of evaluation has increased as has the demand for a higher quality of life. The point is that we are increasing our level of social scrutiny and demand. Furthermore, the very existence of a debate about risk, of which the writers on risk are part, is *in itself* one of the gains of late modernity. It is not so much that modernity has failed to keep its promise to provide a risk-free society as that late modernity has *taken seriously* this promise, has demanded more and realized the greater difficulty of its accomplishment.
>
> (Young 1999: 78; emphases as original)

Summary

Risk plays a central but differential role in the contemporary penal policy characterized by Garland as 'punitive sovereignty', deployed in adaptive strategies of community security on the one hand, and in expressive, punitive penality on the other. Whilst the crime control techniques differ, dispersed and localized in communities in adaptive strategies and highly politicized, legislatively driven, and 'popularized' in sovereign strategies, the underpinning rationale is the problematic of crime control in advanced liberal society. This has been expressed as the 'meta-dilemma' of third way governance: the delicate balance of social inclusion for the 'dangerous classes' without alienating the ontologically insecure, fearful and 'fretful' middle class. This policy objective is set against an increased 'institutionalized crime awareness' and increased demands for security and risk avoidance. The result is a paradoxical awareness of risk coupled with a desire to be free of it.

This paradox is increasingly played out in the crime arena. Everyday life is characterized by 'precariousness and insecurity' (Garland 2001), consequently demands that the state meet its obligations to risk manage are increasingly strident and impatient. In a world in which we must 'take care' and pay the economic and emotional costs of doing so, we are unforgiving of those who perpetuate the risks, and of those professionals who fail to protect us against them. For Garland the salient result has been the institutionalization of a 'collective conscious of crime' or what he terms the 'crime complex of late modernity' (Garland 2001). Constant awareness of crime potential, the constant spectre of victimization, and the constant need to self-care against crime risks produces citizens not only pragmatically adaptive to the daily reality of crime risks, but also unsympathetic to the needs of the offender. Sympathy is replaced by condemnation, and consequently reintegration is seen as both unrealistic and less morally desirable (Garland 2000: 368). In the face of economic and emotional costs, fear and irritation, distinctions between minor and violent predatory crime slides: all crime, any crime is intolerable.

These crime control trends can be characterized as a broader reaction to the pluralism and diversity of postmodern society (Rose 2000). In particular, a retreat through penal measures to fixed certainties: fixing personal identities through risk profiling (Leonard 1997); segregating and fixing in place sections of the population, for example the 'disorderly', the 'under-class' (Simon 1993, 1997, 1998); constructing boundaries through technologies of surveillance and demarcation (Lianos with Douglas 2000; Lyon 2001); and the reduction of threat to civil society from the 'disorderly' by restricting their access to it (Campbell 1993).

Further reading

Feeley, M. and Simon, J. (1992) The new penology: notes on the emerging strategy for corrections, *Criminology*, 30(4): 449–74.

Garland, D. (2001) *The Culture of Crime Control: Crime and Social Order in Contemporary Society*. Oxford: Oxford University Press.

Stenson, K. and Sullivan, R.R. (eds) (2001)*Crime, Risk and Justice: The Politics of Crime Control in Liberal Democracies*. Cullompton, Devon: Willan.

chapter three

Approaches to risk and risk assessment tools

Introduction: approaches to risk and the 'two cultures'

The 'risk business' has been characterized by 'two cultures' (Jasanoff 1993) or two conceptual 'ideal types' (Otway and Thomas 1982), although it is claimed that they are often 'blurred in practice' (Bradbury 1989: 381). These will be referred to as: *artefact risk* and *constructivist or socially constructed risk*. Lupton (1999a) has described this as 'differing logics of risk', deployed not only between experts and 'lay publics' but also between workers and managers in risk-focused agencies (Kemshall 2000).

The relationship between how risk is conceptualized (as artefact or constructivist), and subsequent assessment methods and policies has been much explored (Douglas 1986; Bradbury 1989; Hood et al. 1992; Wynne 1992, 1996; Hood and Jones 1996). Differing conceptual approaches to risk are reflected in the choice and construction of risk assessment tools (Wynne 1992; Hood et al. 1996) and how risk problems are framed and subsequently resolved (Jones 1996; Pratt 1997; Brown 2000).

This chapter will explore these differing conceptualizations of risk and how they are reflected in criminal justice policies and penal strategies, particularly the construction and use of risk assessment tools. As Brown (2000) argues, this enables us to stop 'thinking of risk as a phenomenon that has been similarly conceptualised but differently measured', to something that varies 'in its conceptualisation' (Brown 2000: 95). Thus 'risk' can be used as a 'justificatory proposition' for a number of differing and at times contradictory penal strategies as diverse as cognitive behavioural therapy, preventive sentencing, and selective incapacitation for the most dangerous. Such an approach challenges the traditional, linear approach to risk assessment development in criminal justice presented by commentators such as Bonta (1996) who pose that 'first generation' practitioner intuition has been replaced by second and third generation statistical tools. As Brown contends, such histories are based upon a fundamental misconception: that risk is thought of similarly but measured differently. However, disputes about tool use between frontline workers, policy makers and tool producers are not about the validity or refinement of the tool, they are about the nature of risk and its very measurability (Kemshall 1998, 2000). For probation officers, risk is a 'moveable feast' subject to numerous 'it depends', highly contextualized and highly contingent upon policy demands, legislation and individual case circumstances (Kemshall 1998). In essence, they deploy a *constructivist* conceptualization of risk. Policy makers and tool producers tend to use an *artefact* notion of risk, framing risk within a technical and statistical discourse in which contingency is replaced by probability. The next section will examine some of the key features of these differing approaches to risk, and to its assessment and management.

Artefact risk

In the artefact approach risk is framed as objectively knowable and amenable to probabilistic calculation (Horlick-Jones 1998), for example as a 'physically given attribute of hazardous technologies' (Bradbury 1989: 381). This is epitomized by the early-twentieth-century scientific and engineering approach to risk and the safe management of emerging technological risks such as those within the nuclear industry (discussed in Chapter 1 of this volume; see also Ansell and Wharton 1992). This notion of risk 'has deep roots in the history of science' (Horlick-Jones 1998: 84). It is embedded in empiricism, scientific canons of proof, probabilistic thinking, and a realist epistemology to the study of risk. (Epistemology is defined as the system of rules and values through which researchers explore and know the natural and social world.) Risk is usually dealt with through step-by-step flowchart-style decision making designed for 'repetitive situations' in which ambiguity and uncertainty are reduced to procedural steps (Kemshall et al. 1997) and judgement is replaced by a system approach to decision making. Mathematical and statistical models of prediction (of varying degrees of sophistication) have developed throughout the nineteenth and twentieth centuries extending from the engineering and scientific realms into the social and penal arenas. Technologies of risk assessment are well developed in the commercial and insurance sectors with the market providing a key incentive for the development of reliable procedures for risk measurement and management (Rowe 1977) although the sector is far from infallible on risk assessment.

Artefact risk and the penal realm

In the penal realm this conceptualization of risk is epitomized by the pursuit of statistically valid and predictively useful risk factors for recidivism and for parole violation. This approach is epitomized by the work of Hart (1923) and Burgess (1928, 1929, 1936) in which attempts were made to statistically validate a correlation between particular individual risk factors, recidivism and parole violation. The principles utilized by Burgess still form the core of present-day actuarial parole prediction (Copas et al. 1996). In essence, from the study of a large number of cases certain factors that statistically relate to the violation or success of parole are selected. Burgess selected some 22 factors initially, after which a further examination of cases takes place to establish the sum probabilities for success or failure in each case. An experience table is then constructed and applied to both those cases with a low expectancy of violation and a high expectancy of violation (Burgess 1936: 228–9). In this way the indicators of parole success or failure can be retrospectively validated and applied in terms of statistical probabilities. Commercial insurance utilizes a similar technique.

Typologies of dangerousness, common in the late nineteenth and early twentieth centuries, are also exemplars of this construction of risk. Categorizations and typologies in the social and penal realm based upon the scientific principles of Darwin (1859) were much pursued, for example through the science of eugenics and attempts to identify and categorize 'degeneracy' and 'dangerousness' (Pratt 1997). Statistical methods were used to give the eugenics movement and its notion of inherited criminality and a 'criminal class' scientific respectability (Pratt 1997: 42). In psychiatry 'moral insanity' was reframed in the late nineteenth century as 'congenital deficiency' and habitual criminals were increasingly subjected to the discourse and categorizations of psychiatry (Pratt 1997). This separateness through categorization was extended through what Pratt has described as criminal anthropology in which the degeneracy of habitual criminals justified their exclusion and their classification as irredeemable.

These disciplines contributed to the classification of criminals as well as crimes, and by the early twentieth century a notion of graduated risk rather than either/or classifications such as habitual and non-habitual were devised. Binary classifications were replaced by individual assessments of degree, of both risk and responsibility. Risk was still conceptualized as a quality of the individual, amenable to measurement of extent and degree through identifiable risk factors. The welfarism of the twentieth century reinforced this individualized assessment of risk, both of those 'at risk' and those presenting a risk. By the early twentieth century 'knowability' was seen as the key to 'governability'. While crime could be recorded and recidivism tracked, individual criminals, particularly the problematic 'habituals' could not necessarily be known. Proportionate punishment, even the cumulative and repetitive use of prison sentencing had also failed to stem the tide of recidivism. What was now required was 'a programme of government that would allow the state to intervene as appropriate to the risk that a particular criminal posed, rather than simply match punishment to crimes' (Pratt 1997: 45).

Gravity was replaced by risk, and grave crimes by risky offenders. Sentencing now needed to be matched to 'the risk of a particular offender and his or her potential for endangering others', an individualization of punishment that required the categorization, classification, assessment, and diagnosis of individual offenders (Pratt 1997: 47; see also Garland 1985; Rose 2000; Garland 2001). While neat periodization and sharp discontinuities are not necessarily evident in the history of penality (O'Malley 2000; Garland 2001), the late nineteenth and early twentieth centuries have been identified as a crucial era in the individualization process of penality. O'Malley (2000) has identified nineteenth-century liberal government's preoccupation with the prevention of social danger and preventive governance as significant forerunners in this process, and in particular the regulation of problematic classes through disciplinary technologies of risk management (for example the factory, the prison, the school and the asylum). These institutional settings were also central to the formation, implementation and dissemination of the positivistic human sciences, so crucial to the individualized management of dangerous offenders in the twentieth century: criminology and prisons, psychiatry and asylums, a socializing and instrumental educationalism in schools. Not only did such sciences make the categorization, classification and assessment of offenders easier, but also they contributed to the reconstitution of individual responsibility. While not a new concept, the early twentieth century saw criminal responsibility reframed as a relative standard, and hence individual responsibility for certain acts could be impaired (for example by 'mental retardation', 'feeble-mindedness': Pratt 1997 following Crackanthorpe 1902). Differential responsibility of itself could justify differing sanctions for the same crime, but could also be importantly linked to capacity for change and moral rehabilitation. Penal sanctions aimed to achieve future honesty, but where this could not be achieved the public should be protected from harm – hence preventive and indeterminate sentencing for selected offenders could be justified. The key issue was how to identify those who could be redeemed and those who were too dangerous.

This was also the era of positivistic science and calculability, exemplified in almost every area of life. Actuarial tables, in use for commercial purposes from the late 1700s (Rowe 1977), were based upon statistical calculations of frequency and distribution, but in essence were concerned with the regular and predictable (for example death). Positivistic science manifested itself in a view of the material and social world as amenable to investigation and explanation. A world made calculable through 'the universal science of measurement and order' (Foucault 1989: 56), in which 'there are no mysterious, incalculable forces that come into play' and in which all things can be mastered by calculation (Weber 1949: 139). A calculable individual is of course a predictable individual, and a knowable individual is one that can potentially be disaggregated from a class, for example the dangerous individual from the dangerous class.

Paradoxically, for all their ability to individuate, classify and segregate, the positivistic human sciences had (and still have) 'poor predictive power' and the 'psy' disciplines have been described as the least actuarial (O'Malley 2000: 22, 24). This has resulted in an interesting tension between the scientific *episteme* and risk prediction. While deviations from the norm can be identified they cannot necessarily be predicted. 'Abnormality' and 'deviance' can be diagnosed, that is explained and made known once they have occurred, but their predictability has remained elusive (Grubin and Wingate 1996). The more infrequent a behaviour the less predictable it is, and the most concerning of behaviours are often the most unpredictable. Conversely, commercial insurance has concerned itself with the most likely of events: death. Social insurance has followed a similar format with attention to regular and relatively frequent acts and events, such as unemployment and occupational accidents (Simon 1987), with less frequent risks often remaining in the domain of the 'psy' disciplines and their clinical (that is individual) techniques.

The twentieth century and the era of the welfare state in particular saw a tension between the actuarial approach to social problems and economic life for social policy ends (Daston 1988; O'Malley 2000: 23), and an individualization of risk through clinically based disciplines such as psychiatry.

While science may have plotted the various pathologies and social problems, their amelioration was delivered to and on the individual through largely individualizing disciplines (O'Malley 2000; Garland 2001).

The development and demise of the parole predictor are a good example of this tension with attempts to replace anecdotal, case-based judgement with a statistically validated predictor. The latter is an example of large-scale actuarialism, based upon a large sample of male prisoners and the statistical validation of predictors for 'success' or 'failure' on parole (Burgess 1936; Nuttall et al. 1977), and has been pursued in a number of countries including the USA (Ohlin 1951), Australia (Challinger 1974) and Canada (Nuffield 1982) as well as the UK. However, parole boards are tasked with making individualized decisions and despite the risk-based test introduced by Carlisle (1988), moving away from highly individualized decision-making has proved problematic (Glaser 1975; Polvi and Pease 1991; Weatheritt 2002). Hood and Shute (2000a) have found that contrary to the expectations of the Carlisle Committee the changes in parole introduced by the Criminal Justice Act (CJA) 1991 have resulted in a 'more risk-averse approach than originally expected' (Hood and Shute 2000a: 4). They argue that this is due not only to Home Secretary Directions but also to parole board members' interpretation of them. Their key findings were:

- Under the new system parole had dropped by about one-third.
- About 87 per cent of parolees had conditions attached to their licences (double pre-CJA 1991).
- Parole board members often estimated the risk as higher than the actuarial risk prediction.
- Half of the prisoners in the sample had a low actuarial risk of reconviction for a serious offence in the parole period, yet only half of them were granted parole.

(Hood and Shute 2000a, 2000b)

Weatheritt (2002) has argued that these results are partly explained by the reliance of board members on external information sources such as the probation officer report, and the assumptions and judgements of others (usually based on clinical assessment). Board decision making can then be characterized as largely assumptive, consensual and clinical.

These 'second generation' static risk tools have been replaced by what Bonta (1996) has termed 'third generation' or combined tools in which social dynamic factors are combined with actuarial risk factors. (Third generation tools are discussed later in the chapter.) Dynamic factors can be understood as social, contextual and circumstantial factors pertinent to offending, such as housing and unemployment, although the legitimacy of their use as risk factors is usually supported by larger-scale meta-analyses of those factors most commonly associated with recidivism (Andrews 1995; McGuire and Priestley 1995). Such tools attempt to have the best of both worlds by utilizing meta-analytic research and large-scale actuarialism to generate risk factors within tools that 'structure' assessment, usually through the individualized clinical interviewing of practitioners such as probation officers, prison psychologists and parole officers.

Assessment and categorization have replaced prediction as the main goals of such tools, and their ability to markedly out-predict 'pure' actuarial methods is questionable (Raynor et al. 2000; McIvor et al. 2001). Thus individual offenders are made more 'knowable' (and hence more controllable) although not necessarily more predictable. It is perhaps no coincidence that it has been the most positivistic of the human sciences – psychology – that has most influenced the design of third generation tools and has been instrumental in attempting to bridge the gap between the scientific episteme of risk calculation and the clinically based assessments of mental health and social work. As Walklate (1998) has noted the pursuit of this scientific episteme of risk assessment has framed risk as an essentially forensic concept, that is as a mechanism for risk avoidance and blame attribution. For Walklate this leaves us with 'zero-risk' as the ultimate baseline, and with a pervasive view that risk is negative and undesirable. This emphasis upon risk avoidance results in a preoccupation with *managing* the impacts and distribution of crime risks, not with crime causes – hence a risk-based administrative criminology closely allied to the scientific episteme.

Constructivist risk

By the close of the twentieth century this artefact approach was increasingly challenged by a 'social' view of risk in which the contextual and social nature of risk decision-taking is emphasized. Whilst the broad term constructivist is used the paradigm actually has a number of differing constituents. Lupton (1999a: 35) has characterized these positions as variations along a continuum from 'weak' to 'strong' constructivism rooted in differing conceptualizations of risk.

In *weak constructivism* there is a limited acknowledgement of the role of subjective processes in risk perception and assessment. For example investigations into why lay publics do not act upon expert advice and evaluations of public health campaigns about 'safe sex' or 'drink driving', or why risk assessors fail to risk assess accurately or reliably (Reason 1990). Subjective processes are constructed as an 'impingement' or barrier to effective calculations of objective risk realities, something to be understood in order to be corrected (for example Slovic 1992), and objective risk is predicated as a norm. This 'weak' version of social risk is essentially materialist, and operates in a psychometric paradigm in which attention to the 'social' is merely in passing (Slovic et al. 1985). The 'prudential' and 'rational' actor is still essential to this position, and research tends to focus on the reasons why prudence and rationality are not deployed appropriately in accordance with normative ends (Slovic et al. 1980), for example why people continue to smoke even when the risks are well known and extensively communicated.

Strong constructivism on the other hand poses that 'Risk is always a social product' (Thompson and Wildavsky 1982: 148) of which cultural theory is the main exponent (Douglas 1992). Its emphasis has been on how risks are selected and legitimized for public attention, and on how group membership and risk perception are intrinsically linked. This approach to risk contends that risk is always mediated by the interaction between action and cultural system. Lupton (1999a: 26) has described this as functional structuralism 'interested in how social and cultural structures and systems serve to maintain social order and the status quo'. However, this does not mean that cultural theory ignores disputes; on the contrary:

> Cultural theory can be seen . . . as an account of how particular com-
> munities think about risk . . . and the kinds of controversies and
> disputes that arise within and between them about risk-laden topics
> such as nuclear safety, genetic engineering and crime and punishment.
> (Sparks 2001b: 163)

Social constructivism has similar concerns to cultural theory, and takes as its site of investigation the plurality of risk meanings and the contested nature of risk (Rayner 1992). Rayner for example has examined the differing perceptions and responses to radiation hazards amongst occupational groups in a hospital, and demonstrates how such perceptions are mediated by social processes (for example membership of an occupational group), personal experiences of organizational life (for example trust in the regula-tory system) and the deployment of 'non-expert' knowledge when expert knowledge has fallen into disrepute (Rayner 1986). Competing rationalities on risk are the focus of such research, and in particular how some rationalities gain credibility, acceptance and legitimacy while others do not. Wynne (1982) in a detailed analysis of the Windscale nuclear inquiry found that some discourses of risk were legitimized and held influence while others were easily dismissed. In this debate legitimacy and therefore credibility stemmed from a risk discourse located in a scientific rationality of risk assessment, cost–benefit calculations and an almost unassailable belief that nuclear power was the only possible replacement for diminishing fuel resources. Framings of risk outside this discourse were literally dismissed as ill-informed fringe protests. In the post-Chernobyl era there has been considerable reframing, and the nuclear industry is now seen as highly fallible with risk management procedures likely to fail if left without external regulation (Beck 1992a) and alternative fuel sources are seen as worthy of pursuit. In this approach to risk, risk is always 'historically, socially and politically contingent' (Irwin and Wynne 1996; Wynne 1996).

Summary

The 'risk business' is characterized by two paradigms, albeit 'ideal types' somewhat blurred in their deployment. The risk literature frames them as 'artefact' and 'constructivist' risk (Jasanoff 1993). Within the constructivist approach there are a number of constituents ranged on a continuum from weak to strong constructivism with differing levels of emphasis upon the extent to which risk is *socially constructed*. These differing conceptualizations of risk have implications for how risk is assessed and managed. The next section will consider these epistemologies (systems of knowledge) of risk and their deployment in criminology and crime risk management.

Epistemologies of risk and risk management

Artefact risk and homeostatic risk management

The artefact conceptualization of risk and its realist epistemology has resulted in *homeostatic* risk management (Hood et al. 1992; Hood 1996; Hood and Jones 1996) characterized by prescriptive rules, rigorous system monitoring for compliance to pre-specified criteria, technical control and corrective action, and 'fail-safe' procedures in the event that something goes wrong. There is a presumption for equilibrium in systems with them returning to pre-set norms (Dunsire 1990). Blumstein et al. (1977) have argued for a similar system of stasis and equilibrium in penality, emphasizing the stability of punishment over time 'so that a roughly constant proportion of the population is always undergoing punishment' (Blumstein et al. 1977: 317).

Engineering has a long history of such risk management (Ansell and Wharton 1992), as does the technical approach to 'waste' management in the nuclear industry (Bradbury 1989). Homeostatic risk management presumes that risk is a quantifiable phenomenon and is reducible to step-by-step decision-making, and error is seen as a breakdown of such procedures, human fallibility or irrational decision-making against expert advice (Fischoff et al. 1978; Slovic 1987; Reason 1990). Homeostatic risk systems are usually accompanied by investigative and correctional approaches to risk failures, and seek to regulate the activities of workers (and indeed public) away from risky choices or actions. Information giving, training and socialization are seen as key ingredients of such correctionalism in order to facilitate the prudent, rational worker or the prudent, rational citizen to better (less risky) choices. The HIV/AIDS awareness campaigns of the 1980s urging 'safe sex' and later campaigns to change the injecting habits of intravenous drug users are two examples in the social policy arena. In engineering the tireless pursuit of 'prudent man' on the North Sea oilrigs or the emphasis upon fail-safe procedures in the nuclear industry pre-Chernobyl are other examples.

While the homeostatic and corrective approach to risk has predominance in engineering, it has been transferred to both the social and penal policy realms. In the social policy arena the modernist welfare agenda was based upon the 'soft policing' of deviant groups in line with pre-specified normative ends (Donzelot 1980; Garland 2001). As the century progressed public policy became increasingly preoccupied with lay perceptions of risk and why these were often at odds with official government information. This crystallized around public disquiet and dissent around nuclear risks, public perceptions of other environmental hazards such as toxic waste, and risks emanating from science and technology such as genetically modified foods. Research attempted to establish the key influences on lay perceptions, for example the role of 'dread' and the impact of large-scale involuntary catastrophic disasters in heightening risk perception (Slovic et al. 1980). The work was given added impetus by the 1980s 'AIDS epidemic' and subsequent public health campaigns aimed at correcting risky behaviours followed by increased attention to health promotion in health policy (Department of Health 1992) and the production of what Petersen (1977) has called the 'at-risk self' in need of self-care and self-regulation. This health promotion construction of risk has been particularly influential in framing the risk assessor as a rational choice actor capable of making the correct choice if only the right information is communicated and is properly received (Petersen and Lupton 1996; Lupton 1999a). As Lupton puts it:

> This model relies upon an understanding of the human actor in which there is a linear relationship between knowledge of a risk, developing the attitude that one is at risk and adopting a practice to prevent the risk happening to oneself.
>
> (Lupton 1999a: 21)

Homeostatic risk management and criminology

This model has also been influential in criminology and penal policy and has informed what Young (1986) has called 'administrative criminology'. This work was progressed under New Right government policies throughout the 1980s and mirrors closely similar developments in social and health policy in this era (see Kemshall 2002a for a full discussion). While it was not particularly novel to see offenders as capable of choice (Walklate 1998), the emphasis upon personal responsibility and individual decision making reflected a policy era in which the 'social' as either a causal or explanatory factor was largely eschewed (Rose 1996b). Crime management in this vein has focused on two areas: individual choice and the crime opportunity.

This has framed the emphasis upon the 'situational management' of choices and opportunities rather than upon the causes of crime (Young

1992, 1994) particularly in crime prevention policies. In direct work with offenders the individual has been reconstituted within an economic discourse of choice, an individual making decisions about crime on the grounds of cost–benefit, literally weighing risks against rewards, and treating arrest and punishment as an 'occupational hazard'. The desistance studies (for example Cornish and Clarke 1986) particularly focused on the ingredients of this decision making, attempting to establish what it takes to make an offender stop and in what circumstances costs would outweigh benefits. In crime prevention this translated into policies that increased the chances of getting caught through more intensive surveillance (such as CCTV), making properties more difficult to burglarize or cars more difficult to access – hence raising the cost and diminishing the benefit but also reducing crime opportunities. Whether this reduces crime or merely displaces it to less well protected areas is a matter of some debate, literally displacing risk from 'fortress cities' (Hughes 1998) (this will be discussed further in Chapter 6).

Rational choice theory and the administrative criminology within which it is embedded also fuelled the development of a correctional curriculum in direct interventions with offenders. Introduced under the guise of 'What Works' it reflected disenchantment with the social causes of crime and the failure of what Young (1986) has called the 'social democratic positivism' of the welfare state. Cast within an economic framing of criminal justice (Garland 2001) this 'new rehabilitationism' (Rotman 1990) is not a 'general all-purpose prescription' but is specifically 'targeted towards those individuals most likely to make cost-effective use of this expensive service' (Garland 2001: 176). Central to determining such cost-effectiveness is risk level and the 1990s in particular saw the development of numerous risk assessment tools to determine both risk level and eligibility for cognitive-behavioural interventions (this is discussed in more detail in Chapter 4). This 'risk principle' (McGuire 1995; Home Office and Association of Chief Officers of Probation (ACOP) 1997) is essential to appropriate targeting and effective rationing. It is predicated upon an artefact notion of risk and a normative framing in which risk prediction is presented as an issue of accurate definition and measurement.

The *practice of risk* in criminal justice agencies has also been governed by a homeostatic approach in which prescriptive tools and procedures have steadily replaced professional judgement and discretion (Kemshall et al. 1997; Kemshall 2000). The 1980s and 1990s in particular saw a growing scepticism in the professionalism and expertise of criminal justice personnel and a lack of trust that frontline workers could manage risk appropriately if left to their own devices (for example the 1995 thematic inspection of probation's work with dangerous offenders: Her Majesty's Inspectorate of Probation (HMIP) 1995), coupled with a central government desire for risk aversion in the face of mounting risk management failures (for example

Dunblane – shootings by Thomas Hamilton at Dunblane Primary School on 13 March 1996 when he shot dead sixteen children and one teacher before turning the gun on himself). Clinically based, professional judgement was challenged (if not necessarily wholly replaced) by the importation (usually from across the Atlantic) of decision tools. Such tools could either replace the biased and inconsistent clinical judgements of workers (for example anecdotal parole decisions with the parole predictor: Glaser 1955, 1962, 1975; Copas et al. 1996), or merely structure them towards managerially desired ends (for example the use of risk/need assessment tools in probation: Kemshall 1998). Such tools are introduced in order to replace the vagaries of individualized decision making with formalized tools that can be subject to quality assurance, regulation and audit (Clarke et al. 1994; Kemshall et al. 1997; Parton et al. 1997).

The homeostatic artefact discourse has framed risk as a prescriptive technical task, a matter of appropriate technical competence and not a matter of professional judgement or experiential knowledge (Kemshall 2000). In this climate workers are trained in the technique of the risk tool, and blame is a key tactic in ensuring integrity of use. Lack of consensus and compliance on risk is presented as an issue of blame and enforcement, training and resocialization, for both workers and offenders.

The limits of homeostasis as a risk management approach

The rational choice risk assessor, whether victim, offender or worker, has underpinned the homeostatic approach to risk assessment and subsequent management processes. However, this construct of risk has been challenged by research framed within a constructivist epistemology in which the contingent and contextual nature of risk is emphasized, and the differing perspectives on risk is itself the site of investigation. This work found expression in social science investigations of lay perceptions of environmental risks (Douglas and Wildavsky 1982), and in the 1980s with investigations of how perceptions of risk influenced health behaviours, particularly around HIV/AIDS and condom use (Lupton 1993, 1995; Hart and Boulton 1995), and then intravenous drug use (Bloor 1995). While some of the earlier work was concerned with the accuracy of lay perceptions of health risks, and the failure of lay people to act on expert advice (Robertson 2000), these corrective investigations of 'irrational risks' have been superseded by social theories of risk in which risk is understood as dynamic, negotiated and indeterminate (Adams 1995) and risk is understood as an interaction between individuals and social factors (Rhodes 1997). This work has presented limits to homeostasis and rational choice risk decision-making in the following key areas:

- Choice is not merely individual and risk perceptions and attendant decisions are influenced by group membership and social factors.

Rationality is thus not only plural but also 'situated', and normative rationality may be reasonably circumvented by situated decision-making (Rayner 1986).

- The linear model between knowledge of a risk, attitude to the risk and action to avoid the risk is an ideal-type construct of the psychometric tradition of risk research. The interaction between knowledge, risk perception and subsequent action is far more complex (Lupton 1999a) as evidenced by 'moral panics' on risk and personal choices to continue with risky behaviours in the full knowledge of the facts.
- Choice is itself bounded, particularly by the power and opportunity to do otherwise (Bloor 1995) and perception about whether the choice is desirable and legitimate (Grinyer 1995).
- Homeostatic risk management systems are costly and ineffective in practice. The emphasis upon blame and enforcement (of either workers or offenders) is ultimately self-defeating (Hood 1996). Motivation and commitment is eroded by over-regulation, workers experience 'cognitive dissonance' as they are increasingly alienated from the agency's purpose and mode of operation and offenders are stigmatized and blamed for their own 'irrational choices' and failures to comply (Kemshall 2002b).
- Homeostatic systems are characterized by 'anticipationism' (Hood 1996), that is a constant preoccupation with anticipating and avoiding every eventuality of risk. This tends to result in front-loaded and expensive risk assessment procedures and constant monitoring for compliance. Procedures and policies proliferate on the basis of 'just in case' and organizational responses to risk tend towards the defensive. Practice is overloaded with systems, leaving less time for contact work. Workers then circumvent them in order to get the job done, exposing themselves and their agencies to blame should things go wrong. Expert fail-safe systems are mediated by practice necessity and the 'occupational survival' of workers (Satayamurti 1981; Wynne 1988, 1989, 1996).

In recent crime management developments routine activity theory has recast the rational calculative criminal as an adaptive one and the cost–benefit equation as constantly changing (Ekblom 1997). As Ekblom (2001: 38) puts it: 'crime is always changing' and 'offenders adapt to countermeasures'. Thus crime prevention has a built-in obsolescence. Services, systems and products are constantly open to misuse and offenders 'misbehave in new environments as they emerge' and 'what was once secure against crime is now vulnerable' as criminals adapt and circumstances change (Ekblom 2001: 38). For Ekblom the only way to combat this constant adaptation is through 'crime futures', a constant anticipationism in which planning against crime and designing out opportunities is central. In essence we are all urged to 'think thief' and engage in crime proofing. This is reflected in the government's crime reduction policy 'Turning the Corner' (see www.foresight.gov.uk) in which design against crime is emphasized. This requires risk and impact assessment to be routinely embedded into organizational and personal life, around policies, procedures, designs and systems. It also requires a highly reliable predictive method and one that can predict over time lines in excess of 20 years. Ekblom offers an empirically grounded conceptual framework developed from Cohen and Felson's (1979) 'Routine Activities Theory' in which 11 generic variables are used to plot the possible interactions between offender, situations and potential crime opportunities (see Ekblom 1997, 1999, 2000, 2001 for further details). The long-term efficacy of such an approach remains to be seen. Initially promoted as risk aware and on the grounds of sound anticipationist risk management such approaches are themselves high-risk strategies. High risk because even minor flaws in the calculative models used to anticipate will result in failed crime prevention and will be revealed only with the benefit of hindsight. Such an approach also carries the risk that such a risk-infused approach to almost every walk of life will heighten public awareness of risk, awaken anxieties that are not necessarily reduced, and consequently lower public tolerance of crime, threat and insecurity (Garland 2001).

Social risk and negotiated risk management

Social action theories have reconceptualized risk by framing it as a product of 'social dynamics of particular relationships or situations' (Rhodes 1997: 216). Risk is conceptualized as a negotiated concept and product of social interaction, context specific and bounded by group norms and values (Douglas 1986). This interactive approach recognizes that risk decisions are negotiated and subject to both constraint and opportunity (Bloor 1995). In a study of risky behaviours related to HIV transmission Bloor (1995) investigated the risk decision-making of male prostitutes and intravenous drug users and found that 'habituation' and 'routinization' underpinned risk decisions and that sudden change of such routinized risk-taking was rarely contemplated in the closed world of male prostitutes and their clients. Volition and choice were bounded by group norms and contingent knowledge about both the likelihood of risk (HIV contraction), weighed against knowledge of customer likes and dislikes: condom use tended to discourage customers and lowered earnings. The immediate risk of no money outweighed the future possible risk of HIV. Needle sharing was also an habituated activity, important in group bonding and in offering trust. The implications of such a conceptualization of risk is that power and group processes have a key role in both the exercise of choice and the perception of opportunity, and that risk is a highly interactive and negotiated concept.

Negotiated risk management and criminology

In criminology this social approach to risk is epitomized by work on risk particularly around fear and victimization, and 'social constructivist approaches to fear of crime' in which the 'knowledges, discourses and experiences used by people to construct their notions of risk and fear' are the site of investigation (Lupton 2000: 23). Traditional binary conceptualizations such as 'real' and 'imaginary' fears, 'lay' and 'expert' perceptions of risk are discounted in favour of attention to how such fears and risks are the products of particular, and at times conflicting discourses and 'cultural understanding'. Lupton's studies of fear of crime (set within a paradigm of strong constructivism) for example locate the different and at times paradoxical fears of crime presented by respondents within the broader 'normalization of crime' and subjective responsibility for crime risk avoidance of late modernity (Lupton 2000; see also Lupton 1999b; Lupton and Tulloch 1999; Garland 2001). Crime was seen as frequent and therefore highly likely to happen 'someday', but also random in terms of who, where and when it might strike. This pervasive risk, particularly of property crime, was paralleled by increased anxiety about the randomness of personal assaults and higher perceptions of vulnerability particularly for women in public spaces. This produced a paradoxical response to crime: a fatalism about pervasive property crime, a fact of late modern life against which one could insure; and an increased personal calculativeness about personal violence and public spaces. Respondents had a dual approach to crime, fatalism around the likelihood of crime, combined with caution and increased responsibility for self-protection against threats to the person.

This more recent attention to the relationship between discourse and practice is important for reframing risk in criminology (Sparks 2000). As Lupton (1999a: 15) puts it, 'discourses delimit and make possible what can be said and done about phenomena such as risk' in effect an organizing frame within which some risks gain both legitimacy and saliency. Within this epistemological framing of risk the focus is not on individual risk management, but on how some risks are chosen for attention while others are not. In essence, this involves attention to the meaning and symbolic significance of risk classifications and the penal subject they constitute, and the political rationalities and strategies that underpin them (Sparks 2001b).

Recent commentators have also explored how differing conceptions of risk can be held and deployed by differing players within the criminal justice system at the same time. Brown (2000) for example has contrasted the differing concepts of risk held by penal policy makers and the judiciary. He notes that policy makers hold a *fluid* concept of risk which frames risk as a changeable but measurable entity, particularly through risk profiles and factors. Risk can go up or down, but it is essentially knowable through formalized assessment tools ranging from statistically based predictive tools to structured interviewing schedules. Brown's fluid risk is coterminous with the artefact risk of the broader risk literature. Brown poses that such a conceptualization of risk is at odds with the *categorical* risk held by the judiciary. Categorical risk is defined by a combination of legal and political processes and definitions. For example the framing of serious risk and danger through offence type independent of the behaviour and character of the offender, expressed by mandatory 'three strikes and you're out' sentencing, bifurcated sentencing in the UK following the Criminal Justice Act 1991, and selective incapacitation. Within this approach, judicial commonsense judgements of risk to the public have been used to justify sentencing to 'protect the public' and are little influenced by actuarial risk assessments. This can produce some high-risk responses to presenting offences of apparently low risk, either on the grounds of 'likely risk of serious harm to the public' (Criminal Justice Act 1991, section 2(2)(b)) or when the 'third strike' is of significantly less risk than the preceding two offences.

Fluid and categorical risk differ both epistemologically and ontologically. Brown (2000) locates fluid risk in scientific and causal notions of risk and within an essentially positivistic epistemology. Categorical risk is located in an essentialist approach to risk, seeing risk as 'intellectually' and 'intuitively' knowable independent of assessment methods, and located within a constructivist epistemology in which both political and judicial processes play a significant role. Fluid risk exhibits a rationalist ontology in which the individual is literally 'made up' by the statistical aggregates of actuarialism (Hacking 1986) and the insights of clinical judgement. (Ontology is concerned with the nature and existence of reality, and in this context the nature of the natural and social world, for example how the social world and the individual within it are conceptualized.) Categorical risk exhibits an essentialist ontology in which basic human qualities are imputed, for example evil, and are routinely deployed as part of common-sense knowledge about offenders. The British judiciary for example see their freedom to deploy such common-sense in sentencing as essential. The legitimacy of this common-sense knowledge is not to be found in science, but in the 'social and institutional order from which it emerges' (Brown 2000: 103). Pratt (1997) for example examines how this commonsense knowledge has been deployed in the development of policy on dangerousness from the nineteenth century. Essential to this legitimacy are conceptions of moral worthiness and belonging, and consequently definitions of those offenders who are 'beyond the pale' or demonized as 'monsters in our midst' (Simon 1998).

Summary

Differing epistemologies of risk can be discerned in criminological theorizing and in subsequent constructions of offenders, victims, criminal acts and crime control responses. The positivistic episteme of artefact risk is embedded in rational choice theory and administrative criminology, and in direct work with offenders in an increasing correctional curriculum of interventions. Social constructions of risk have been particularly influential around victimization, fear of crime, and crime control, and provide a mechanism for exploring the discursive power of risk and risk conflicts.

There is potential for social theories of risk to chart how risks gain legitimacy and saliency, and more importantly to facilitate reflective dialogue between differing perceptions of risk (Lupton 1999b, 2000; Lupton and Tulloch 1999). Epistemological analysis of risk also enables a consideration of risk tools as examples of *risk conceptualization* rather than as mere methodological refinement (Brown 2000). It is to risk tools that the final section of this chapter now turns.

Risk assessment tools

The history of risk tools has been characterized as an attempt to 'tame chance' and reduce uncertainty through the use of formalized methods of assessment and calculation (Hacking 1987, 1990; Reddy 1996). Bonta (1996) for example has presented this history as a 'generational' development towards ever more accurate tools in which intuitive judgement has gradually been replaced by formalized tools generated by scientific knowledge. He contends that differentiating offenders has a long history and is not only crucial 'to rehabilitation but essential for good correctional practices' (Bonta 1996: 18). He defines first generation tools as 'subjective assessment, professional judgement, intuition and gut-feelings' and second generation tools as systematic and empirically grounded (Bonta 1996: 19). In essence, a distinction between the clinical assessment of professionals, and the actuarial assessment of statistically based formal tools. The clinical method is essentially a diagnostic technique with roots in mental health and psychiatry (Monahan 1981), individualistic and most often associated with social casework types of treatment. The method has been significantly discredited on the grounds of bias and high error rates by numerous studies (see Kemshall 1996 for a review), although it still continues to be used as professional judgement by assessors in criminal justice (Kemshall 1998) and as common sense by sentencers. More recent tools have attempted to structure clinical assessments to enhance explanations of behaviour, assessments of motivation, and likely response to treatability.

Actuarial tools

Actuarial risk assessment has its roots in the insurance industry and is based upon statistical calculations of probability. This type of risk prediction is based upon predicting an individual's likely behaviour from the behaviour of others in similar circumstances, or predicting risk on the basis of an individual's similarity to others who have proved to be risky in the past. Parole predictors were the first real attempt to provide such empirically grounded and statistically valid tools (Burgess 1928) and the twentieth century saw various prediction tables for parole (Gottfredson and Gottfredson 1985, 1993; Copas et al. 1996). The emphasis upon static historical factors has been seen as the key limitation of such tools. While they differentiate between high and low risk of recidivism or parole violation, they do not indicate areas for potential change, guide treatment plans or assist in the measurement of change (Bonta 1996). They also fail to adequately assist criminal justice personnel tasked with making individual decisions as they fail to disaggregate the individual from the group. While more accurate than clinical assessment (Quinsey et al. 1998), the actuarial approach does have its difficulties, most notably:

- statistical fallacy
- the limits of meta-analysis
- low base rates.

Statistical fallacy

Actuarial risk assessment is based upon a comparison of the similarities of an individual's profile to the aggregated knowledge of past events. However, this methodology has been challenged, not least by the 'statistical fallacy' (Dingwall 1989) in which the transfer of generalized information from a population to an individual is seen as problematic. In reviewing a number of risk prediction studies, Grubin and Wingate (1996: 353) identified that empirical evidence from one population does not necessarily translate to another, and that most prediction scores cluster at around the 40 per cent mark (the Offender Group Reconviction Score has claimed 71.4 per cent: Copas et al. 1994). This has been particularly acute in transferring group information from largely white, male prison populations to women and ethnic minorities. Grubin and Wingate (1996: 351) argue that even if 40 per cent represented 'a significant improvement over chance, [it] is not particularly helpful to those who must make decisions about release.' Such predictions merely state that 40 cases in 100 are a potential risk, and risk *in any individual case* cannot be reliably predicted. This raises the spectre of *false positives* and *false negatives*, that is cases that are falsely predicted as positive for risk, and cases falsely predicted as no risk (Moore 1996). In addition to lacking individual sensitivity, such tools cannot graduate risk along a continuum and tend to differentiate in broad categories of low–high risk, or low, medium and high risk. This again proves problematic for practitioners concerned with degrees of risk, and needing to differentiate between cases for resource allocation and case management priorities. In addition, classification profiles need to change as what is known about offender groups changes over time. Insurance companies for example revise both their actuarial tables and their premiums over time in response to changing events (for example increased likelihood of flooding due to climate change). Actuarial tools that fail to change and respond become outdated very quickly.

The limits of meta-analysis

Meta-analysis has been increasingly used to generate actuarial predictors. Meta-analysis is a statistically based technique that analyses the outcomes of a large volume of primary research studies. These outcomes are then aggregated in order to establish which factors and outcomes have the most statistical significance for risk prediction (McGuire 1997). This technique has been increasingly deployed to establish dynamic risk factors, that is those factors which change over time or that can be made to change through treatment and intervention (Quinsey et al. 1998). However, the technique has been challenged, not least because complex outcome measures of individual studies are often simplistically aggregated and categorized for ease of comparative analysis (Copas 1995; Mair 1997) and the selection of the original studies has been open to accusations of bias (Losel 1995; McIvor 1997). In addition, meta-analysis cannot demonstrate 'multi-variant effects' (Grubin and Wingate 1996), that is, it cannot identify how dynamic factors may be interacting, or distinguish between the weight of impact between particular factors. As Jones (1996) has put it, risk predictors should be independent of each other and add to the 'overall, additive risk score'. However, risk predictors are 'often highly inter-correlated', making some variables redundant and their inclusion 'inefficient and misleading' (Jones 1996: 67).

Low base rates

Low base rates also present difficulties for actuarial risk assessment (Gottfredson and Gottfredson 1993; Kemshall 2001). The base rate is the known frequency of a behaviour occurring within the population as a whole. The base rate is key to accurate predictions of behaviour in similar cases. For behaviours with low base rates such as child abuse or sexual offending, predictions made without reference to the relevant base rate can result in error. In effect, the correlation coefficient is adversely limited by low base rates. Data based on infrequently occurring behaviour has low predictive utility. This problem has been particularly acute in mental health and the prediction of violence amongst mentally disordered patients. Recent statistical developments have attempted to compensate for this problem through the Relative Operating Characteristic (ROC: Mossman 1994; Rice and Harris 1995) by enabling statistical predictions free from base rate limitations. According to Mossman's re-evaluation of some 58 data sets from 44 studies, this has substantially increased the accuracy of actuarial predictions of violence in mental health settings.

Actuarial prediction has also been seen as limited in terms of both explanation and assessment of treatability (Grubin and Wingate 1996). In essence they predict behaviours but do not explain them (Pollock et al. 1989). Bonta (1996) for example sees classifying for treatability as the defining characteristic of third generation tools.

The Offender Group Reconviction Score: an example

The Offender Group Reconviction Score (OGRS) is a key example of a statistical predictor in criminal justice, and exemplifies some of the above difficulties. OGRS reflected early concerns with recidivism following the CJA 1991, in particular with calculations of recidivism risks to inform parole decisions after the Carlisle (1988) report, and the combination of proportional and bifurcated sentencing introduced by the Act. The tool began life as a statistical predictor of parole recidivism, and calculated statistically aggregated risks of reconviction. While not originally intended for use in the individualized assessment of pre-sentence reports (J. Copas, personal communication), its potential as a risk tool for court assessments was seized upon by the Home Office (Probation Services Division 1996). While the Home Office recognized OGRS as 'no more than an aid to the judgement of probation officers in preparing PSRs' and that it 'cannot substitute for that judgement' (Probation Services Division 1996 para. 6.7), probation officers perceived its introduction somewhat differently. The National Association of Probation Officers rejected the tool on the grounds that it was an imposed replacement for professional judgement, and a poor one at that (Fletcher 1995; *The Independent* 24 July 1995: 1). Whilst the tool was resisted by the workforce on both professional and ideological grounds, there was also suspicion that the actuarial tools were being intro- duced as an evaluative tool for probation practice, literally to measure service impact upon recidivism rates (Humphrey et al. 1992), and to evaluate the impact of pre-sentence reports in the courts (Roberts and Robinson 1997). Almost immediately concerns were raised over the tool's ability to predict accurately the risk of recidivism and with the methodological difficulties in transferring an actuarially based tool to individualized assess- ment (Copas et al. 1994: 96; Lloyd et al. 1994; ACOP 1995; Vennard 1996; Mair 1997).

Third generation tools: the introduction of criminogenic need

The 1970s saw the development of a number of psychologically based classification systems aimed at classifying offenders in terms of treatment responsiveness, with the Wisconsin classification system becoming the most widely used in the USA (Baird 1981; Harris 1994). Initially such tools were inventories of need and made no claim to predict risk (Clements 1986; Bonta 1996). However, the Wisconsin system, and the Client Management Classification (CMC) system in Texas did classify offenders for supervision dependent upon score thresholds and attempted to score for both risk and need. This tool refinement is not merely a matter of knowledge or methodological developments, but can be located within broader criminal justice and penal policy trends in the USA from the late 1970s onwards. Most notably desires to provide increased cost-effective interventions, targeting and rationing of precious resources (Flynn 1978) and an increased bifurcatory approach to both the use of custody and intensive community supervision resources (Greenwood and Abrahamse 1982). Jones (1996) identifies a number of crucial factors in the recent emphasis upon risk prediction in criminal justice:

- Cost.
- Research studies on 'career criminals' and the recognition that some criminals are disproportionately responsible for crime, hence the desire to identify them accurately.
- A need for equity and appropriateness in sentencing.
- A desire to control/change behaviour: if you want to control behaviour you have to be able to predict it.
- An expansion in electronic databases and electronic statistical packages in the 1980s providing more general access to statistical prediction packages.
- A change of emphasis to selective incapacitation in the face of 'nothing works'.

(Jones 1996: 33–4)

While the purpose of tools was still couched in the language of rehabilitation, cost was also seen as relevant:

There is an acceptance of the need to deliver rehabilitation services if we are to manage risk. Furthermore, treatment services cannot be given to everyone because of the costs involved, nor can they be randomly assigned as in a lottery. Treatment must be matched to the 'needs' of the offender.

(Bonta 1996: 22)

In effect, these tools were developed for targeting, intervention rationing and change measurement. However, not all needs were to be included, but only those 'linked to criminal behaviour':

Criminogenic needs are linked to criminal behaviour. If we alter these needs, then we can change the likelihood of criminal behaviour. Thus criminogenic needs are actually risk predictors, but they are dynamic in nature rather than static . . . The importance of criminogenic needs or dynamic risk factors lies in the fact that they may serve as targets for correctional intervention. They form the treatment goals for staff who counsel offenders, run treatment programs, and in general, attempt to reduce the risk of future criminal behaviour. Thus third-generation offender assessments are inextricably linked to rehabilitation and control efforts.

(Bonta 1996: 23, 27)

Thus need was reframed by the language of risk, and only certain needs were legitimized for concern and intervention (Gendreau and Andrews 1990; Aubrey and Hough 1997). While presented within the framework of rehabilitation, the 1970s also saw the New Right reaction against rehabilitation on the grounds of cost and Martinson's (1974) 'nothing works'. Rehabilitation was reframed as 'correctional rehabilitation' under what Rotman (1990) has called a 'New Rehabilitationism' (see Chapter 4 in this volume). Such interventions were

to reduce recidivism. Criminogenic needs are the intermediary links to recidivism. For the correctional interventionist, programs that target criminogenic needs form one of the basic approaches to reducing crime.

(Bonta 1996: 29)

Tools such as the Level of Service Inventory – Revised (LSI–R) (Andrews and Bonta 1995) have played a key role in targeting offenders for correctional rehabilitation and the development of such tools has been supported by governments keen to improve intervention effectiveness and lower criminal justice costs. (The LSI–R for example was supported by the Ministry of the Solicitor General in Canada, and James Bonta held the position of Chief of Corrections Research from 1990.) Criminogenic needs have been championed for their introduction of social, dynamic factors into risk assessment; however, the assessment of such factors is not without problems. Quinsey et al. (1998) have noted that such assessments are bound to be more complex (and therefore more prone to error) due to the complex and variable nature of dynamic factors. The accurate weighting of factors and how they may interact has also proved problematic (Raynor 1997a), exacerbated by the fact that many are compiled from different sources, and prone to subjective assessor bias, and are heavily reliant upon key information being available (for example up to date and accurate information on social networks and environment). While May's (1999) study of over 7000 offenders concluded that dynamic factors could not out-predict criminal history, offenders with 'multiple problems' were more at risk. Dynamic factors such as drug misuse, accommodation and employment were found to have a 'clear link' to reconviction and social factors were particularly helpful for predicting reconviction in those cases with little criminal history (May 1999: 26, 38). However, May found that some dynamic factors such as ethnicity and being a survivor of abuse were in fact static factors and that the delineation between static and dynamic factors was not always clear. The distinction between risk prediction and prioritizing needs for supervision interventions is an important one, and subsequent evaluation demonstrated that structured risk/needs tool and statistically based actuarial predictors predicted reconviction at around or slightly above the 60 per cent mark (Raynor et al. 2000). The length and time required by workers to complete most of the tools remained a problem, and recommendations were made for shorter versions of the main tools to be developed without compromising accuracy. McIvor et al.'s (2001) study in Scotland found that OGRS and LSI–R were broadly similar in their performance as predictive tools, but that OGRS 'was better able than LSI–R to correctly differentiate between offenders with a medium and high risk of re-offending' and that effectiveness with specific groups of offenders such as sex offenders 'remained to be assessed' (McIvor et al. 2001: 1).

Offender Assessment System

The Home Office risk predictor for the Probation Service is a further example of government researchers devising a tool in response to a policy imperative to assess and categorize offenders' recidivism risk (Home Office 2001a). The tool, labelled the Offender Assessment System (OASys) is based upon social learning theory, assesses risk factors across a number of domains and combines actuarial and dynamic risk factors (Raynor 2002). A number of key strands can be discerned in the design of the tool: actuarial predictors from the Offender Group Reconviction Score for risk prediction designed by Copas et al. (1994) and used by some probation areas from the mid-1990s, dynamic risk factors derived from tools such as the LSI–R, Home Office studies on reconviction, research literature on 'what works' with offenders, and literature reviews on dangerousness (Clark 2002; Raynor 2002). The tool 'has been designed from research evidence to meet a comprehensive specification and to take into account user preferences and requirements' (Home Office 2001a: 8). The latter were taken into account through the use of surveys of user views, the establishment of a user group and extensive piloting of use (Home Office 2001a; Clark 2002). The development team also tried to take into account user views on the use of risk assessment tools (Aubrey and Hough 1997; Aye Maung and Hammond 2000) and from this seven key requirements were identified:

- Face validity, that is, it is clear to offender and assessor why items have been included.
- Clear definitions: terms are clearly defined and unambiguous to promote consistency of use across assessors.
- A simple scoring system: a binary scoring system based on yes/no answers is used.

- Evidence boxes for assessors to justify their ratings and answers.
- A self-assessment section for offenders to make their own input.
- Resource lean tool and 'time friendly' for staff.
- The tool should complement current practice.

(From *OASys*: Home Office 2001a: 9–10)

The current figures for reconviction prediction are 69.2 per cent representing a 37.4 per cent improvement over chance, although this is still less than OGRS at 71.4 per cent and 41.9 per cent respectively (Clark 2002). While the tool does have a separate risk of harm section, this has been less extensively evaluated, and is the least actuarial in construction (in part reflecting traditional base rate problems in this area). The tool's major contribution is in the area of criminogenic needs assessment and the targeting of offenders for accredited programmes of intervention in both prison and probation settings.

Summary

The risk principle and the responsivity principle are also key ingredients in third generation tools. In effect the tools attempt to categorize the risk probabilities for recidivism in order to match treatments to risk levels. Low intensity services for low risk, and more intensive treatments for high risk – a principle proven by research to be effective in the reduction of recidivism (Andrews et al. 1990; Andrews and Bonta 1994). Tools have also increasingly paid attention to 'responsivity', that is the learning style of the offender and programmes should be matched to this learning style (McGuire and Priestley 1995).

The key 'selling point' of third generation tools is their combined nature – of both static actuarial factors and dynamic social factors, and their usefulness in targeting criminogenic needs for intervention (Bonta 1996). In these tools criminogenic needs have come to function as 'risk markers' (O'Malley 2001b) in essence having a need makes you a risk. However, some risk factors are seen as more amenable to change than others, and interventions have largely crystallized around cognitive-behavioural programmes targeting behaviours and 'thinking patterns' rather than those arising from social conditions and underlying conditions of social disadvantage (Rodger 2000; Vanstone 2000; Kemshall 2002b). The emphasis is rather upon transforming 'irresponsible' and transgressive citizens into responsible and self-managing ones, in effect transformation to active and enterprising citizens (Dean 1995; Rose 2000; see also Chapter 4 in this volume). The difficulty in the direct alleviation of risk factors has resulted in what O'Malley has described as the emergence of the 'protective factor' as 'part of a process of risk sequencing that defines precise strategies for governing risk in ways that do not address the prime risk factor itself' (O'Malley 2001b: 99). He suggests that this occurs for two reasons: risk factors are by nature imprecise and difficult to target, and many risk factors are not amenable to minimization. One is risk marked but one cannot necessarily be changed. For those offenders with intractable risk markers or whose 'responsivity' cannot be matched by an intervention style harsher punitive measures are justified (Garland 2001). This can quickly become what O'Malley has called the 'criminology of the Other' which 'consigns such outsiders not to punishment per se, but to incapacitating exclusion' (O'Malley 2001b: 94).

The tools have also played a key role in regulating practice amongst criminal justice personnel and providing a mechanism for both evaluating change and evaluating the respective efficacy of differing interventions and 'treatment modalities' (McGuire and Priestley 1995; Bonta 1996). This evaluative mechanism has inscribed such tools within the managerialist agenda of New Right penal policy (Vanstone 2000) and within the quantitative methodologies of the positivistic human sciences (O'Malley 2001b). The tools have pursued both an artefact notion of risk and a normatively corrective stance to the activities of both offenders and workers.

The challenge of sexual and violent offenders

While third generation tools proved to have some usefulness in predicting general recidivism and categorizing offenders for treatment interventions (Ditchfield 1997; Raynor 1997a, 1997b) their ability to predict the harmful reoffending of sexual and violent offenders has been more limited (Raynor et al. 2000; McIvor et al. 2001). Both categories of offender have proved challenging to risk tools. Their low base rates have made the development of actuarially reliable risk tools difficult, and the heterogeneity of offending within both groups has made the generation of key dynamic and social factors difficult to generate. However, it is these categories of offenders that criminal justice personnel most need to risk assess and predict both future likelihood of offending and level of seriousness or harm. It is these cases that pose the most threat to the credibility of justice personnel and their agencies, and the most threat to the public, but it is these cases that can be the most difficult to predict (Walker 1996).

Sexual offenders and relevant tools

While a number of tools have been developed in the USA (for a full review see Kemshall 2001) and Canada, Grubin (1998) notes that only two have been extensively evaluated in Britain and the USA:

- the Rapid Risk Assessment for Sex Offence Recidivism (RRASOR: Hanson 1997)

- the Structured Anchored Clinical Judgement (SACJ: Thornton and Travers 1991). This was updated in 2000 by David Thornton into MATRIX 2000 (discussed on p. 74).

This section will concentrate on the RRASOR and SACJ due to their more extensive evaluation and use within Britain (Hanson and Thornton 2000), and in particular their use by police and probation in work with sex offenders (reviewed in more detail in Chapters 4 and 5 in this volume). The recent comparison and combination of these two tools to form the STATIC 99 and latterly the MATRIX 2000 will also be explored. (Details of all four tools can be found in Chapter 4 of Kemshall 2001.)

RRASOR

This is essentially an actuarially based tool that weights key variables in terms of their predictive utility as discerned from Hanson and Bussiere's (1998) meta-analysis, with four items finally chosen for their predictive accuracy for sex offence recidivism:

- the number of past offence convictions or charges (with additional weight given to sex offence history)
- age of the offender is less than 25
- offender is unrelated to the victim
- gender of the victim

(Summary of key indicators from Hanson 1997)

Based upon the scoring of these items the tool can distinguish between high and low risk 'with a validated distinction between an 80 per cent "low" and "middle" risk group and a 20 per cent "high" risk group' (Kemshall 2001: 25; see also Hanson 1997; Grubin 1998).

However, the tool is heavily based upon static actuarial factors and is useful as an initial screening tool but has had limited success in tracking changes in risk status over time (for example as a result of prison or community based treatment programmes) or in more sensitive grading of offenders (Kemshall 2001). These limits were addressed initially by the SACJ.

SACJ

The SACJ incorporated dynamic risk factors and operated as a 'step-wise' system rather than as a 'simple summation of weighted items' (Hanson and Thornton 2000: 121) comprising:

- Stage 1: initial actuarially based screening
- Stage 2: a more in-depth analysis of aggravating factors
- Stage 3: careful monitoring of offender performance over time to note the impact of treatment on risky dispositions.

Thus a key distinction between screening and in-depth assessment was made and incorporated into the overall process. However, administration of the whole tool proved resource hungry, particularly for police personnel in the new sex offender registration units, and stage 3 often had limited relevance to newly convicted or newly released sex offenders (Maguire et al. 2001). In effect, SACJ MIN based upon stages 1 and 2 came into use, recommended by the Association of Chief Police Officers (1999) as an initial screening tool for use in sex offender registration units. However, as the registration units referred all high risk sex offenders to the newly formed Multi-Agency Public Protection Panels (MAPPPs) it was found that the SACJ and SACJ MIN catapulted too many offenders into the high-risk category making the subsequent business of the MAPPPs unmanageable (Maguire et al. 2001). Further refinement for both predictability and manageability was required, and the RRASOR and the SACJ were subsequently compared and combined to produce the STATIC 99 (Hanson and Thornton 1999), evaluated as outperforming both although Hanson and Thornton (2000: 129) noted that the 'incremental improvement of the STATIC 99 was relatively small'.

MATRIX 2000

Since the comparison of RRASOR and SACJ and the development of STATIC 99 for use in Canada, Thornton has updated the SACJ into MATRIX 2000 and this tool has been rapidly adopted by police forces for sex offender assessment (Risk Assessment and Management of Sex Offenders Police Conference, Cheltenham, 19–20 October 2000). The tool is also gaining increased use in the Probation Service. The tool represents an important improvement on the SACJ as it provides for greater accuracy and refinement of the high-risk category thus enabling more accurate targeting of very high-risk offenders, and has been extended to a second version covering violent offenders. Whilst the tool has yet to be subject to extensive peer reviewed published evaluations, it has been validated retrospectively against a 20-year follow-up of reconvictions and found to identify high-risk offenders of whom 60 per cent were reconvicted. Similar findings have been found for a sample of violent offenders (Grubin 2000).

The tools have, however, been developed and validated against male offenders and often male prisoners, and have a limited transferability to other groups. (At the time of writing David Thornton was Head of the Prison Psychological Service in England and Wales.) As Cooke et al. (2001) have argued, risk tools must be able to predict well in the community as well as in institutions. These tools are also designed to predict recidivism and not levels of likely seriousness or harm – a key concern to criminal justice personnel tasked with decisions of release, community location, treatment interventions and victim safety.

Violent offenders and relevant tools

Traditionally violence prediction has been plagued by unacceptable levels of unreliability (Monahan 1981) and practitioners have been resistant to prediction on the grounds of both possible litigation and ethics (Walker 1996). The research literature on dangerousness and the development of assessment tools for violence prediction derive predominantly from the mental health arena and reflect psychiatric concerns to predict dangerousness accurately. Assessment tools have therefore been developed largely for use with mental health in-patients, psychiatric assessments at point of sentence, or prisoners under consideration for parole. Research populations have been largely male and institutionalized, and transferability to other offenders is acknowledged as problematic (Hagell 1998). The tools vary in their 'definitions, purposes and the quality of evaluation' (Hagell 1998: 69) and consequently the reliability and accuracy of predictions have been questioned (Menzies et al. 1994). The lack of homogeneity of violent offending means that assessment tools either are highly specific to particular groups or take a broad brush approach to a largely disparate group and this remains a significant barrier to the development of a single all-embracing assessment tool. Pure actuarial scales in particular have low transferability across settings and groups (Cooke et al. 2001). Tools have largely been generated from institutional groups, either prisons or mental hospitals, but 'the balance between individual determinants and situational determinants of violence may be different in prisons settings than in community settings' (Cooke et al. 2001: 116), and 'situational factors may be more influential in generating violence than individual factors' (Cooke 1991; Ditchfield 1991; Cooke 2000).

This section will examine those assessment tools most discussed in the research literature in the USA, Canada and the UK, and focus on those most likely to have relevance to the assessment of violent offenders by criminal justice personnel. The assessment tools will be discussed in three main groups: actuarial tools, structured clinical tools and classification trees.

Actuarial tools for violent offender assessment

The Violence Risk Assessment Guide (VRAG: Quinsey et al. 1998) is the most widely used actuarial tool for violence offence recidivism (Cooke 2000). The VRAG was developed in Canada based upon patients detained in secure hospitals between 1965 and 1980, and has been the subject of extensive evaluation (Quinsey et al. 1998). The VRAG contains 12 items:

- Revised Psychopathy Checklist score
- Elementary School Maladjustment score
- Meets DSM-IV (American Psychiatric Association 1994) criteria for any personality disorder
- Age at time of index offence

- Separation from either parent (except death) under age 16
- Failure on prior conditional release
- Nonviolent offence history score (using the Cormier-Lang scale)
- Never married
- Meets DSM-III criteria for schizophrenia
- Most serious victim injury (from the index offence)
- Alcohol abuse score
- Female victim in the index offence.

(Quinsey et al. 1998: 147)

The factors are scored using a weighting system 'that calculates the weight on the basis of how different the individual is from the base rate' (Quinsey et al. 1998: 147). Based upon a number of evaluations (Harris et al. 1993; Quinsey et al. 1995; Rice and Harris 1995) the VRAG has an adjusted ROC score between 0.73 and 0.77. The VRAG score is used to assign individuals to one of nine risk categories (or 'bins' as Quinsey et al. 1995 designate them) and individual's 'actual risk scores' do not differ 'by more than one "bin" from his obtained score' (Quinsey et al. 1995: 150). The VRAG is subject to ongoing evaluation (Quinsey et al. 1998) and has established a reputation for predictive accuracy (Cooke 2000), but as with the RRASOR for sex offenders it cannot 'provide any guidance on how that risk might be managed' (Cooke et al. 2001: 116). In order to bridge the gap to risk management structured tools have been preferred, with the HCR-20 (Historical Clinical Risk-20) for example recently adopted by the Scottish Prison Service (Cooke et al. 2001).

As with other actuarial tools the VRAG does have recognized limits. The tool does not include any assessment or prediction of the nature, severity, imminence and frequency of future violence (Cooke 2000). In addition, statements of probability recidivism over long time periods (for example five, seven or ten years) do not assist individual case managers or panels in planning risk management strategies in individual cases where issues of severity and imminence can be more important. Finally, the VRAG encourages assessors to ignore clinical and dynamic factors outside the 12 items even in the face of research that may show their relevance to violent behaviour (Hart 1999; Cooke 2000). It is difficult to see that such decisions would be defensible in the light of risk assessment failures.

Structured clinical tools for violent offender assessment

In an important comparative study of three assessment tools, the VRAG, PCL–R (Psychopathy Checklist – Revised) and HCR-20, Cooke et al. (2001: 116–17) have argued that 'risk assessment should entail more than prediction, it should entail consideration of what can be done to avert further violence in the future'. Structured assessment tools combining static actuarial factors and dynamic ones have the most efficacy in indicating treatment plans and guiding practitioner interventions, not least because they guide practitioner judgement to the 'risk factors that have received empirical support in the literature' and they engage the assessor more readily in the assessment process (Cooke et al. 2001: 13). Judgements are therefore individualized but more valid as they are rooted in 'empirically validated, structured decisions' and can take account of particular and 'idiosyncratic risk markers' (Douglas et al. 1999: 156). Such tools are seen as crucial to consistency of risk assessment practice. From a number of tools on both sides of the Atlantic three tools have emerged as front-runners:

- Violence Prediction Scheme (VPS)
- HCR-20
- PCL-R.

The Violence Prediction Scheme (Webster et al. 1994) combines 10 dynamic items with 12 actuarial items from the VRAG. However, while the dynamic factors are intended to identify areas of intervention, they have added very little to the predictive utility of the VRAG (Webster et al. 1994: 57). The PCL-R and its various derivatives is a structured interviewing tool for use in forensic settings and aims to predict the future risk of violence by psychopaths (Hare 1991; Hare and Hart 1993; Hart et al. 1994). While not originally designed to predict violence per se, it has been contended that the scale can measure the most important factor in the risk of predatory violence: psychopathy (Hare 2000). Various studies have indicated that the PCL–R can accurately identify psychopathy amongst forensic patients (Hare 1991; Cooke and Michie 1999), and that it has transferability to other offender populations such as women and ethnic minorities (Brown and Forth 1997; Cooke 1998; Hare 1998). Its use has however been largely confined to forensic settings and its reliable use requires well-trained assessors.

To date the most systematic structured tool for the assessment of violence is the HCR-20 (Webster et al. 1995, 1997). The assessment combines historical factors that have a track record in predicting risk, with clinical variables such as respondent insight, attitude, motivation to change and to treatment, stability and general symptomology. In addition, the assessment tool has the value-added component of structuring the assessor's attention towards case management plans, motivation to change and likely compliance, individual coping mechanisms, and the feasibility of the risk management plan (for a full review of factors see Webster et al. 1997: 11).

Although initially formulated as an aide-memoire in order to make practitioner decisions transparent (Webster et al. 1997: 5, 73), the predictive validity of the HCR-20 has been evaluated with persons 'scoring above the HCR-20 median were 6 to 13 times more likely to be violent than those scoring below the median' (Douglas et al. 1999: 917). The HCR-20 in this evaluative study was found to add incremental validity to the Psychopathy

Checklist – Screening Version (PCL-SV), although the sample was restricted to civil psychiatric patients. This research importantly validated the importance of the Historical and Risk Management Scales (with the Clinical Scale having a limited significance to short-term risk prediction), and the dynamic factors were seen as particularly pertinent to the ongoing assessment of risk. Cooke's (2000) short review of the HCR-20 indicates that these findings have been supported by Klassen's evaluation of the Historical Scale of the HCR-20 which found a moderate strength correlation to inpatient violence by civil psychiatric patients (Klassen 1999); a further study by Strand et al. (1999) which found that the HCR-20 was related to violence; and Wintrup's (1996) study which found a moderate strength correlation to patients who committed violence after their release from secure forensic settings. However, limits to this study were acknowledged. The small scale of the sample (193 patients) over a relatively short time frame (626 days) does require longer follow-up particularly post-discharge. Although recently adopted by the Scottish Prison Service, the tool has been almost exclusively applied in the mental health arena. As with other methods, severity and impact of offending are less well covered (Douglas et al. 1999), although the tool does indicate key areas for treatment and intervention (Cooke et al. 2001).

Classification trees

A more recent development has been around classification trees, particularly to help practitioners in the assessment of high risk in clinical settings. The Iterative Classification Tree (ICT) takes a binary approach to risk decision making with assessors following a pre-set guide through a series of options. The questions are empirically and theoretically grounded, and each question is dependent upon the answer to the preceding one. The model starts with initial screening (for example using the PCL–R) and the classification is refined through the questioning process. The ICT is designed to assist practitioners with the use of actuarial data in clinical settings in a resource lean manner (Monahan et al. 2000: 312). The ICT 'partitioned 72.6 per cent of a sample of discharged psychiatric patients into one of two categories with regard to their risk of violence to others during the first 20 weeks after discharge' (Monahan et al. 2000: 317). However, as Monahan et al. (2000: 312) point out, this approach can only classify individuals as either high or low risk. A number of individuals remain unclassified, and as Cooke (2000: 154) states: 'It is these individuals, whose risk level is equivocal, with whom the assessor needs most assistance' (see also Cooke et al. 2001: 12). However, this approach does attempt to recognize the contingent nature of risk and its dependency upon a number of 'it depends' and to mimic this approach to risk in practice settings through the decision tree. While factors remain empirically grounded, the binary nature of the classification may prove a key limit, not only in grading risks, but also in restricting the question and answer options of practitioners. While classification trees attempt to avoid the mechanistic approach of actuarial methods, and attempt to push the boundary of structured interviewing assessment tools to better capture the nature of risk in assessment settings, contingency and context are limited to binary options. In this sense, they do not severely challenge the prevailing episteme of risk tools or the technical methodologies in which it is expressed.

Jones (1996) has argued that risk prediction tools are not the 'value-free' objective tools that emerge from their technical representation. Rather, 'risk instruments inevitably reflect a series of policy and value decisions including the choice of variables, cutoff points, and relative values given to false positives and false negatives' although in both their development and subsequent adoption this 'is often unrecognised or ignored' (Jones 1996: 34). He suggests that the mechanisms, knowledge base and processes by which risk prediction and assessment tools are developed should be subject to high standards of visibility and accountability. Arguably this should include explicit reference to the policy imperatives that have informed the formation and adoption of the tool, the value framing of the tool (for example are false positives seen as more acceptable than false negatives, is the tool designed to ensure selective incapacitation or protect human rights) and a clear expression of the prevailing episteme within which the tool is cast and why it is prioritized over any other. While pure actuarialism has been superseded by 'combined' tools, the approach is still underpinned by the use of aggregates (derived from meta-analysis) and probabilistic thinking (Auerhahn 1999).

Concluding summary

Differing conceptualizations and epistemologies of risk can be discerned in both the generation of risk assessment tools and subsequent risk management approaches, and in broader criminological theorizing on crime risk management. The 'two cultures' have been framed as a positivistic and arte-fact approach to risk embedded within a scientific and technical episteme, and a constructed and mediated framing of risk located within a constructivist episteme. The development of risk tools can be seen in a broader context than the mere improvement of risk methodologies. Early statistical predictors reflect both the imperatives of criminal justice to accurately classify and respond to habitual criminals (Pratt 1997) and the methodological techniques of actuarialism expanding into many areas of policy at that time (Rowe 1977). Third generation tools are rooted in more recent criminal justice trends to evaluate interventions, promote evidence-based treatments, classify and target offenders for change programmes, and allocate scarce resources in a rational and transparent manner (Bonta 1996; Jones 1996). Sexual and violent offenders have presented a particular challenge to risk assessment tools, not least due to low base rates and the difficulty in grounding them sufficiently in actuarial factors. However, it is these offences and the assessment of 'risk of harm' that tends to attract most public attention and media coverage, particularly when things go wrong. This has seen intense activity by researchers, often employed or funded by government departments, to design and validate risk assessment tools for these offence types.

Further reading

Kemshall, H. (2001) *Risk Assessment and Management of Known Sexual and Violent Offenders: A Review of Current Issues*. Police Research Series 140. London: Home Office. For a full review of current risk assessment tools see Chapter 3.

Lupton, D. (1999) *Risk*. London: Routledge. For a review of current theoretical approaches to risk see Chapter 2.

chapter four

Risk, dangerousness and the Probation Service

Introduction

The Probation Service has been one of the central agencies (along with the police) in both the identification of dangerous offenders and in their subsequent management (Kemshall 1998; Nash 1999). Changes in the policy objectives and practice of Probation have long been linked to broader shifts in penal policy (Hudson 1993, 1996) and the Probation Service has long demonstrated its ability to adapt to the shifting sands of the law and order agenda (McWilliams 1987, 1992a, 1992b). For most of the twentieth century the Probation Service was rooted in the rehabilitative ideal of the 'penal-welfare complex' (Garland 2001), a central agency in the 'normalisation' of offenders (Garland 1985). However, by the 1970s the 'rehabilitative ideal' was under severe challenge, not least by Martinson's (1974) famous contention that 'nothing works' (although actually better understood as 'some things work'), and a lack of confidence in the efficacy of treatment for offenders. This sea-change was indicative of a broader challenge to the legitimacy and desirability of offender rehabilitation (Robinson 1999) and a crisis of confidence in modern corrections and its individualized sentencing (Garland 2001).

A crisis of confidence

By the 1980s the Probation Service was experiencing a crisis of confidence about its role in the modernist penal agenda. The 'treatment paradigm' was critiqued as a vehicle for oppressive, compulsory and largely ineffectual interventions (Raynor 1980) and low impact upon crime rates and individual recidivism (Davies 1974). The demise of the treatment paradigm post-Martinson (1974) is well documented (Bean 1976; Folkard et al. 1976; Hudson 1987) and will not be extensively reviewed here. The Probation Service found itself in a vulnerable position: costs had grown with a 123 per cent increase in financial resources between 1983 and 1992 and while the overall workload had increased, individual officer caseloads had diminished (Mair 1996: 25). However, growth was not accompanied by effectiveness (Folkard et al. 1976), and in this climate there were increasing academic and professionally based calls for a 'non-treatment paradigm' and sentencing to justice (Bottoms and McWilliams 1979; Raynor 1980; Tutt and Giller 1984). Both approaches were important: the non-treatment paradigm for its emphasis upon mutuality in problem definition and collaboration between officer and offender in problem-solving; and the justice approach for its avoidance of net-widening, systemic approach to the justice system and attempts to influence sentencers to non-custodial options. In reality, such 'steers' were often resented and circumvented by sentencers, particularly magistrates, and practitioners oscillated between 'treatment' and 'non-treatment' ideologies in their assessments (Hardiker 1977).

The legislative and policy context: the Probation Service and the 'discovery' of the dangerous offender

However, a number of key principles were established for probation work in this period. The most significant for the Probation Service's later role in risk management were bifurcation in sentencing policy:

- a managed and strategic approach to criminal justice
- a recognition of the Probation Service's place in a multi-agency, systemic and managed approach to penal matters (Faulkner 1989; Mair 1996).

The latter was epitomized by increased executive control of the Probation Service and imposed accountability to central government (McWilliams 1987; G. Smith 1996). This period saw the introduction of bifurcation or a twin-track approach to sentencing (Bottoms 1977) in which a distinction was made between serious and non-serious offenders. The former were defined as those most likely to reoffend, and while bifurcation was not explicitly posed in terms of dangerousness, an important principle of sentencing on the grounds of seriousness was introduced. The Criminal Justice Act 1982 expressed this dichotomy between serious and non-serious offending, and reflected a growing New Right preoccupation with both spiralling crime rates and crime costs, and the high cost and perceived failure of deterrence (Baxter and Nuttall 1975; Bottoms 1977; Flynn 1978; Hudson 1993). However, it is not unusual for persistent offending and recidivism to become conflated with seriousness in the practical operation of bifurcation, for example in late-nineteenth-century penal policy (Pratt 1997) and throughout the 1980s (Nash 1999). Habitual criminals are subject to a process of 'dangerization' in which the constant, persistent and unknowable threat of crime reduces public tolerance and meshes notions of seriousness, persistence and dangerousness in both public policy and public conscious-ness (Garland 2000). This conflation was influential in New Right penal policy during the 1980s and 1990s, and has influenced much of the Probation Service's approach to risk and danger (Kemshall 1998). In policy terms this has been described as a period of 'swings and roundabouts' (Nash 1999), characterized by an oscillation between bifurcation on the one hand, and punitive populism on the other. In less than ten years the Criminal Justice Act 1991 provided a clearer distinction between offences against the person and the 'risk of serious harm' on the one hand, and property offences on the other (Wasik and Taylor 1991). Persistent offenders were to be subject to the just deserts of proportionate sentencing, and preventative sentencing on the basis of serious harm was to be restricted to violent, sexual and drug offenders. Cavadino and Dignan (1997) have dubbed this 'punitive bifurcation': a combination of just deserts punishment and bifurcated seriousness.

The Criminal Justice Act 1991 and the emergence of public protection

The 1991 Act provided the Probation Service with a new and challenging remit (Home Office 1990; Faulkner 2001) to move 'centre stage' (Faulkner 1989) and to 'prevent reoffending' and protect 'the public from serious harm' (Home Office 1990: 2). In an era of New Right erosion of the public sector, financial constraint, increased executive control, and the demise of the rehabilitative ideal the Probation Service had little choice about embracing this remit despite the resistance of frontline workers (Kemshall 1993; Worrall 1997). In the decade that followed public protection replaced social work values and rehabilitation as the key driver of probation work (Pitts 1992; ACOP 1994; Kemshall 1995; Nellis 1995) although there would be attempts to reconstitute rehabilitation as 'helping' (McWilliams and Pease 1990), 'non-treatment' problem-solving (Raynor and Vanstone 1994) and more recently as cognitively based intervention programmes (Robinson 1999).

The Criminal Justice Act 1991 was concerned with two contradictory objectives: reduction in the use of custody and 'being tough on crime' (Nash 1999). In effect, the reduction in the use of custody for less serious offenders was obscured by the tougher policy on those offenders for whom there was little public sympathy: sexual, violent and drug offenders, an 'early sign that certain offenders were to be isolated within the criminal justice system for special attention' and of an increasing policy of targeted preventative sentencing (Nash 1999: 45). The intellectual and policy colonialism from the USA also continued, not only to Britain but also to other anglophone countries such as Australia and New Zealand with penal policy increasingly underpinned by risk, dangerousness, and selective incapacitation (Meek 1995; Pratt 1995, 1997, 2000d; Brown 1996). Just deserts and bifurcation were meshed in both policy and legislation in an uneasy partnership that was tested by the increased harshness of the penal climate throughout the 1990s and the combination of proportionality and protection was increasingly strained (Pratt 1997).

While the service had long dealt with risk, for example parole violation risks or those emanating from child protection (National Association of Probation Officers (NAPO) 1977; McWilliams 1987), risk reduction was defined as a task that should be compatible with the traditional casework principles of 'advise, assist and befriend' and broader social work aims (NAPO 1977). The probation officer was cast as the 'offender's champion' against an overly anxious and blaming community wary of risk – a position that was to inform the subsequent value debates on risk throughout the 1990s (Kemshall 2000). In just over ten years the Home Office had issued 'protective guidelines' to chief officers on the registration of 'Potentially Dangerous Offenders' (Home Office 1988). This followed a number of HMIP-driven area reviews of work with dangerous offenders in the 1980s and cases that had attracted 'adverse criticism'. In the absence of central guidance, local services developed a plethora of registration policies and practices (Shaw 1991) and a cautious and defensive approach to risk emphasizing control, public protection and staff safety took hold (Kemshall 1998). Registration procedures also varied in their definition of 'dangerous offender' and while risk was increasingly central to probation work assessment tools and procedures were embryonic. Risk and danger were identified with mental disorder, assaults on staff, and parole violations despite evidence to the contrary (Brown 1996; Ryan 1996). Interestingly Shaw's study found little registration of sex offenders, in sharp contrast to the review by Her Majesty's Inspectorate of Probation some five years later (HMIP 1995) and the reframing of sex offenders as dangerous by the late 1990s (Cobley 2000). By the time of the Inspectorate's thematic report on dangerous offenders (HMIP 1995) there were already tensions and disputes within the service about the nature of risk and the legitimacy of the task (Kemshall 1995). The Inspectorate's report identified various shortcomings, and combined with various Probation Circulars and guidance (for example Probation Services Division 1994; 1999) and a detailed analysis of 'serious incidents' (Probation Services Division 1997) gave the view that the service could not act competently on risk if left to its own devices. ('Serious incidents' are offences resulting in death or grave injury committed by an offender subject to Probation Service supervision. The service is required to make a full report to the Home Office, and these are subject to analysis and review. In one instance this resulted in newspaper coverage stating that a murder per week is committed by someone subject to probation supervision.)

'Expedient managerialism' was the vehicle through which the new economic rationality of penality was legitimized and delivered. The dual concerns of recidivism and dangerousness, meshed in legislation and policy, were conflated in the subsequent ACOP (1994) statement, fuelling a conceptual confusion that has been frequently repeated at Home Office and service level (Kemshall 1996, 1997a, 1997b, 1998), and reinforced by subsequent Home Office National Standards for probation practice in which the distinction between seriousness and likelihood lacked clarity and force and the desirability of assessing risk 'in all cases' was emphasized (Home Office 1995a: 11).

Summary

The Probation Service's response to risk and dangerous offenders throughout the 1990s can be characterized as a period of risk aversion, enforced repositioning and blame avoidance, and a more proactive engagement with the 'politics of punishment' and value for money (Wallis 1997). The risk agenda was largely centrally and managerially driven, seen by most chief officers and central government policy makers as a question of accountability, staff compliance and effective resocialization through training (Lawrie 1996, 1997; G. Smith 1996), with a few more liberal voices drawing attention to organizational and cultural issues in implementation (Mackenzie 1996). By the time of the Inspectorate's conference on 'Public

Protection' in 1996 the tone was set and the new raison d'être for the service was embedded in the new three year plan (Home Office 1996a) and the subsequent publication of the government's crime strategy *Protecting the Public: The Government's Strategy on Crime in England and Wales* (Home Office 1996b).

From dangerous to predatory: the rise of the predatory paedophile

The CJA 1991 distinguished between those offenders for whom pro-portionality was appropriate, and those offenders for whom preventative (custodial) sentencing could be justified on the grounds of protecting 'the public from serious harm' (section 2(2)b). Serious harm was defined in section 31(3) as 'protecting the public from death or serious personal injury, whether physical or psychological, occasioned by further such offences committed by the [defendant]' (Wasik and Taylor 1991), although the criteria for dangerousness and the uncertainty of risk prediction as a basis for disproportionate sentencing has been heavily critiqued (Wood 1988; von Hirsch and Ashworth 1996). The efficacy of such sentencing to reduce harmful offending (Pratt 1997) and appropriately target the right offenders has been questioned: persistent property offenders and par-ticularly burglars have most usually attracted such sentences (Dingwall 1998). Importantly the Act targeted sex offenders for special attention, for example section 44 amended existing parole arrangements to allow for the extension of the supervisory term until the completion date of the ori-ginal prison sentence, and it was sex offenders, and more particularly paedophiles, who were to dominate the penal agenda of the late 1990s. While the 1980s saw criticism of police, probation and crown prosecution service for failing to take sexual crimes seriously (Worrall 1997), the 1990s saw a growing penal preoccupation with sex offenders, and in particular sex offending against children. The latter was highlighted by a series of high-profile cases and the spectre of organized and pervasive paedophilia in society at large, for example 'satanic abuse', and the Butler-Schloss (1988) inquiry in Cleveland. As Cobley (2000) says, 'Paedophile' has become a 'household word', illustrated by a computer search of news-paper articles that revealed its use in '712 articles in six leading British newspapers' in the first four months of 1998, 'whereas the word had only appeared 1,312 times in total in the 4 year period between 1992–1995' (Cobley 2000: 2).

Detection and conviction rose in the 1980s and 1990s, more sex offenders were imprisoned (Worrall 1997), and the balance between community sentences and custody was tilted in favour of more prison sentences (Hebenton and Thomas 1996, 1997). While the Probation Service had only a small percentage of those sentenced on community supervision (between 12 and 15 per cent: Worrall 1997: 119), it undertook this work with vigour.

Intensive group work and individualized programmes were developed, often requiring considerable probation officer resources (McEwan and Sullivan 1996), and the service found that this was one area of work where staff had little difficulty in prioritizing victims and abandoning 'advise, assist and befriend' in favour of 'challenge and change'. Sex offenders were also one area of work where the risk agenda was most easily accepted and where the service was at pains to demonstrate the effectiveness of its community management arrangements (Gocke 1995; Nash 1999).

Although there has been a 100 per cent increase in notifiable sex offences between 1955 and 1999, the 37,492 notifiable offences recorded by the police between 1998 and 1999 in Britain sexual offences account for less than 1 per cent of all notifiable offences recorded (Cobley 2000; Home Office 2000b). Against this backdrop sex offenders still came to dominate the political and penal policy agenda of the late twentieth century and resulted in a 'criminal apartheid' approach towards them (Soothill and Francis 1997a, 1997b; Soothill et al. 1998). The implications for the Probation Service were significant. Work with sex offenders assisted managers and policy makers in justifying the risk agenda to staff (HMIP 1998) – after all who could dispute the moral desirability of protecting children? In effect victims became the new client and offenders became the site of management. Restrictions such as monitoring, tagging and tracking were legitimized on the grounds of protection and risk. The significance of the work to the Probation Service and its political importance were reflected in the HMIP (1998) report *Exercising Constant Vigilance: The Role of the Probation Service in Protecting the Public from Sex Offenders* (HMIP 1998). Little distinction was made between types of sex offences and levels of harm, and the emphasis upon the work significantly outweighed its actual volume on the service caseload where it comprised 3 per cent of the probation supervision cases, and 9 per cent of the through-care caseload (HMIP 1998: 31).

The construction of the paedophile

The penal policy focus on sex offenders also opened up the distance between victim and offender, and offender and society and the rights and citizenship of offenders is consequently diminished (Faulkner 2001; Garland 2001). This distance has been exacerbated by the construction of the 'predatory paedophile' – the spectre of an invisible stranger in our midst preying on vulnerable children, often linked to the fear of child homicide (Wilczynski and Sinclair 1999). In part a media-constructed moral panic (Thompson 1998; Kitzinger 1999a, 1999b), this construction plays on stranger-danger. Paradoxically, most children and women who suffer abuse are abused in their own homes by men they know (Ehrlich 1998).

Media coverage tends to be largely stereotypical with little attention to causation (Kitzinger and Skidmore 1995), with the 'predominant image' of abusers as 'bad', 'mad', or 'sad' (Wilczynski and Sinclair 1999: 276). Abusers are presented as 'sex beasts' but also as 'moral tales' and 'barometers of the state of the nation' (Soothill and Soothill 1993: 19; Wilczynski and Sinclair 1999: 276).

While the 1980s constructed the 'rapist' as the most dangerous sex offender, the 1990s elevated the paedophile, particularly the predatory paedophile, to this position (Cowburn and Dominelli 2001). Kitzinger (1999b) identifies the roots in the mid-1980s and the key impetus given by the BBC *Childwatch* programme and the inception of ChildLine. However, public attention was given focus and expression by sex offender releases from prison, relocation in the community and central government policy initiatives around the sex offender register (Thomas 2001). In effect, policy objectives aimed at reducing risk inadvertently unleashed it. This initiated a 'right to know' campaign and severe vigilante action in 1996 and 1997 and both the news and policy agendas were quickly hijacked (Kitzinger 1999b; Thomas 2001). The subsequent panic around 'paedophiles in the community' was fuelled by the image of children as innocent victims. This is no coincidence. Jackson and Scott (1999: 86) have argued that children and childhood are constructed as 'innocent' spaces deserving of protection, and as such are a constant site of anxiety for parents and society at large. (Paradoxically the murder of James Bulger in 1993 and the subsequent trial of Robert Thompson and Jon Venables resulted in extensive media coverage that portrayed children as evil and childhood as a source of potential threat: see for example James and Jenks 1996; Muncie 1999.) Kitzinger (1996) notes from focus groups with parents in the early 1990s that the paedophile was a key fear etched in the consciousness of parents. This was exacerbated by a feeling of siege in some communities, with council house tenants often feeling that they were asked to accept a disproportionate level of risk, especially on 'sink estates' (see for example Walters 2001). Clandestine rehousing of paedophiles against the wishes of local residents did not always endear professionals and experts to communities.

In an era of increased personal responsibility for risk and a location of risk in any 'Other' (Giddens 1991; Craze and Moynihan 1994; Furedi 1997) it is not surprising that predatory paedophiles have become the constant terror of the twenty-first century. This has been exacerbated by the increased location of childhood and its appropriate regulation to the private, family domain – a domain responsibilized through discourses of risk and vulnerability (Moss et al. 2000; Kemshall 2002b). Sex offending and paedophilia have in effect been meshed (Soothill et al. 1998). While concerns with the dangerous and the invisible ex-offender in our midst have been perennial (Radzinowicz and Hood 1986; Pratt 1997; Radzinowicz 1999), postmodern society holds the 'spectre of the mobile and anonymous sexual offender' as particularly demonic (Hebenton and Thomas 1996: 429), and as Soothill and Walby (1991) put it: 'sex crime sells'.

The 'textual outlaw' of the non-familial paedophiles has been constructed as a demon to be 'put under surveillance, punished, contained and constrained' (A. Young 1996: 9). Their media coverage is often accompanied by 'alarmist reactions to crime' and what Welch et al. (1997: 486) have described as an 'escalating vocabulary of punitive motives' in which ever harsher penal policies against the dangerous are advocated. Sanders and Lyon (1995) have described this as 'repetitive retribution' and illustrates the 'significant impact on major policy decisions' that can ensue (Muncie 1999: 182).

The challenge for the Probation Service

Concern with the predatory paedophile has presented the Probation Service with a severe challenge: how to effectively manage in the community offenders who are perceived as beyond the pale and unworthy of community reintegration. Sex offenders are also an area in which the coexistence of the new penology of risk and 'popular punitiveness' can most easily be discerned. As Simon (1998) puts it, while the new penology is concerned with risk, populist punitiveness is 'obsessed' with dangerousness.

Simon argues that this tension is managed in practice by an 'acoustic divide', in effect a division between political soundbites and the actual activities of penal professionals who ameliorate its worst excesses (for example the attempts by both the Association of Chief Officers of Probation and the National Association of Probation Officers to influence the *News of the World* 'name and shame' campaign in the summer of 2000 following the murder of Sarah Payne). This describes the late 1990s penal policy response to sex offenders within most of the anglophone countries (Simon 1998; Pratt 2000b; Sparks 2001a), and in Britain the key role of the Probation Service in both implementing populist soundbites and attempting to ameliorate their worst excesses. By the turn of the century the new penology of risk and a populist punitiveness centred around sex offenders had merged in the following:

- The Sex Offenders Act 1997 which provided for a sex offender register designed to monitor and track such offenders (Plotnikoff and Woolfson 2000).
- The Crime and Disorder Act 1998 which provided for a Sex Offender Order (full details are provided in Kemshall 2001: 6–7).
- Amendments to the Sex Offenders Act 1997 provided in the Criminal Justice and Court Services (CJCS) Act 2000 – this included the requirement to notify foreign travel, increased the penalty for non-registration, gave additional powers for photographs and finger-printing of offenders, and shortened the period for initial registration to 72 hours.
- Statutory provision for joint risk assessment and management by police

and probation in sections 67 and 68 of the CJCS Act 2000 and the official creation of Multi-Agency Public Protection Panels.

- To offset further calls for a British equivalent of the USA's Megan's Law (discussed below) the Home Secretary announced in December 2001 that representatives of local communities (as yet it is not known how they will be appointed) will be allowed to sit as members of MAPPPs in order to express a local community view on risk management and resettlement plans. These individuals will not be permitted to reveal details of individual offenders or their whereabouts to other community members.
- Section 67 of the CJCS Act 2000 requires MAPPPs to publish an annual report of their activities and thus ensure greater accountability, although individual offender details are not to be revealed.

The Probation Circular *Early Warning Mechanism for the Release or Discharge of Potentially Dangerous Offenders* (Probation Services Division 1999) also placed a duty on chief probation officers to establish an early warning system to the Home Office of those offenders due for release from prison or hospital where high-profile cases were likely to present media scrutiny of accommodation or supervision plans. While the Home Office did not seek to engage in the management of individual cases as this was 'beyond the resources of the Home Office and contrary to the strategic aim of embedding risk management in local inter-agency partnerships', central information was seen as important in establishing the size of the problem and providing reports to ministers 'so that they can have a fuller picture than at present of problems to come and can consider handling and presentational issues' (Probation Services Division 1999: 3).

These developments were given added impetus by subsequent high-profile cases that attracted unprecedented media coverage and in some instances vigilante action and community disquiet (for example the cases of Robert Oliver and Sydney Cooke, who were released to public outcry and vigilante action after serving approximately eight years for the abduction, buggery and manslaughter of a 14-year-old boy) (Kitzinger 1999a, 1999b). The murder of Sarah Payne in the summer of 2000 stimulated intense media debate about the appropriate monitoring of paedophiles and led to calls for 'Sarah's Law' (a UK version of the American Megan's Law), whereby the local community would have a right to be informed of the names and addresses of people with convictions for sexual offences. It also led to a campaign by the *News of the World* to 'name and shame paedophiles'. The campaign, which resulted in public disorder and vigilante action (some against wrongly identified people) in several towns, was eventually suspended after protests from police and probation officers that such media attention and its aftermath served only to drive offenders 'underground' (Kemshall and Maguire 2002). The National Association for the

Care and Resettlement of Offenders for example described the *News of the World* reporting as 'grossly irresponsible' and the Association of Chief Police Officers stated that it would 'put children's lives at risk by driving sexual offenders underground' (Thomas 2001: 103; see also *Guardian* 24 July 2000: 1). This campaign also highlighted the growing divide between professionals and public in penal matters and a growing assertion, especially through the media, that common sense should prevail and that parents had 'the right to know'. This campaign resulted in some compromises from the government, although not a Sarah's Law. In particular, proposals to tighten the operation of and extend the remit of the sex offender register (Home Office 2000a), and proposals to reform the law in respect of sex offenders (Home Office 2001b, 2001c). This was exacerbated by calls from the opposition for more extensive measures, including the possibility of life imprisonment for sex offenders (*Sunday Times*, 13 August 2000: 1).

The subsequent trial and conviction of Roy Whiting in December 2001, a man on the sex offender register and known to the local MAPPP, rekindled calls for a Sarah's Law and again challenged the expertise and professionalism of those agencies tasked with the community risk management of sex offenders. In this instance the media coverage was less inflammatory, with both sides of the argument for community notification receiving more considered and largely professional (rather than media) comment. (See, for example, www.bbc.co.uk/news 'Do we need a "Sarah's Law?"' (13 December 2001), with Michelle Elliott the director of *Kidscape* arguing that it would work for the most dangerous paedophiles, and those such as Harry Fletcher of the National Association of Probation Officers arguing that it would fuel vigilante action and lead some offenders to avoid registration.) Home Office Ministers have generally argued that a Sarah's Law would be 'unworkable' (see Beverley Hughes' remarks on the same website), particularly as offenders might merely move their activities to another area where they would not be known, a situation exacerbated by the 110,000 offenders currently on the register and the impracticability of providing all parents with useful information on all offenders. Important and difficult practical questions are also beginning to be considered, such as what information might be given out, to whom, and in what form; about which kinds of offenders, and of what level of risk; and how might parents and communities be supported to respond appropriately to the information they are given. These are crucial issues if any future Sarah's Law is not to become a vigilante's charter, and if community notification is not to become community retribution (Kemshall and Maguire 2002).

The 1990s also saw a further significant development imported from the USA: the idea that 'Prison Works' and the notion of selective incapacitation for serious habitual recidivists as well as for the most dangerous

(Greenwood and Abrahamse 1982; Greenwood and Turner 1987; Greenwood et al. 1996; Murray 1997).

Public and politicians became familiar with the baseball idiom of 'three strikes and you're out'. In the UK this policy was aimed at property offences, particularly burglary. Violent and sexual offenders were also targeted for special measures and public protection was prioritized over proportionality. Despite concerns that mandatory sentencing would in effect pull the tariff for all crimes upwards and result in gross inequities in sentencing (Clarkson 1997; Nash 1999), the Crime Sentences Act 1997 introduced mandatory life sentences for a second offence of the following:

- attempting, conspiring or inciting to commit murder or soliciting murder
- manslaughter
- wounding or causing grievous bodily harm with intent (a section 18 wounding)
- rape or attempt to commit rape
- intercourse with a girl under 13
- possession of a firearm with intent to injure, use of a firearm to resist arrest, or carrying a firearm with criminal intent
- robbery where during the commission of the offence the defendant had in his/her possession a firearm or imitation firearm within the meaning of the Firearms Act 1968

Except in exceptional circumstances where judges have the power to overrule.

(from Teggin 1998)

Summary

In this climate the Probation Service has had a key role in the following areas:

- the assessment of risk in *all* cases
- proposing sentencing options to the courts on the basis of risk and allocating the use of supervision resources and treatment programmes on the grounds of risk
- the identification and segregation of 'potentially dangerous offenders' for special attention and increased management and surveillance
- increased attention to sex offenders, particularly paedophiles, both on community supervision and post-release
- joint work with police and other significant agencies through Multi-Agency Public Protection Panels.

Risk in probation practice and policy can be understood as a 'pragmatic' adaptation to the new penality of the New Right in the 1980s and 1990s.

However, the Probation Service has had to respond to a fluctuating and at times contradictory penal environment in which populist punitiveness has played a significant role, particularly in the late 1990s with regard to sex offenders and more broadly in relation to 'potentially dangerous offenders'. However, to characterize the service as merely reacting to penal policy winds, and as an agent within a broader 'inexorable logic of risk' is to oversimplify matters. This presumes that significant 'firewalls' to policy implementation did not exist, and it underestimates the role of both workers and staff as important sites of both mediation and resistance (Lynch 2000; O'Malley 2000, 2001b). The remainder of the chapter will explore these issues in relation to one significant area of risk practice for the Probation Service: the work of MAPPPS.

Risk and Multi-Agency Public Protection Panels[1]

Multi-Agency Public Protection Panels

MAPPPs were formally named and given legislative force by sections 67 and 68 of the Criminal Justice and Court Services Act 2000. The Act placed a duty upon chief police officers and chief probation officers to implement inter-agency arrangements for the assessment and management 'of the risks posed by sexual and violent offenders' (Home Office 2001b, 2002a). (The definition of sexual or violent offences for the purposes of sections 67 and 68 are set out in Annex A of *Further Guidance (1)*, Home Office 2002a.) However, inter-agency arrangements between police and probation had existed since the late 1980s (for example West Yorkshire Police and Probation Services), and were fuelled by the Home Office letter to chief probation officers on the identification and registration of dangerous offenders (Home Office 1988; Shaw 1996). These largely informal arrangements were expanded in the mid-1990s through the use of formal protocols that attempted to establish clear remits for panel operation, and inter-agency panels began to incorporate other key agencies such as social services and housing. Arrangements for joint working with dangerous offenders were given impetus throughout the 1990s by the following key factors:

- Increasing policy, media and public attention to sex offenders, particularly paedophiles, and various studies that established the extent of the problem both nationally and internationally (see for example Grubin 1998).
- High-profile cases, particularly those that contributed to the growing moral panic around paedophile rings, satanic abuse and stranger-danger (Thompson 1998; Kitzinger 1999a, 1999b).
- Individual cases that raised public awareness and discontent, particularly with release arrangements from prison and the perceived failure of

community agencies to manage such offenders effectively (for example the case of Sydney Cooke).

- Home Office disquiet with the volume of 'serious incidents' within the Probation Service caseload, that is the number of offenders committing serious offences such as murder or rape while subject to supervision, 891 in a three year period (HMIP 2000).
- Developments in the USA (and to a lesser extent in Canada) around Megan's Law (disclosure of sex offender details to communities) 'tracking' systems to monitor the whereabouts of sex offenders in the community, and 'special measures' for those deemed to pose an unacceptable risk (Hebenton and Thomas 1997; Kanka 2000; Petrunik 2002).
- Broader criminal justice policy to achieve 'joined-up' responses to crime, particularly through the Crime and Disorder Act 1998 and increased attempts to join-up and coordinate policy under the New Labour government's modernization programme (Faulkner 2001).

Key legislation and policy developments

The Home Office Special Conference in 1997 on 'Inter-Agency Work with Dangerous Offenders: Sharing Information to Manage Risk' began to formalize inter-agency work and attempted to tackle the pressing issues around disclosure to third parties, confidentiality, and duty of care to potential victims (Home Office Special Conference Unit 1997). The Sex Offender Act 1997 attempted to clarify these issues, and provided a statutory requirement for almost all sex offenders to register their address with the police within 14 days of caution of conviction (for a review of requirements see Kemshall 2001: 6). Sex offender registration aims to deter recidivism, provide community awareness and public protection (Rudin 1996). However, the efficacy of sex offender registration has been questioned (Tewksbury 2002). Whilst Plotnikoff and Woolfson (2000) found that 94.7 per cent of UK sex offenders are compliant with registration requirements, the longer existence of registers in the USA has enabled research into registration outcomes. Zevitz and Farkas (2000a, 2000b) claim that there may be negative effects in terms of community anxiety and vigilantism. The subsequent marginalization of sex offenders has also been seen as detrimental to their potential reintegration and avoidance of future sex offending (Prentky 1996). Schram and Milloy (1995) have suggested that there is no statistically significant difference between those sex offenders subject to registration and community notification and those who are not.

The Sex Offender Act 1997 did not specify police duties following registration, but many police services began to extend registration into surveillance and community management of sex offenders (Maguire et al.

2001). In some cases this was extended to offenders not subject to any statutory supervision or control, and in some cases to offenders under suspicion but not convicted. Police personnel considered that such activities were constrained by the lack of powers of entry into the homes of sex offenders, and by a lack of legal sanction and control for those who did not respond to the risk management provided under the umbrella of the sex offender register (Maguire et al. 2001).

This situation was partly rectified by the Crime and Disorder Act 1998, which removed registration anomalies and brought approximately 100,000 offenders under the registration procedures and also introduced the Sex Offender Order for offenders whose behaviour justified more intrusive measures (Power 1998, 1999). Sex Offender Orders were aimed at those offenders whose behaviour warranted more intrusive measures and negative prohibitions (such as restricting access to victims) in order to protect the public, and while requiring only civil standards of proof carried up to a five year custodial sentence for breach. (For the current uptake and use of Orders see Knock and Thomas 2002.) The Act was subsequently amended by the Criminal Justice and Court Services Act 2000, including an increase in the penalty for non-registration, a requirement to notify foreign travel, provisions for photographs and fingerprinting, and a shortening of the period allowed prior to initial registration to 72 hours. Parallel to these developments was the enactment of section 58 of the Crime and Disorder Act 1998, which gave courts the power to impose an extended post-release supervision to offenders convicted of a sexual or violent offence where the custodial sentence is four years or more. (These extended licences can apply to sex offenders for up to ten years, and for violent offenders for up to five years, although for a violent offender the combined period cannot exceed the maximum sentence for the offence.) The risk arising from those deemed both dangerous and suffering a 'severe personality disorder' also received attention (prompted by the murder of Lin and Megan Russell by Michael Stone), with proposals to restrict the release from prison or hospital of those deemed untreatable but still dangerous (Home Office 1999). The cumulative impact of this legislation was an increased responsibility upon both police and probation to identify and assess those offenders for whom special measures of selective incarceration or intensive community surveillance could be justified. This has required both formal cooperation and the development of risk tools and techniques to aid assessment (Kemshall 2001).

However, extensive empirical research commissioned by the Home Office carried out between November 1998 and October 1999 found varying degrees of formal cooperation and varying approaches to risk assessment and risk management (Kemshall and Maguire 2001; Maguire et al. 2001). (For an account of both methodology and range of data collected see Maguire et al. 2001: 5–7.) Whilst MAPPPs are 'risk driven' to the extent that their remit is bounded by risk concerns and are informed by both policy and legislation aimed at 'high-risk' and 'dangerous' offenders, practices and procedures do not bear out a wholesale shift to actuarialism. In essence, the system is concerned with risk, but is not totally predicated upon formalized actuarial practices.

This is evidenced by findings in the following areas:

- The use of subjective and professional judgements alongside of, and at times, in place of actuarial tools.
- The movable nature of risk classifications and thresholds.
- The role of professional values and occupational culture in risk practice.

Professional judgement versus actuarial tool

The period of MAPPP development was characterized by key developments and revisions in the Home Office sponsored sex offender assessment tool: the Structured Anchored Clinical Judgement (SACJ: Hanson and Thornton 2000; see Kemshall 2001 for a full review), and various attempts to launch a national consistent tool for sex offender risk prediction. For the police such a tool was attractive, particularly for those dealing with the high volume of sex offenders requiring registration, and in determining those offenders who required special, inter-agency measures of community management. In some instances, the tool enabled the downgrading of risk assessment to civilian workers, releasing police officers from work perceived as essentially administrative. While the ease and speed of use of the SACJ made it attractive, it remained essentially a screening tool, enabling police personnel to triage sex offenders for attention, and for referral to the MAPPPs. However, professional and subjective judgements have continued to play a key role in risk assessment. Initially, the screening tool catapulted unmanageable volumes of offenders into the high-risk category, leading to an upward revision of thresholds in order to manage numbers at MAPPPs (a process subsequently addressed by revisions in the tool). There was no evidence that any risk tool replaced professional judgement, rather professional judgement was used to confirm or revise actuarial risk scores. Whilst MAPPPs recognized the need to make risk assessments against clear criteria, this did not necessarily mean risk scores based upon actuarial tools. Whilst actuarial tools were used to target assessments, these could be overridden by clinical judgement, and assessments during MAPPP meetings were characterized by individualized clinical judgements and case presentations from individual workers. This tended to give MAPPPs an anecdotal feel. Little if any reference was made to actuarial scores during MAPPP meetings, a position exacerbated by the differing risk tools used by police and probation. While actuarial tools have gained a growing role in the initial filtering process and sex offender registration, MAPPP meetings are seen as the arena for in-depth assessment and as such remain the preserve of expert, clinically based risk assessment. Despite the recent formation of the Home Office Dangerous Offenders Unit there has been little central guidance to MAPPPs on decision making, and MAPPP risk assessments are not subject to any minimum standards. At present, while legislation requires annual reports of panel activities, the *actual practices* of MAPPPs remain beyond public scrutiny. Following the trial and conviction of Roy Whiting for the murder of Sarah Payne, the Home Secretary suggested that MAPPPs may be required to include lay members in order to enhance public confidence (Kemshall and Maguire 2002).

Risk classification and risk thresholds

In addition to risk prediction the role of actuarial tools is to classify risk, usually in terms of low, medium and high. The failure of any tool to do so satisfactorily is likely to lead to resource pressure and actions from practitioners and managers to recategorize in order to more effectively ration scarce resources. In effect, the availability (or perceived availability) of resources determines the risk categorization. Within probation risk thresholds have proved problematic, both for internally registering dangerous offenders and for referrals to MAPPPs (Maguire et al. 2001), exacerbated by the lack of a commonly used risk tool between probation and police. Prior to the creation of the National Probation Service and the implementation of the Offender Assessment System (Home Office 2001a) local services also operated varying systems to identify and assess dangerous offenders, and used varying criteria to justify referrals to local MAPPPs. These variations were informed not only by resource issues, but also by defensive decision-making and blame avoidance, and the use of MAPPPs to access resources from other agencies that would otherwise be withheld (Kemshall 1998; Kemshall and Maguire 2001). Similar issues exist for police personnel, with sex offender registration units often attached to busy vice units, and senior police personnel left to make difficult individual decisions about how to prioritize work and how to allocate local budgets across competing demands. This has become increasingly associated with value for money evaluations of MAPPP work, and particularly of the high cost of risk management, for example intensive surveillance of offenders, and the high costs associated with regular panel attendance for senior personnel (Maguire et al. 2001). MAPPP meetings have also felt the pressure as numbers have risen and panels have been swamped by both new referrals and the backlog of case reviews. In such circumstances it is not surprising that pure actuarialism gives way to 'occupational survival' (Satayamurti 1981) and a street-wise approach to policy implementation (Maynard-Moody et al. 1990). Even within highly hierarchical and bureaucratic organizations like police and probation, policy implementation is prone to adaptation by the workforce just in order to survive and 'get the job done' (Maynard-Moody et al. 1990).

Professional values and occupational culture

Probation in particular played an important role in the modernist penal-welfare agenda, and within this pursued individualized case by case assessment and allowed workers considerable discretion within the exercise of their professional judgement. This approach to decision-making was taken into MAPPPs, replicated by other agencies such as social services and health whose workers operated within similar parameters. This tended to give MAPPPs a rather anecdotal feel. However, the transition to the community management of high volumes of sex offenders has been challenging to the traditional reactive style of policing, not least because risk management outcomes can be difficult to evaluate and MAPPPs are perceived to take a disproportionate volume of resource for what is provided (Kemshall and Maguire 2001). For the police other risks were often more immediate and more pressing (for example street robberies and burglaries), and the disproportionate amount of time that could be taken by one high-profile case was questioned. Both frontline and management decisions on risk need to be placed within this broader context of workplace demand and discretion, a context in which both probation and police practitioners mediated and diluted the managerial imperative of actuarialism. In particular the tactic of 'mere containment' (that is merely monitoring and holding offenders within the community without any long-term impact on behaviour) was doubted as either effective or as publicly acceptable (Kemshall and Maguire 2001; Maguire et al. 2001).

Summary

Given their creation as an inter-agency risk assessment and risk management forum MAPPPs could be expected to be a prime example of actuarialism and the new penality. However, the empirical reality of practice does not entirely bear out the broader policy or ideological trends of the new penology. There is a key difference between developments that are 'risk driven' in principle and risk delivered on the ground, and MAPPPs are illustrative of this difference. Tool use and risk classification in particular have proved to be important sites of worker and manager mediation, and traditional practices are adapted to new demands rather than replaced. In this area of practice, actuarialism and a risk-based penality has had an adaptive and evolutionary impact rather than a transformative one.

Conclusion: risk and rehabilitation in Probation-transformation or accommodation?

The emergence of a 'new rehabilitationism'

The Probation Service has survived the challenging climate of 'law and order', New Right managerialism, and the 'politics of punishment' (Nellis 1999; Nash 2000), although at some cost to traditional values and working practices (Nellis 1995). 'Public protection' has become a key objective of the Probation Service, particularly from dangerous offenders and predatory paedophiles. Within this discourse, risk has been a key feature, and in particular risk to the most vulnerable section of society – children. As such it has been difficult for the Probation Service to resist it (Nash 2000). While the most far-reaching demands in the name of public protection have been largely resisted by both the Association of Chief Officers of Probation and the Association of Chief Police Officers, the formation of a national service in 2001 firmly placed probation as an arm of the Home Office and diminished the ability of the service to resist or challenge central policy steers.

There can be little doubt that risk and public protection have transformed the work and character of the probation service; however, the extent to which the discourse of need and rehabilitation has been replaced by risk and actuarial risk management continues to be debated (Kemshall et al. 1997; Robinson 1999, 2002). While the contention that the probation service has been totally refigured by risk may be overstated, the welfarism of 'advise, assist and befriend' has been superseded by an economic rationality of crime management and a risk-driven agenda in which 'rehabilitation is increasingly inscribed in a framework of risk rather than a framework of welfare' (Garland 2001: 176). This is evidenced by an increased bifurcation of policy and practice in probation that separates 'dangerous offenders' from those who present a risk of reoffending but not a 'risk of serious harm', and subjects such dangerous offenders to special measures. For the remainder, probation practice has been reframed as largely correctional with risk playing a key role in establishing eligibility for cognitive-behavioural programmes and targeting offenders more efficiently for interventions. In this sense, risk is both a rationing and a targeting mechanism within an economic discourse of probation practice (Garland 1997b). Risk then has different functions within this bifurcation: efficient targeting of the many, and a justificatory role in an expressive populist penality for the few. It has also been argued that need and rehabilitation have been reintroduced to the probation agenda through their reinscription as risks, characterized as a 'New Rehabilitationism' driven by 'risk classifications' (Rotman 1990; Robinson 1999). Certainly the strange linguistic hybrid of 'criminogenic need' attempts to legitimize needs only in so far as they contribute to offending (Aubrey and Hough 1997), and also seems to function as an ideological hybrid between the world of welfare needs and the world of risk and correction, a hybrid that serves to make some staff more comfortable with the risk agenda (Kemshall 1998). While social factors seem to enter by the 'back door' (Raynor 1997b, 1999), new rehabilitationism stresses self-management and the inculcation of self-controls. This individualizing discourse has served to restrict interventions to the personal domain of individual change and away from broader issues of social structure (Hannah-Moffat and Shaw 1999).

While some commentators such as Robinson (1999, 2002) see the new rehabilitationism as a potential vehicle of compatibility between risk and need, and between risk management and rehabilitation, her caution that the operational reality of practice may not bear this out is welcome. Risk classifications for example are still subject to the residual autonomy and discretion of probation officers (Kemshall et al. 2002) and criminogenic risk/need tools are not always used with integrity (Beaumont et al. 2001). While risk classifications and subsequent targeting are driven by the principle of eligibility (the offender meets the risk score), probation officers are also concerned with issues of suitability (is the offender suitable for the programme, willing and motivated), and with viability (can the offender get there, does it fit with their lifestyle and so on) (Kemshall et al. 2002). These are essentially individualized assessments that are set against the aggregated assessments from risk scores. While for policy makers targeting may mean targeting groups of offenders on the basis of risk thresholds, for probation officers it means targeting an individual for an appropriate intervention (Kemshall et al. 2002). Hence risk and targeting are understood and deployed differently. This can make the operation of any case management system based upon 'risk bands' very difficult to achieve.

The discourse of risk has also served to reinscribe the causes of crime as risks, those factors seen to predispose a person to criminal behaviour, and more importantly inscribes the means by which an individual may be prevented from criminal acts as resilience (Faulkner 2001: 99). This not only can serve to justify early and preventive interventions, particularly with young offenders, but also serves to responsibilize individuals and communities for their own crime management (Rose 2000). Within probation this is epitomized by the cognitive-behavioural programmes of effective practice that seek to build resilience to criminal behaviour and choices while teaching self-risk management and correcting 'thinking deficits' (Kemshall 2002b; Raynor 2002). 'What works' can be understood as part of a broader social and criminal justice policy agenda of citizen re-moralization and responsibilization under New Labour (Drakeford and Vanstone 2000; Kemshall 2002b). In essence New Labour inherited a penal policy in which the social causes of crime were eschewed, and penal policy represented a shift from a rehabilitative society to an exclusionary one (Young 1998, 1999: Rodger 2000). In a climate in which 'what counts is what works' the recycling of any conservative policy deemed to have utility was accepted (Labour Party 1997). 'Blairism' has been infused with an emphasis upon self-reliance and responsibilization, epitomized by Blair's statement that it is a 'something for something society' in which there are 'no rights without responsibilities' (Blair 1998: 4). In essence, the 'responsible citizen' is required to self-manage and exercise prudential choices towards socially desirable ends within an overarching principle of self-regulation. The responsible citizen will make the required choice. Those who do not are recast as risky and blameworthy, in need of re-moralization and correction. Offenders are of course a key group in this re-moralization agenda, and the probation service is a key moral engineer in its delivery (Gibbs et al. 1992). This has resulted in a new bifurcation in 'Third Way' penality between those who can be remoralized and socially included, and those who cannot and are consequently subject to increased exclusionary and risk management techniques such as preventative custody and zero-tolerance policing (Sullivan 2001). (While it is recognized that the term 'Third Way' is open to debate and interpretation, the usage here is derived from Giddens' thesis in *The Third Way* (1998b) and the expression given to it by New Labour in the UK: see Blair 1998.) In probation the choice is more usually between those who comply with programmes, and those who become the subject of breach and enforcement.

While cognitive behavioural programmes are only one part of a broader crime reduction strategy in which the government has promised to be 'tough on crime and tough on the causes of crime' (Blair 1993, 2002; see also Vanstone 2000), individual deficits have more often been targeted than structural issues, and the 'pathfinder' programme and national curriculum of effective practice has largely been defined in individualistic and corrective terms. The emphasis upon coerced compliance and a standardized national curriculum has already resulted in high attrition rates and national recognition that targets may not subsequently be met (National Probation Service 2001: 22–6). The linkage of enforcement to effective programmes has changed the status and meaning of such rehabilitative processes, with effective practice as a complementary strategy to more overt risk management tactics such as preventative sentencing and intensive community risk management (Kemshall 2002b). In this 'new rehabilitationism' it is not risk management and rehabilitation that are 'partners in crime' (Robinson 1999: 427), it is *risk and responsibilization*.

Summary

Contemporary criminal justice is often contradictory and oscillates between an economic rationalist approach sited upon the entrepreneurial self (both the law-abiding citizen who should avoid risks, and the rational choice offender) and an expressive rationality concerned with populism and the regulation of dangerous others (Pratt 1995, 1996, 2000b; O'Malley 2000, 2001a, 2001b; Garland 2001). This 'schizophrenic' criminal justice (Sullivan 2001) is evidenced in probation by the bifurcation between dangerous offenders and reoffending risk, and between those who will comply with re-moralization and those who will not. Consequently risk is deployed differently in probation practice, and as Brown (2000: 106) expresses it about penal policy generally, risk 'emerge[s] from more than one system of thought'. Within probation this has led to a difference between politically and policy framed risks and their actual operational deployment in the agency (Kemshall 1998; Kemshall and Maguire 2001; Robinson 2002). The Probation Service is now confirmed in its role as a public protection agency, directly accountable to the Home Secretary, with 'protection of the public', the 'reduction of reoffending' and the 'proper punishment of offenders' all statutory duties given by the Criminal Justice and Court Services Act 2000. Increased accountability, fiscal control and centrally driven policy-making do not leave a lot of room for manoeuvre, and the scope for continued resistance and firewalls to risk-based practice is being steadily eroded. While the Probation Service has a long history of reinvention in the face of policy change (McWilliams 1987), the prospects for further reinvention should public protection and effective practice fail are bleak.

Note

1 This section is based upon research conducted with Professor Mike Maguire, Dr Lesley Noaks, Dr Emma Wincup, Karen Sharpe and Rob Jago for the Home Office Policing and Reducing Crime Unit, subsequently published as Police Research Series paper 139, and upon a further publication with Professor Maguire in *Punishment and Society*, 2001, and subsequent research on value for money and evaluation of MAPPPs by the author.

Further reading

Kemshall, H. (1998) *Risk in Probation Practice*. Aldershot: Ashgate.
For reviews of legislative and policy developments in the 1980s and 1990s see: Cavadino, M., Crow, I. and Dignan, J. (2000) *Criminal Justice 2000*. Winchester: Waterside Press.
Dunbar, I. and Langdon, A. (1998) *Tough Justice Sentencing and Penal Policies in the 1990s*. London: Blackstone Press.
Nash, M. (1999) *Police, Probation and Protecting the Public*. London: Blackstone Press.

chapter five

Risk and policing

Introduction

Recent analyses of policing in Britain have explored the challenges and restructuring posed by late modernity. Central to such analyses have been issues of security, risk and governance (Johnston 2000). The formation and operation of a bureaucratically organized police force has been seen as essential to the development and consolidation of the modern nation-state (McMullan 1987; Dandeker 1990; Johnston 2000), providing security against internal threat. Johnston for example points out that explanations for the emergence of a modern police force have been seen 'as a response to the problems of crime and disorder arising under capitalist industrialisation and urbanisation' (Johnston 2000: 11), particularly within the Anglo-American model. He divides these analyses into two broad approaches: 'orthodox' or conservative, and 'revisionist' or class-based (see also Reiner 2000). The orthodox view sees the emergence of a modern police force as a response to the inefficiency and inability of traditional policing systems to manage the escalating crime problem (Reiner 2000). The revisionist view sees the major impetus as the requirement to discipline and regulate the working class (Spitzer and Scull 1977). In this approach, policing became part of a 'wider process in which the costs of reproduction of labour power were socialized through the collective provision of health, welfare and protection' (Johnston 2000: 12).

However, Johnston warns against an overly teleological and functional approach to police history, not least on the grounds that the Anglo-American model does not reflect the diversity of policing at both local and global levels, and breaks between 'old' and 'new' are rarely that well defined (Johnston 1992, 2000). While seeking to avoid simplistic social determinism, many leading analysts agree that the 'hallmark of the modern state' is the 'monopolisation of legitimate force in its territory' and that 'policing is at the heart of the functioning of the state' (Reiner 1992: 762). In this sense changes in policing are affected by broader 'changes in the social order' (Reiner 1992: 762). Johnston for example sees the impact of globalization as significant for policing, particularly economic, social and state restructuring under the post-Fordism of late modernity (as discussed earlier in this volume). In brief, his argument in two key themes dominate the 'social plurality' of late modern societies such as Britain: mass consumption and the commodification of all aspects of life, and a growing preoccupation with risk and security. He sees the commodification of security, particularly around 'consumption locales' such as shopping malls, as a key meshing of both preoccupations. Security itself is prone to inexhaustible growth, a major prerequisite of capitalist markets:

> the success of consumer capitalism is based upon the indefinite expansion of demand rather than the satisfaction of need. As Spitzer (1987) points out, the objective consumption of security – through the provision of bars, bolts, alarms . . . CCTV cameras and razor wire – is unlikely to satiate the demand for subjective security. Indeed, such are the contradictions of consumption that the more security we consume, the less secure we may feel.
>
> (Johnston 2000: 23)

This of course is the paradox of risk eloquently presented by Beck (1992a, 1992b) and reviewed in Chapter 1 of this volume.

While Johnston (2000) warns against a teleological understanding of risk-based policing in late modernity, he provides a detailed analysis of risk-oriented policing in which both sociological and advanced liberal theorizing on risk is used. In this analysis policing is characterized by both risk-based *and* disciplinary approaches, and detailed empirical evidence is provided of risk-based police practice in particular areas, for example zero-tolerance policing. This chapter will examine current trends in policing and the extent to which they are evidence of an increasingly risk-infused approach to public policing in the UK.

However, before embarking upon this, the broader issue of transformation or continuity in policing will be addressed.

Late modern policing: transformation or continuity?

In a seminal article, Bayley and Shearing (1996) argued that:

> Modern democratic countries like the United States, Britain and Canada have reached a watershed in the evolution of their systems of crime control and law enforcement. Future generations will look back on our era as a time when one system of policing ended and another took place.
> (Bayley and Shearing 1996: 585)

Along with other commentators, they identify the following as key to current changes in the policing systems of western societies:

- developments in actuarial justice (Feeley and Simon 1992, 1994)
- the availability of new technologies and the growth of risk-based information systems (Ericson and Haggerty 1997)
- the globalization of crime and policing (Sheptycki 1997)
- the growth of private security and the end of state monopoly on policing (Shearing and Stenning 1987; Bayley and Shearing 1996; Loader 1999, Loader and Sparks 2002)
- changes in police organization, management and accountability (Jones and Newburn 1994; Jones et al. 1994)
- a crisis of identity (Bayley and Shearing 1996)
- the challenges of postmodern society and policing in 'a millennial malaise' coupled with and the end of the 'Golden Age of Policing' (Reiner 1992).

Both the significance of these factors and the extent to which changes in policing practices represent transformation or continuity has been hotly disputed (see for example Jones and Newburn 2002). The counter-argument focuses on the following areas:

- the extent to which the 'transformation thesis' has global application or is restricted to the USA
- the extent to which the public policing monopoly has been broken
- the extent to which policing has fragmented or is a displacement of policing to other formalised processes of social control.
> (from Jones and Newburn 2002)

Part of the dispute arises from the use of terminology in which police and policing are often conflated (Johnston 1992). As Johnston (2000: 8) puts it:

'policing, a social function' is used interchangeably with 'police, a specific body of personnel'. Police and the function of policing are not necessarily synonymous: 'policing may be carried out by a diverse array of people and techniques of which the modern police is only one' (Reiner 1997a: 1005).

The activities of policing can be provided through diverse personnel and agencies. However, as Johnston (2000: 8) points out, the avoidance of a reductionist definition has often led to 'an expansive one', hence policing is readily equated with social control. In turn this runs the risk of devaluing the concept of social control, turning it into what Cohen has called a 'Mickey Mouse concept' (Cohen 1985; Johnston 2000). Bayley and Shearing attempt to capture this balance in their article by stating that: 'the scope of our discussion is bigger than the breadbox of the police but smaller than the elephant of social control. Our focus is on the self-conscious process whereby societies designate and authorize people to create public safety' (Bayley and Shearing 1996: 586). By drawing on key literature Johnston (2000) provides a useful definition of policing comprising the following elements:

- Policing as a purposive activity designed to produce security through 'the creation of systems of surveillance coupled with the threat of sanctions' (Reiner 1997a: 1005).
- Such policing activities can take place through agencies other than the police force, including commercial and private police.
- Other forms of social control can be included in so far as they are 'organised forms of order maintenance, peacekeeping, crime investigation and prevention, and other forms of investigation – which may involve a conscious exercise of coercive power' (Jones and Newburn 1998: 18; 2002).
- Policing is about the 'assurance' and provision of security (Shearing 1992), although this does not necessarily guarantee that it will be achieved (Reiner 1997a).
- Security is a contentious notion – whose security is secured and for what purpose? Hence policing is not necessarily a consensual activity.
- Policing is concerned with governance, that is the regulation of conduct through rule, and as such need not take place solely through the state or state agencies.

(from Johnston 2000: 8–10; see also Shearing 1992;
Bayley and Shearing 1996; Reiner 1997a, 1997b;
Jones and Newburn 1998, 2002)

The transformation thesis as expressed by Bayley and Shearing (1996) rests on two key contentions:

- the demise of the public police monopoly and the increase in other modes of policing

- the search by the public police for an identity, particularly as expressed in developments like 'community policing'.

Evidence for the former comes from two sources: the increase in private security provision since the 1960s, and the increased role for informal modes of social control and the displacement of crime management to citizens through mechanisms such as Neighbourhood Watch (Bayley and Shearing 1996: 586–7). Evidence for the latter comes from the increased pursuit of community policing in the face of ineffectiveness in general detection and crime reduction strategies. Bayley and Shearing express it thus:

> Its philosophy is straightforward: the police cannot successfully prevent or investigate crime, without the willing participation of the public, therefore police should transform communities from being passive consumers of police protection to active co-producers of community safety. Community policing changes the orientation of the police and represents a sharp break with the past. Community policing transforms the police from being an emergency squad in the fight against crime to becoming a primary diagnostician and treatment co-ordinators.
>
> (Bayley and Shearing 1996: 588)

In practice, community policing has taken three key forms:

- A pragmatic response to strained community relationships, usually in ethnic minority communities and usually after significant levels of conflict (such as the Handsworth (Birmingham) riots in the 1980s). This has been described as a 'largely cosmetic exercise masking reluctance to make major changes when entrenched patrol and investigation methods have failed' (Fielding 1995: 25).
- A mechanism for developing communication with key groups (often described as 'hard to reach') in which a 'common good' is defined (for example a crackdown on drug-trafficking in a neighbourhood).
- To enhance information gathering in locales in order to facilitate more effective crime-oriented policing such as targeting of habitual burglars and drug-traffickers. This can also include what is referred to as 'order-maintenance policing' in which the 'disorderly, unruly, and disturbing behaviour of people in public places, whether lawful or not' is challenged. This is pursued partly as a public relations exercise to reassure the public, and to set zero-tolerance thresholds for crime. This has been called 'community policing with a hard edge' (Bayley and Shearing 1996: 589; see also Weatheritt 1983, 1986, 1987, 1988; Fielding 1995, 2002).

While the issue of community policing will be more fully explored later in this chapter, the key to Bayley and Shearing's (1996: 595) contention is that the pluralization and dispersal of policing has increased 'the informal regulatory control of crime' in which 'social pressure rather than law ensures discipline'. In this scenario the spectre of community policing they draw is rather bleak:

> Seen in these terms, community policing, which is community-based crime prevention under governmental auspices, is a contradiction in terms. It requires the police, who are bound by law, to lead communities in informal surveillance, analysis, and treatment. Community policing is a license for police to intervene in the private life of individuals. It harnesses the coercive power of the state to social amelioration. This represents an expansion of police power, and is much more in keeping with the continental European than with the Anglo-American traditions of policing. Community policing may be an answer to the dualism brought by pluralizing but at the risk of encouraging the 'vigilantism of the majority' (Johnston 1994).
>
> (Bayley and Shearing 1996: 595)

The key rebuttal to the transformation thesis comes from Jones and Newburn (2002). In brief, they argue that the 'Golden Age of Policing' associated with the public police monopoly is largely myth rather than reality (see Reiner 1992). The notion of consensual policing was achieved at a time of social harmony and stable economic and social conditions in the early postwar years, although as Reiner (1992: 763) points out, the *Dixon of Dock Green* imagery hid the reality that policing of the social and economically marginal was conflictual even in the rosy era of the 1950s. For Jones and Newburn (2002) the demise of stable social and economic conditions at the close of the twentieth century has resulted in the weakening of informal social controls leading to increased pressure 'upon public policing services' and a greater exposure of the myth of state effectiveness in crime control. They also dispute the contention that public policing has been subject to pluralization and fragmentation. By drawing on nineteenth- and twentieth-century material they demonstrate that a public monopoly of policing in Britain did not exist, and that the expansion of private security began prior to the 1960s, although to a lesser extent in Britain than in the USA. Importantly they point out that much private policing has taken place in public spaces, for example shopping malls, and as such is highly visible. The key issue may well be the visibility and profile of private security, rather than its volume, and for Jones and Newburn (2002: 134) there is 'considerable continuity as well as change'. Noaks (2000: 145) for example in an analysis of private policing in residential areas notes that the shift from public to private services 'has been a gradual process rather than an abrupt separation' located within the broader privatization of public services pursued under the New Right. However, the higher levels of satisfaction with the surveillance levels provided by private policing leads Noaks

(2000) to suggest that the relationship between public and private policing does need to be addressed.

Has public policing changed?

Are there discernible changes in public policing, and if so, how fundamental and 'epochal' are they? Commentators within the governmentality approach see a fundamental shift from what O'Malley and Palmer (1996) have called Keynesian policing based upon a welfarist agenda of reformative discipline and concerned with governing the 'social' to post-Keynesian policing based upon responsibilized communities and shared responsibility for crime management.

In brief, O'Malley and Palmer (1996) identify the key elements of Keynesian policing as:

- Public dependency upon professional expertise, for example upon the welfare net, and dependence upon professional, public policing as part of this wider network of state services.
- 'Welfare policing' linked to pathological notions of crime causation, notions prevalent within the welfare state (see also Gordon 1987).
- An acceptance of public policing as a key mechanism in ensuring social stability and order.

They identify the key features of post-Keynesian policing as:

- Weakened dependence upon the professional expertise of the public police, including a willingness to purchase policing services from elsewhere.
- The replacement of the 'social' and the 'state' with neo-liberal notions such as the 'active community'. This is paralleled by promulgation of a non-interventionist state within which both the individual and the community are constructed as active consumers of security and active agents in crime risk management.
- The dominance of the market and the prioritizing of market efficiency in public service provision.
- The replacement of bureaucracy in public services with performance management, characterized by audit and accountability.
- The replacement of trust with audit (Rose 1993; Power 1999), public regulation and transparency (Osborne 1993), and increased attention to the governance (that is regulation of conduct) of the police (Jones et al. 1994; McLaughlin 1994; Jones and Newburn 1997).

(from O'Malley and Palmer 1996: 141–2;
see also Keat 1991: 1; McMullan 1998)

In policy and practice terms this has led to an emphasis upon local initiatives and responses, and the promulgation of active and enterprising communities working in *partnership* with the police to achieve community-based crime management. Central to this approach is the notion of the responsibilized and rational choice community as well as the rational choice individual (as discussed in Chapter 3 in this volume), capable of making well-informed choices about risk if appropriately trained and if exposed to the correct information. For O'Malley and Palmer (1996) this combination of 'partnership' and 'shared responsibility' has led to a delicate balance between police expertise and professionalism expressed as 'proactive leadership' on the one hand, and increased responsibilization of the public on the other – the latter to be achieved through training and socialization into the skills of community crime management (O'Malley and Palmer 1996: 144). Such training is seen as essential for individuals and communities 'made dependent' through welfarism, and is essential for the micro government 'at a distance' of neo-liberal regimes (Rose 1996a, 1996b). The rational choice approach to risk underpins such policing. Rational actors will embrace shared responsibility and the proactive leadership of the police as it is in their best interests to do so. This epitomizes the two central features of post-Keynesian policing: an economic framing of crime risk and its effective management; and the responsibilization of individuals and communities in crime control. Post-Keynesian 'community policing increasingly centres around the police force's responsiveness to private and local demands, expressed in the communal consultation with committees of residents or local business people' (O'Malley and Palmer 1996: 149; see also Stenson 1993).

Post-Keynesian policing: rhetoric or reality?

While broad claims are made for a transformation in policing, it is important to review the extent to which they are expressed in 'material form' (Garland 1996). Based upon various empirical studies, O'Malley and Palmer (1996) identify several areas in which 'resistance' and 'firewalls' exist:

- Community policing does not enjoy wholehearted support within the police. In particular, the police do not like to consult or share power, and the culture of police dominance is difficult to break (McConville and Shepherd 1992; McLaughlin and Murji 1993; Bennett 1994). Community policing is thus reduced to rhetoric (Beyer 1991), and consultation used merely as a vehicle for expressing police views (Moir and Moir 1992; Bennett 1994).
- Resistance is not merely a rank-and-file issue. Chief constables have also been targeted for increased control and accountability (see Home Office 1994a; Jones and Newburn 1997), and public policing has been increasingly exposed to the managerialism of New Right approaches to public sector management (Hood 1991; Leishman et al. 1996). While

some chief constables have welcomed the opportunity to become 'change managers' (O'Malley and Palmer 1996; see also Etter and Palmer 1995), impact has been uneven and the relationship between central government control and local management has remained difficult (Jones and Newburn 1997). As Johnston (2000: 81) puts it: 'Managerialism is unable to expunge politics from policing' not least because newly empowered consumers articulate various and often competing demands that have to be prioritized. Sometimes decisions over such priorities are local, sometimes they are centrally imposed (Johnston 2000). Such disputes are particularly acute in local communities characterized by diversity and pluralism, and where local concerns are not commensurate with centrally set crime management priorities.

- Disputes over priorities are exacerbated by pressure for cost-effectiveness and performance management, resulting in the pursuit of 'perverse incentives' (easily cleared up crimes for example rather than those that most concern the community), and the 'civilianization of the police' and deployment of officers to targeted policing rather than visible (and community reassuring) policing. While this may initially leave public police to do 'real' police work, it also opens the door to police provision from other sources, including the private sector.
- Policing, even high-profile 'real' policing, is open to competition. O'Malley and Palmer (1996) note the redeployment of national security forces to domestic policing matters as external threats have fallen (for example MI5 attention to drug-trafficking: Cohen 1996). The long-term impact of such trends on public policing is difficult to gauge; however, there is potential for the police to lose market share at both the high and low ends of its task range, possibly exacerbating the 'crisis of identity' identified by Bayley and Shearing (1996). The response to such a crisis is not preordained (O'Malley 1999a) and policing has more than one possible future (Johnston 2000).
- The impact of audit and increased accountability is also variable, both within the UK and across the anglophone countries (Reiner and Cross 1991; Moir and Eijkman 1992; Jones and Newburn 1997). Hence national and local responses to marketization may vary, and the extent of post-Keynesian policing may differ in practice.

(adapted from O'Malley and Palmer 1996; see also
Jones and Newburn 1997, 2002; Johnston 2000;
Reiner 2000)

The extent of transformation and restructuring is far from clear cut, and while broad trends can be identified, their implementation is somewhat variable. Leishman et al. (1996) draw attention to the 'policing policy network' as a site of resistance to the Conservative agenda of police reform in

1990s Britain for example. The New Public Management (NPM) agenda of the Posen and Cassels inquiries (Home Office 1994b, 1995a (Posen); Police Foundation and Policy Studies Institute (PSI) 1994 (Cassels)) were not fully executed. Leishman et al. (1996: 17) put this down to the fact that 'an attempt to bring markets into networks and consequently redistribute power, may encounter resistance from entrenched interests within policy networks, thus blunting the thrust of reform'.

In this analysis the fragmented and vested interest nature of the police policy network itself provides a firewall against central government plans, epitomized by highly vocal police staff associations and their capacity to gain public sympathy and support (Leishman et al. 1996). More recently, attempts to create community support officers and increase the privatization of the police under the Police Reform Bill has met resistance from police, public and the Lords, for whom the new 'semi-police' are unacceptable (*The Times*, 26 April 2002: 12). However, Leishman et al. (1996) identify four key areas in the restructuring of the police:

- The increased centralization of the police (Loveday 1991, 1994, 1995, 1996), reflected in increased central government control of the police through the Inspectorate and the Audit Commission in particular, and a number of key national initiatives such as the development of the police national computer. The Police and Magistrates' Courts Act (PMCA) 1994 laid 'down key national objectives supported by performance indicators for the police' and a reporting system to ensure that local objectives are in line with national ones (see also Jones and Newburn 1997).

- Paradoxically, decentralization has also occurred with the police exercising 'greater managerial and operational autonomy within an increasingly centralised policy and operational framework'. In essence, central government 'steering' and the police 'rowing' (Osborne and Gaebler 1993). PMCA 1994 requires chief constables to draw up local plans but they must be commensurate 'with the national policing objectives set by the Home Secretary'. Strategic decisions remain central, with operational ones increasingly devolved.

- Privatization has continued, and in Britain with little difference between Conservative and Labour governments on this key issue (Johnston 2000; Reiner 2000). Leishman et al. (1996: 22) see privatization as taking four key forms: 'load-shedding; compulsory competitive tendering and contracting-out; charging for services; imitating private sector management styles'. Load-shedding is reflected in the increased use of civilian workers in police tasks (for example the use of such workers to maintain sex offender registers), and the expansion of private policing and the private security sector (see also Bayley and Shearing 1996). Prisoner escort duties are an example of contracting-out, and recently leaked material on the Prison Reform Bill suggests that there are plans to contract out detention officers with the power to carry out intimate searches (*The Times*, 26 April 2002: 12). While charging for services is less developed, there is certainly more emphasis upon budgeting, financial management and value for money issues. Finally the impact of NPM has continued with the introduction of private sector management values, techniques and language, with the Sheehy report giving chief constables the 'right to manage' (Home Office, Northern Ireland Office and Scottish Office 1993).

- Increased 'Europeanization' of the police has also been identified (Leishman et al. 1996). However, the evidence for this trend is weaker (van Reenen 1989; Robertson 1994; Sheptycki 1995; Johnston 2000). Whilst greater European integration presents increased crime opportunities (for example trafficking in illegal immigrants, drugs and counterfeit goods) and requires increased European cooperation to deal with them, Britain has looked across the Atlantic to the USA for models of police practice and governance rather more than it has looked to Europe (Hebenton and Thomas 1995). As Johnston (2000: 122) puts it: 'the transnationalization of policing in no way implies homogenization'.

(adapted from Leishman et al. 1996: 20–4)

While Leishman et al. (1996: 25) point out that 'it is far easier to say where we came from than where we are going', it is possible to discern at the present time (seven years after their publication) that there is evidence of a move to a 'new policing order'. Its manifestation in 'material forms' (Garland 1996) may be variable and mediated by various firewalls and sites of resistance, and the transformation may be more cumulative than epochal (Jones and Newburn 2002). However, there are significant changes in the form and nature of public policing that can be placed within broader economic, structural and social changes, coalescing in what Reiner (2000: 200) has called a 'new political and social configuration, with profound implications for crime, order and policing'. Of particular significance are the weakening of traditional social bonds and informal mechanisms of social control (Newburn 1992; Jones and Newburn 2002), rising crime rates, increased social exclusion, and the erosion of social welfarism and its 'soft' social controls (Reiner 2000). The 'hollowing out' of the state and the increased immiseration of the so-called underclass in post-Fordist capitalism have had profound implications for policing, not least in terms of its legitimacy and effectiveness as a social control mechanism. As Reiner (2000: 78) points out, policing has always fallen disproportionately on the economically inactive and those excluded from full citizenship (see also Waddington 1999). However, this has been exacerbated by the 'structural inevitability' of long-term unemployment that disproportionately affects young males and black people. Whilst Reiner warns against linking crime and unemployment in any simplistic way, he does contend that 'the structurally generated formation of a completely marginalised segment of society is a major source of the huge growth recently of crime, disorder, and tensions around policing (N. Davies 1998)' (Reiner 2000: 79).

Legitimacy is strained by conflictual rather than consensual policing, exacerbated by 'institutional racism' (MacPherson 1999) and the failure to uphold the rights of black victims (for example Stephen Lawrence, and the more recent police failures in the case of the murder of Damilola Taylor). In this climate community policing is perceived not so much as a partnership in which collective interests and needs are identified and met, but is rather about 'policing communities of risk' (Johnston 1997, 2000: 55). Pluralism and diversity challenge the consensual nature of policing, if indeed any 'Golden Age' did exist (see Reiner 1992, 2000), and policing becomes increasingly politicized. (The 'myth of the British bobby' and the 'Golden Age' of policing are explored in Reiner 1992, 2000.) Nor is legitimacy merely contested by the underclass. As Reiner points out, the 'chattering classes', engaged in what they see as legitimate political protest particularly in the 1980s and 1990s, have been increasingly subjected to police regulation. This has resulted in critical questioning of the police role and its legitimacy from those whose support could traditionally be counted on. Such questioning has extended to the efficiency and effectiveness of the police in delivering its main promise: crime reduction and crime control.

Summary

The preceding section examined the extent of changes in contemporary policing and the public police. While there is dispute about the extent to which such changes are 'epochal', key trends and characteristics can be discerned. There is evidence that the social, economic and structural changes in post-welfare western societies, particularly anglophone societies, have had a profound impact upon the public police and the nature of policing. While what O'Malley and Palmer (1996) call post-Keynesian policing may still be an emerging form, subject to various firewalls and sites of resistance, there are significant features already present in contemporary policing. The rest of the chapter will examine these emerging features in more detail through a closer examination of risk-based policing, including in the following areas:

- community policing
- surveillance and intelligence-led policing
- zero-tolerance policing (ZTP).

Risk-based policing

Analyses of risk-based policing have been located within broader analyses of changes in crime management, in particular the move from disciplinary to actuarially based practices of crime control (Simon 1988; Feeley and Simon 1992, 1994; see also Chapters 2 and 3 in this volume). In brief, such analyses posit that attention to individual behaviour change and offender rehabilitation typical of disciplinary techniques is superseded by attention to the aggregate assessment and regulation of risky groups through anticipatory strategies of risk assessment, prevention and exclusion. Central to such an approach is the rational actor, capable of rational assessment and 'weighing up the risks, potential gains and potential costs, and then committing an offence only when the benefits are perceived to outweigh the losses' (O'Malley 1992: 264). Victims and communities are similarly 'rationalized', assessing risks and taking avoidance action, or working in partnership with the police to develop local risk management plans (Felson 1998). As Johnston (2000: 56) puts it: 'risk management is actuarial, proactive and anticipatory, the application of those principles requiring the collation and analysis of information obtained through the systematic surveillance of those at risk or likely to cause risk'.

In his seminal work Johnston (2000) identifies key exemplars of risk-based policing: community policing, intelligence-led policing and zero-tolerance policing, although Johnston is at pains to argue that current police practice and policy is a hybrid of both disciplinary and actuarial practices.

Risk and community policing

As stated earlier, community policing has taken three key forms: public relations with minority communities and a response to the severe challenges of policing diversity and pluralism; partnerships to tackle specific problems (for example drug-dealing in particular neighbourhoods) and 'hard-edged' community policing based upon intelligence-led policing and targeting (see Fielding 1995, 2002). It is also worth noting that while community policing has emerged to some extent from the contemporary 'crisis in policing' (Fielding 2002), the public are not necessarily disengaged from policing or critical of the existence of policing per se, rather the key issues are the 'justness' of policing and the effectiveness of its performance in crime reduction (Fielding 2002: 150). Community policing has attempted to bridge the gap in both arenas.

The inception of community policing is most often associated with John Alderson (1979, 1982), the Chief Constable of Devon and Cornwall, who advocated a closer working relationship between police and local communities. However, the development can be located within broader late 1970s and 1980s trends towards more systemic approaches to crime management (Tutt and Giller 1984), and a move from what has been labelled as 'situational crime prevention' (Clarke and Mayhew 1980; Clarke 1992) to 'social crime prevention' (Clarke 1981) – although in practice and policy terms these distinctions have often been blurred (Bottoms 1990; Jones et al. 1994). Laycock and Heal (1989: 320) for example describe how Home Office training on crime prevention reflected this change from 'the previous locks and bars emphasis towards community involvement, crime pattern analysis and inter-agency work'. Certainly the 1980s saw a nationally driven agenda on crime prevention (Home Office 1984b) including the launch of the Safer Cities Programme and Crime Concern (Jones et al. 1994).

Situational crime prevention has its roots in rational theory approaches to crime and particularly crime control (as discussed in Chapter 3 in this volume), in which 'crime arises from an interaction between dispositions, perceived opportunities, and perceived risks (Clarke 1992)' (Jones et al. 1994: 57). In essence, situational crime prevention concentrates on the reduction of crime opportunities usually through the manipulation of environmental factors (such as street lighting, CCTV, 'locks and bars') rather than 'programmes of action which will help change people's attitudes to offending, encourage respect for law and reduce the wish to commit crimes' (Weatheritt 1986: 57, quoted in Jones et al. 1994: 56). Social crime prevention is rooted in social control theories of crime in which social bonds and informal mechanisms of social control are reinforced and communities in effect 'police' themselves more effectively (Jones et al. 1994). The Safer Cities initiative epitomized this approach (Home Office 1984b, 1991). The policy and practice boundary between situational crime prevention and social crime prevention became increasingly permeable throughout the 1980s (Bottoms 1990), resulting in what Hope and Shaw (1988) have labelled 'community-based crime prevention'. This occurred within a growing national agenda that stressed the responsibility for crime prevention was a task for the 'whole community' (Jones et al. 1994: 58; see also Home Office 1991; Chapter 6 in this volume). Central to this notion was the idea of 'community policing' and 'partnership' between communities and police (Fielding 1995).

Partnership and community

Johnston (2000) locates the preoccupation with partnership from the 1980s onwards within broader New Right concerns to 'roll back the state' and advanced liberal concerns to responsibilize citizenship (Johnston 2000: 48, 146). He expresses the problem thus:

> The difficulty for politicians, having mobilized active citizens, is how to contain them within the bounds of central state authority when that very authority is undermined by governmental diversity. Under late

modern conditions there is the probability that acts of autonomous citizenship will increase and the possibility that acts of responsible citizenship will mutate into autonomous forms. Contrary to the dominant view (encapsulated in the 'community policing' and 'partnership models'), the challenge is not only how to mobilize and manage responsible citizens – a task which, in any case, becomes more and more difficult under late modern conditions – but, also, how to incorporate autonomous citizens so that their actions do not degenerate into arbitrary violence and injustice.

(Johnston 2000: 146)

Stenson (1993) for example sees community policing not only as a reaction to inefficient reactive law enforcement, but also as a solution to the more 'intractable problem' of policing the inner cities and minority communities (Stenson 1993: 373). While the term 'community' and its bedfellow 'partnership' have become key terms in the social policy discourse of managing 'troubled' and 'excluded' communities, in practical terms they have been used to close the gap between police and communities and as a pragmatic solution to policing the growing urban crisis without recourse to increasingly reactive, overt and potentially repressive policing (Stenson 1993). Interestingly, Stenson locates early forms of community policing within the Keynesian agenda, with community policing taking the place of the welfare-based institutions of regulation and discipline (for example youth services and social work). Notions of 'serving the community', policing in the public interest and taking a collective approach to risks were strong (Alderson 1982). Whilst the appropriation of community policing to the neo-liberal agenda was by no means predetermined (O'Malley 1992), Stenson argues that community policing has become less concerned with the 'service ethic' and more concerned with problem communities and 'bolstering the preconditions for effective self-policing' (Stenson 1993: 382). Two key issues have provided a catalyst for this agenda: the deteriorating relationship between police and ethnic communities particularly following the 1980s urban riots (McLaughlin 1991; Johnston 2000; Reiner 2000) and the perceived inability of the police to do anything about youth crime and the loss of communal spaces to hostile youth (Campbell 1993; Loader 1996). For Stenson this presents peculiar tensions for policing, in particular how to regulate marginalized groups without exacerbating conflict and adding to their unmanageability. This takes policing into the realm of normative government (Grimshaw and Jefferson 1987), re-educating and remoralizing the marginal towards the 'goals of the social collectivity' (Stenson 1993: 384; see also Miller and Rose 1988, 1992). However, this potentially leaves the police caught between particular communal norms of local communities and wider social norms, and between the accepted norms of society and those of the marginalized. In an era of increasing diversity and lack of trust in professional bodies, the ability of the police to adjudicate between competing norms and between different community interest groups is hampered. Thus 'community' and 'partnership' are themselves contested and problematized concepts (McLaughlin 1994), with the police caught between the 'decent public', the 'rough and respectable' members of the community and increasingly marginalized groups such as young black men (McConville and Shepherd 1992).

Partnership has also been advocated as an innovative approach to crime control (see also Chapter 6 in this volume). As Crawford (2001: 60) puts it: 'an holistic approach to crime and disorder which is problem-focused rather than bureaucracy premised'. However, the diversity of organizations involved has presented practical problems to partnership, resulting in the fragmentation of service delivery and dispersal of accountability (Crawford 2001; Kemshall and Maguire 2001). Paradoxically, while Crime and Disorder partnerships have proliferated, citizens have become more detached from local politics and community activities (Giddens 1990, 1991; Lash 1990; Crawford 1998; Hughes 1998). This results in statutory agencies filling the 'gap', providing leadership and training for those citizens and communities prepared to take on the duties and responsibilities of active citizenship (Blair 1995; Fielding 1995). Rhetorically central control is dispersed to local partnerships and networks, but practically central control is exercised through guidance and audit (Power 1999; Crawford 2001). Partnerships thus find themselves constantly caught between the demands of locale and the 'steers' of central government.

The rhetoric and the reality

Community policing has been dismissed as 'ill-defined' (McLaughlin 1994), pragmatically co-opted to various governmentality agendas (Stenson 1993) and philosophically and empirically ungrounded (Weatheritt 1983). However, as Fielding (1995) notes, its pragmatic and symbolic appeal to policy makers and politicians has not waned (see also Rosenbaum 1994). For Reiner this is merely a myth to promote the notion of effective policing based on 'consent and cooperation' in which policing is constructed as a 'social service delivering good works to a harmonious community of satisfied customers' (Reiner 2000: 108). As Reiner is quick to point out, most policing occurs in conditions of disharmony and contradiction. To some extent, community policing can be understood as a response to such disharmony, particularly in its symbolic functions. For example by ameliorating the worst excesses of 'repressive' policing and in relegitimizing the role of the police in 'distanced' communities. In essence, community policing plays a mediating role between police and public, a mechanism for negotiating and re-enforcing order, hence Banton labelled officers on patrol as *peace* officers rather than law enforcement officers (Banton 1964; Fielding 1995).

However, this presents community policing with its most difficult paradox: the need to 'reconstitute collective communities' with 'collective sentiments' within a society characterized by diversity and plural norms (Johnston 2000: 54). An impossible aim (Mastrofski 1991), epitomized by the difficulty in achieving a consensus about the term 'community policing' and its underlying philosophy (Bennett 1994). While state led in conception and inception, community policing is flawed on two levels: internally by police lack of commitment and underlying culture (McConville and Shepherd 1992), and externally by the structural and social changes engendered by late modernity (Johnston 2000; Reiner 2000). The community requiring policing is in fact a pluralistic heterogeneous community of competing interests. Johnston (1997) argues that the primary response to this has been a shift from community policing of a 'community of collective sentiment' to community policing of communities that are not only 'at risk' but also pose a risk. Community policing is quickly transformed into 'watching communities' (McConville and Shepherd 1992), in which 'information gathering, anticipatory engagement, proactive intervention, systematic surveillance' form a key part of crime management strategies (Johnston 2000: 57). Community policing is quickly co-opted to such strategies as a mechanism for gaining trust, information and intelligence (Gordon 1984).

Intelligence-led policing

Crime control and crime management have been increasingly framed in economic terms (Audit Commission 1993; Sheehy 1993) with police accountability becoming 'calculative and contractual' (Reiner 1993). The 1990s saw managerialism take hold of the public police, not least with greater central control of objectives and performance indicators (McLaughlin 1996), changes to the governance of the police in the Police and Magistrates' Court Act 1994 resulting in increased centralization (Jones and Newburn 1997), and police performance was subjected to cost–benefit calculations (Stockdale et al. 1999) and evidence-led evaluations (Tilley 2001). The Audit Commission (1993: 2) urged the police to be more proactive in its work and introduced the notion of targeting criminals and 'information-led policing'. 'Proactivity' as initially conceived referred to the 'strategic deployment of resources in order to target "criminally active" individuals, so as to obtain evidence for a successful prosecution' (Audit Commission 1993, 1996; Maguire and John 1995; Stockdale et al. 1999: 5). This strategic action was to be intelligence driven in contrast to reactive, demand-led policing. However, as Stockdale et al. (1999) note, the terms proactive and intelligence led have been used interchangeably, and at policy and practice level have taken numerous forms ranging from force-wide proactivity, to proaction only for certain problematic crimes or locales. The strategy also implies a different balance between proactive and reactive policing and a more calculated and rational approach to resource allocation. Stockdale et al. (1997: 7) classify proactivity into three types: specific operations or initiatives, functional changes, and changes in ethos.

Johnston (2000) has argued that this development was given impetus by the commercial security sector and its more risk-infused approach to crime management, in particular the emphasis upon anticipatory and proactive strategies. While the case may be over-stated, it is possible to discern key features such as:

- cost–benefit calculations, for example of detectability and whether the case is worth pursuing
- the redeployment of expertise from the security services to intelligence-led policing
- the growth of surveillance technologies and the use of surveillance to gather key information
- the growth of information technologies such as computer data storage and collation
- the construction of police as 'information brokers', particularly in multi-agency arrangements for crime management, and the role of police officers in collecting, collating and disseminating risk information.

(see Shearing and Stenning 1981; Ericson 1994;
Ericson and Haggerty 1997; Johnston 2000)

Ericson and Haggerty (1997: 18) have critically argued that policing has become significantly risk-infused and present detailed empirical evidence for a transition from traditional policing focused on 'deviance, control and order' to a focus on 'risk, surveillance, and security'. They express it thus: 'The concern is less with the labelling of deviants as outsiders and more on developing a risk-profile knowledge of individuals to ascertain and manage their place in institutions' (Ericson and Haggerty 1997: 18).

Ericson and Haggerty (1997: 18) argue that law enforcement is itself changed, from 'deterrence-based law enforcement towards compliance-based law enforcement'. In other words, setting acceptable risk standards and proactively identifying and monitoring those likely to breach them (such as sex offenders in the community: see Chapter 4 in this volume). In this approach 'deviance' is a normal expectation of the system, a risk hazard to be identified and managed. The system is essentially anticipationist: continually collecting risk information, carrying out risk assessments and exchanging them. Reichman (1986) has described this as 'front-loading' risk assessment, often at the expense of risk management (Kemshall 1998). The focus on risk assessment and attendant information gathering and exchange has also made the boundaries between public police and private security, and between police and other state agencies more permeable, exacerbated by computer-based exchanges and shared databases (Ericson 1994; Ericson and Haggerty 1997; Kemshall and Maguire 2001, 2002).

For Ericson and Haggerty what characterizes this communication is its risk nature, located in virtual space, and the dispersed responsibility for risk it engenders. Responsibility for risk management is dispersed to other agencies (such as Probation), or directly to voluntary groups (such as Neighbourhood Watch) or communities themselves. Problem-solving, community and intelligence-led policing mesh in a logic of risk based on prevention, anticipation and proactivity. As Maguire (2000) states, what they have in common is their *'strategic, future-oriented and targeted* approach to crime control' comprising assessment and management of *'developing problems or risks'* within a system of proactive and intelligence-led policing (Maguire 2000: 316 emphases as original).

Ericson (1994: 162) has described this as the transformation of community policing to communications policing. In essence, a community panopticon delivered by computer chip in which surveillance is routine, remote and automatic, under the watchful, comforting eye of CCTV (Lyon 2001). The community panopticon is legitimized by the notion of consensual community policing in which 'the police are expected to work with local institutions and organisations to help them look after their own risk management' (Ericson and Haggerty 1997: 67).

This approach was crystallized in the Crime and Disorder Act 1998, which placed a statutory duty on the police and local authorities to formulate and implement crime reduction and community safety strategies (Crawford 1998; see also chapter 6 in this volume). This approach to crime risk management has the following key features:

- a problem-oriented approach to crime management
- evidence led and dependent upon information collection, analysis and management
- crime analysis and targeting
- local surveys and auditing
- consultation with communities
- a partnership approach to delivery
- a cycle of planning, implementation, evaluation and review.

(Crawford 1998, 1999; Hough and Tilley 1998; Matthews and Pitts 2001)

Zero-tolerance policing

While ostensibly concerned with low-level crime, zero-tolerance policing does embody the risk features of proactivity and anticipationism. Informed by Wilson and Kelling's (1982, 1989) 'broken windows' thesis, it has in practice also been concerned with the reclamation of threatened spaces (Campbell 1993) and the targeting of problematic persons such as youth and unemployed people. Robustly and aggressively implemented in the USA (for example New York: Bratton 1997), Ray Mallon's initiative in

Middlesbrough is the UK's most famous example. ZTP has two central concerns: the reinforcement of discipline on disorderly communities through a 'civilizing process' most usually targeted at problematic youth or other marginalized persons, and a concern with improvements to quality of life for the majority of residents in a local area. Such policing aims to restore confidence in the police, but more importantly to mobilize 'decent citizens' to address crime within their midst (for example around drug-dealing) and to engage the 'respectable majority' in local crime management (Dennis and Mallon 1997; Johnston 2000). Over-robust ZTP has been criticized for precipitating community disorder and urban riots (Scarman 1981; Crawford 1998), and as short-term policing that merely displaces risk rather than eradicates it (Pollard 1997), usually to those areas least able to bear it (Walklate and Evans 1999).

In its most extensive form it has been integrated with intelligence gathering, profiling and targeting of key criminals, and problem-solving 'crime busting' around particular offences such as drug-dealing (Bratton 1997; Dennis and Mallon 1997). For Johnston this results in the meshing of ZTP within wider risk-based police practices, although its actual operation on the ground may combine both 'disciplinary and risk based techniques' (Johnston 2000: 68).

While most often associated in the media with 'quality of life' offences, ZTP has had a more extensive application. Most notably intelligence led and targeted policing linked to management reforms and a more strategic approach to policing (Bratton 1997; Johnston 2000). For Bratton this has meant the replacement of traditional policing techniques such as 'rapid response', 'random patrol' and 'reactive investigation' with the new techniques of community policing: 'partnership', 'problem-solving', and 'prevention' (Bratton 1997: 32), and strategically based 'crime fighting' using extensive computerized databases of key information. It is the latter approach that has taken the greatest hold within the UK (the Hartlepool initiative notwithstanding) and aggressive ZTP has transmuted into a subtler problem-solving policing with emphasis upon 'identifying and tackling the root causes of crime, disorder and fear in conjunction with our partners in the community' (Pollard 1997: 60). However, the term 'community' has been seen as increasingly problematic (Walklate and Evans 1999), based upon presumptions of 'collective sentiment' and homogeneity that rarely exist in late modernity (Johnston 2000), and prone to stereotypical characterizations of 'strong' communities in wealthy areas, and 'weak' communities in areas of low income and diversity (Walklate and Evans 1999). For Johnston this transforms the rhetoric of community policing as 'collective sentiment' to the reality of community policing as risk containment, policing boundaries of risk between communities and literally managing risk in place.

Conclusion: new risks, new policing?

There is growing evidence for risk-based policing, although as with other areas of criminal justice the transformation is by no means wholesale. While the social, economic and cultural conditions of post-Keynesian and post-Fordism have had a significant impact on public policing (Reiner 2000), their expression in the 'material forms' of policing are often complex and affected by firewalls of resistance (Garland 1996; O'Malley 2000, 2001b). At the micro-level, change in police practices can be variable, with national policy and objectives subject to local context, frontline interpretation and worker resistance (Johnston 1987; Maguire 2000). At the national level the vested interest groups within the 'police policy network' continue to exercise considerable power (Leishman et al. 1996). At the policy level, the provision of security within an increasingly diverse and risk-infused society poses considerable problems for the state (Garland 1996, 2000, 2001; Johnston 2000; Sparks 2001a; Loader and Sparks 2002). While the state attempts to 'steer' and not 'row', in practice the agencies of criminal justice have experienced state oscillation between 'government at a distance' and the overt use of state power (Garland 1996, 2000, 2001). The public police has been no exception (Jones and Newburn 1997; Johnston 2000; Reiner 2000). Johnston has succinctly expressed the key challenge for the police in the twenty-first century:

> How, under the diverse circumstances of late modernity, and without the traditional assurances of state sovereignty, can good governance be achieved? How, in other words, can plurality be managed so as to ensure effective and efficient administration while also maintaining desired standards of democratic accountability and equity?
>
> (Johnston 2000: 162)

In essence, this is a question about the equitable and appropriate provision of security in a society characterized by differential perceptions of and exposure to risk. At least three strategies can be discerned in response to this conundrum:

- bifurcation of crime control between economic and pragmatic responses to 'everyday' crime on the one hand
- expressive punishment of the few on the other (Garland 1996)
- dispersal of risk management through responsibilization and partnership
- the displacement of risk burdens (usually through the purchase of private security by the more affluent and the active containment of communities of risk).

Policing is increasingly inscribed in these strategies. However, these responses to the conundrum of 'risk society' carry risk, not least for policing practice. The dispersal and weakening of accountability for crime risk management, notably through partnerships, has the potential to undermine democratic governance and transparency (Ericson and Haggerty 1997; Kemshall and Maguire 2001). Fragmentation rather than joined-up responses may be the perverse result and control is exercised through audit and managerialism (Crawford 2001). Responsibilization and the displacement of risk burdens, usually to those least able to carry them, exacerbate existing inequalities and oppression. Policing diversity becomes increasingly problematic, particularly as responsibilization strategies emphasize the 'common good' (but whose good is that?), and presume towards homogeneous communities of shared interest. Those who do not share in or contribute to the common good are excluded, and policing is increasingly used to target and exclude them (ZTP for example), and to patrol the borders between those who present risks and those who demand security and risk avoidance. The result is a spiral of demand for security and low risk that cannot be met, either by public or private policing. Paradoxically the provision of security has a built-in obsolescence: there is never quite enough of it, and zero risk can never be achieved. If only we purchase just a little more security we will be that little bit safer. Loader (1997a, 1997b, 1999) has argued that this results in an insatiable public demand for security, fuelled by 'fear of crime' and the vested interest of those commercial interests providing it. In this scenario, demand will always outstrip supply, and for Loader the issue is the management of demand not how to increase the supply. Supply-led policy is likely to result in more extensive and invasive policing, with the potential to erode rights and civil liberties as proactivity on risk is prioritized above individual freedoms. However, the management of demand is no easy task. The key issue for the public police in the twenty-first century is likely to be how to manage and mediate competing desires for risk avoidance and security within the context of low public tolerance for risk. As Johnston (2000: 177) puts it: 'This . . . will demand an end to the dominant assumption – shared by the police and their academic critics alike – that risks are, invariably, "bad things".'

Further reading

Johnston, L. (2000) *Policing Britain: Risk, Security and Governance*. London: Longman.
Reiner, R. (2000) *The Politics of the Police*, 3rd edn. Oxford: Oxford University Press.

chapter six

Risk and crime prevention

Introduction

Crime prevention has been described as a 'growth industry' (Hughes 1998) with prevention becoming a dominant central government approach to crime since the early 1970s (Bottoms and Wiles 1996) accompanied by expansion in the private security industry. Hughes (1998: 13) has described it a 'chameleon concept' open to varying interpretations but in practice mostly concerned with 'crimes of the street' (Walklate 1996). In principle and practice the emphasis is upon the prevention of crime rather than the punishment of offenders, and represents a move from reactionary to preventative crime control (Jones et al. 1994). Whilst the extent of this paradigm shift is debated (see Hughes 1998: Chapter 1), crime prevention policy can be placed within broader criminal justice trends such as economic and efficient crime control, pragmatic prevention in place of 'nothing works', and emerging risk based on other than disciplinary techniques of social control (Bottoms 1990; Muncie et al. 1994; Sutton 1994; Crawford 2001).

The term has been subject to varying definitions and interpretations throughout its history, with early policy and practices characterized as 'situational' concerned with the reduction of crime opportunities through the 'locks and bars' approach, and 'social' or 'community' crime prevention based upon local initiatives to change social environments or patterns of offending behaviour (Hughes 1998). In practice there has often been much slippage between the two. A more recent characterization has been offered by Bottoms and Wiles (1996) in which they identify four approaches to crime prevention:

- opportunity reduction strategies such as the use of alarms, locks, technologies, Neighbourhood Watch
- monitoring and targeting, such as intelligence-led policing, CCTV, local information gathering
- the use of partnerships and networks, both public and private, to enhance social regulation and order
- early prevention of, and diversion from, criminality, usually through early screening and targeting of children and youngsters and the use of targeted programmes.

(Bottoms and Wiles 1996: 7–10; Hughes 1998: 22)

The origins of crime prevention have been located within the pragmatic and administrative approach to criminal justice adopted under the New Right from the late 1970s onwards (Young 1994). The approach is characterized by the pragmatic management of crime and its impact rather than a concern with its causes and their eradication. Rational choice theory has been crucial to the development of crime prevention (Clarke and Mayhew 1980; Clarke and Cornish 1983; Cornish and Clarke 1986). The theory poses the offender as a rational, calculating actor, capable of calculating costs and benefits of criminal activities (as discussed in Chapter 3 in this volume). As O'Malley (1992: 264) puts it, *homo criminalis* is replaced by the 'amoral rational choice individual' of *homo economicus*, a product of the insurance industry and an industry with a vested interest in situational crime prevention. In essence, raising the costs and lowering the benefits deter criminal behaviours and make 'opportunities' less attractive. This has been supported by work on 'defensible space' and controlling or planning environments to 'design out crime' (Newman 1972). As Hughes (1998: 63) puts it, the focus has moved from the offender to the 'spatial and temporal aspects of crime. It focuses on the opportunities to commit crime, and is thus offence-based'.

Crime prevention as a risk-based discourse

Recent commentators have argued that Cornish and Clarke's (1986: 4) 'situational man' has become 'risky man' and victims have been transformed into 'at risk' citizens (O'Malley 1992, 1994). Garland (2001) has described crime prevention thus:

> the beginnings of a new crime control establishment that draws upon the new criminologies of everyday life to guide its actions and mould its techniques. And while this new infrastructure has definite relations to the institutions of criminal justice – especially to the police and proba-tion which sponsor or administer many of the major initiatives – it should not be regarded as merely an annex or extension of the trad-itional criminal justice system . . . The new infrastructure is strongly oriented towards a set of objectives and priorities – prevention, secur-ity, harm-reduction, loss-reduction, fear-reduction – that are quite different from the traditional goals of prosecution, punishment and 'criminal justice'.
>
> (Garland 2001: 17)

Garland has described these as 'preventative partnerships' aimed at re-educating and remoralizing local communities towards their own policing and risk management. Commentators have therefore located crime preven-tion policy and its dramatic rise within the advanced liberal agenda of social regulation in post-Keynesian societies (O'Malley 1992; Garland 2000, 2001; Rose 2000). Preventative partnerships displace responsibility for crime control from the state to communities, and particularly to networks and public–private partnerships (Crawford 2001). Crime reduction is now the responsibility of individual citizens, communities and commercial institutions. As such crime prevention has been located in a broader penal policy trend towards responsibilization of citizens and communities for crime risk management (Gamble 1988; O'Malley 1992; Stenson 1993). As Crawford (1991: 25) remarks: 'Responsibility for the crime problem, according to governmental strategies, is now everyone's. It is shared property.'

Not withstanding the emphasis upon responsibilization, the individual subject is largely eschewed. As Cohen (1985) puts it:

> No-one is interested in inner thoughts . . . the 'game is up' for all pol-icies directed to the criminal as an individual, either in terms of detec-tion (blaming and punishing) or causation (finding motivational and

causal chains) . . . The talk now is about 'spatial' and 'temporal' aspects of crime, about systems, behaviour sequences, ecology, defensible space . . . target hardening.

(Cohen 1985: 146–8)

Prevention is favoured over rehabilitation, and approaches to crime become both risk infused and future oriented. Crime must be identified and prevented before it can occur. This involves the risk assessment of crime opportunities and risk management strategies to reduce opportunities and to alter the cost–benefit ratio on offer to the offender. For O'Malley (2001b) this transforms offenders into targets, and the social conditions of offending are removed or reinscribed as risk markers (see also Hannah-Moffat 1999). Personal responsibility for criminality is prioritized over social causes, blame and responsibility take the place of explanation, and criminal justice is effectively divorced from social justice (O'Malley 1992). For O'Malley this enables a punitive climate and excluding incapacitation to sit alongside crime prevention. Those who do not make the correct rational choice and who continue to pose a risk can be targeted for exclusion (for example sex offenders).

Victims are also constructed as rational choice actors, able to choose risk-avoiding or risk-taking behaviours, thus introducing the notion that victims can be careless and collude in their own victimization. In this world victims can also purchase risk protection, if necessary from private sources and enhancing self-protection is seen as the responsibility of good citizens (Geason and Wilson 1989).

Third way crime prevention

The focus on crime prevention has continued under the 'third way' of New Labour. As Stenson and Edwards (2001: 68) express it, the 'core meta-dilemma of "third way" governance' is how to regulate an increasingly pluralist and diverse population without alienating those who must pay for it, and who perceive themselves to be most threatened. Crime risks are accepted by policy makers, public and academics alike as an ever present and key feature of late modern life (Garland 2000), likely to increase as the social and economic dislocations of globalization and post-Fordism take hold. The management of such changes and the reintegration of the socially excluded within severe economic constraints is a key challenge for most western economies. Two responses to this dilemma can be discerned, particularly within the crime prevention field:

- Targeting communities for regeneration, re-education and re-moralization and to revitalize communities through the promotion of social solidarity, inclusion and social capital in those areas deemed to be high risk and problematic (Stenson and Watt 1999).

- The use of partnership, public and private, and the generation of various statutory and voluntary networks at local level to responsibilize not only local agencies but also local citizens towards more locally informed and proactive crime prevention strategies, and the use of informal mechanisms of social control (Crawford 1999, 2001; Stenson and Edwards 2001).

The Crime and Disorder Act 1998 formed 'community safety partnerships' tasked with forming and implementing 'community safety strategies' (Crawford 1998: 58), and focused on tackling crime locally, dealing with disorder, particularly crime and disorder associated with youth. Responsibility for crime management was effectively displaced to locales. However, this has not necessarily resulted in lack of government control of penal responses to crime. Smith (2002) for example has seen the Act as an extension of the 'carceral archipelago' and the 'micro-politics of social control' (Smith 2002: 24, 26).

Community and partnership are thus key features of crime prevention, and it is to these two notions that we now turn.

Community and communitarianism

As Hughes (1998: 105) puts it, community, like prevention, can be understood as a 'feelgood' word, carrying a normative assumption that communities are a 'good thing' and that nostalgic longings for traditional communities have a place in contemporary policy. These assumptions are evidenced in Etzioni's (1994, 1995, 1997) moral conservative communitarianism which emphasizes the re-establishment of homogeneous communities as a means to combat crime. Moral consensus, particularly around traditional conservative values, and the promotion of civil obligation as mechanisms for combating crime in local communities. Crime control is seen as a matter of social cohesion, but expressed as a matter to be addressed through social obligation and moral fibre (see also Murray 1990, 1996; Dennis 1993, 1997). Etzioni's (1997) emphasis upon community rather than the state, and upon responsibility rather than dependency, has had a profound impact upon both welfare and crime policy. Disadvantage does not excuse either criminality, or exclude individuals or communities from responsibility. Despite its appeals to community, this approach reinforces privatized and individual risk bearing rather than a collective approach to risk, and has the potential to exclude those deemed beyond moral re-education. Etzioni's position has been critiqued on a number of grounds, and the most pertinent will be reviewed here.

Jordan (1992, 1996) argues that neo-liberal policies have resulted in two types of communities: communities of choice and communities of fate.

Communities of choice are characterized by consumer choice (for example to purchase homes and live there), high income, security and the ability to make positive choices about risk (for example the choice to live in gated communities). Communities of fate are characterized by enforced residence in locales through lack of social mobility and opportunity, lack of informed and positive choice on risk (for example young men engaged in collective high-risk activities) and high exposure to the risks presented by others (for example theft and burglary), resulting in what Hughes (1998: 115) has called a 'dualized society'. This raises the issue of community capacity and resource to take the risk burden. As Crawford (1998) puts it, obligations imply resources, but resources are structurally and economically constrained. The rhetoric of crime prevention has often stressed partnership requiring empowerment of communities and the sharing of power between local people and statutory agencies. However, practice has rarely achieved this, and statutory agencies have a poor record on empowerment (O'Malley 1992; Crawford 1998, 1999, 2001).

Crawford (1998) has also argued that communities cannot be forced into homogeneity (notwithstanding Jordan's ideal types) and many communities are characterized by pluralism and diversity. Cultural and social heterogeneity has been seen as problematic for social order and cohesion, and a source of risk to social compliance: 'It is assumed that what "disorganised communities" need is more "community". Put another way, there is a relationship between a lack of "community" and the existence of high levels of crime' (Crawford 1998: 129).

Crawford is able to argue that a causal link between 'improved' communities and lower crime is not proven, and some very well-organized communities such as the Mafia are highly criminogenic. However, such assumptions about community underpin much crime prevention policy and practice, resulting in a 'community defence' model most clearly expressed in Wilson and Kelling's (1982) 'broken windows' thesis. Crawford (1998) sees the ultimate expression of this as 'defensive exclusivity':

> This can produce 'spirals of ghettoisation' . . . whereby communities increasingly form themselves, and construct their boundaries, around concerns and anxieties about crime. There is an important defensive logic within many community crime prevention strategies. Hence, 'defensive exclusivity' can become a powerful dynamic in the formation and sustenance of communal existence, such that communities may increasingly come together less for what they share in common and more for what they fear.
>
> (Crawford 1998: 264)

One outcome of this is exclusion of certain individuals from communities, and the lowering of tolerance about risk (Walklate and Evans 1999). This in turn is fed by what Loader (1997a, 1997b) and others have called the 'anxiety market' (Davis 1990; Crawford 1998) in which the desire for security and low risk is insatiable. A further perverse outcome is that security becomes a 'club good' rather than a 'public good', accessible only by some and those most in need of it are often those who cannot get it (Crawford 1998). However, it is these communities that are seen as most in need of responsibilization (Dennis 1997). More recent work has suggested that patterns of local social networks are more useful than the notion of community (Bottoms and Wiles 1996) with an emphasis upon understanding local crime patterns, local crime careers and interaction between criminals in a locality (Rosenbaum 1988). Velez (2001) in a study of 60 urban neighbourhoods argues that 'disadvantaged neighbourhoods' plagued by high crime do not necessarily have to be disempowered. He argues that such communities are capable of securing resources and the commitment of 'public social control', that is external resources and ties to local government and police that can have an impact upon victimization. He cautions against assuming that disadvantaged neighbourhoods are apathetic and alienated from the political apparatus, and that they can be understood as 'politically viable contexts' (Velez 2001: 858).

Community crime prevention is hence both paradoxical and problematic. Paradoxical because appeals are made to community but responsibilization strategies that are dependent upon individual risk choices are employed. Heterogeneity is problematized and yet the solution of imposed homogeneity tends towards the ghettoization of 'defensive exclusivity' and the production of further problematic communities.

Partnership

The notion of partnership is a significant part of the crime prevention rhetoric through which the public are 'summoned into being active co-producers of crime prevention and public safety' (Crawford 1998: 169), and the 1990s saw the proliferation of partnerships across all public sector services. In crime, partnerships were seen as a key mechanism in moving crime control from 'bureaucracy' to being 'problem-centred'. The partnership approach was given impetus by the Morgan report (1991). This allocated responsibilities to differing statutory agencies and attempted to provide a coherent structure for the delivery of crime prevention. However, the piecemeal approach continued through much of the 1990s with differing agencies such as police and probation pursuing differing strategies and approaches, and some initiatives such as Safer Cities falling by the wayside. (For a detailed history of the partnership approach see Crawford 1999: Chapter 2.)

The roots of partnership have been attributed to the following:

- systems failure, in particular the lack of a joined-up and coherent approach to crime
- the impact of New Public Management, particularly the emphasis upon problem-centred crime control, targeted and clear rationales for resource allocation
- 'hollowing out of the state' and 'government at a distance', and dispersal of crime risks from the state
- dispersal of discipline, extending social regulation and disciplinary controls into the social body and social realm from the penal realm through the use of actuarial risk techniques for managing in place rather than normalizing.

(Cohen 1979; Gamble 1986; O'Malley 1992; Crawford 1998, 1999; Rose 2000; Garland 2001)

Crawford (1999) has described this as a 'partial explanation' and has made some important additions:

- a crisis in state legitimacy and responsibility for crime control
- the extension of the private sphere
- tensions arising from the demands of managerialism.

Legitimacy and responsibility

Crawford (1999) argues that social, economic and cultural uncertainties have led to a crisis of legitimacy for the state and its agencies (for example the police) and that 'Crime, as a symbol of an old uncertainty – social disorder – strikes even deeper to the core of this malaise' (Crawford 1999: 75). Confidence in the state's ability to deliver order and security are thus undermined, resulting in what Crawford (following Beetham 1991) calls 'legitimacy deficits'. In essence, difficulties arise where shared public beliefs do not underpin state objectives, or where the processes for achieving such objectives are not publicly supported (Mudd 1984; Crawford 1999). Policing, particularly as questioned by the 'protesting' middle class and by ethnic divisions, is a case in point (Reiner 2000). In addition, the ability and legitimacy of the welfare state to deliver, both socially and economically, has been severely challenged since the late 1970s (Rodger 2000), with much social policy displaced to the criminal realm and the move to a 'law and order' society in the absence of a welfare safety net (Hall 1979; Rodger 2000). This has been labelled the 'free market and the strong state' (Gamble 1979) of the New Right, but the strong state is increasingly seen to have failed, particularly in the area of crime control (Garland 1985, 1996). Hence the state is keen to emphasize that it alone cannot be responsible for crime reduction and responsibilization strategies are increasingly introduced (Garland 2000, 2001; Loader and Sparks 2002). Individual prudentialism becomes the underpinning principle of crime management (O'Malley 1992, 2000, 2001b).

The extension of the private sphere

While the debate over the extent and impact of private policing continues (Jones and Newburn 1998, 2002; Johnston 2000), and the transformative power of the private security industry is still under analysis (Loader 1997a, 1997b, 1999; Johnston 2001), the broader concept of privatization has been recognized as an important influence on crime policy (Crawford 1999). Crawford identifies four key ingredients:

- The use of markets in public service delivery and the commercialization of state services, for example the use of private security firms in the provision of community safety. Garland (2001: 17) has referred to this as the commercialization of civil society and the end of state monopolization of crime control.
- 'Civilianization' of public services, for example of the police and the use of volunteer personnel and agencies in criminal justice (such as victim support).
- The increase in privately and corporately governed spaces, for example gated communities, shopping malls and a more insurance-based and economic approach to policing. Policing defends such spaces rather than contributes to an overall moral good. Citizens, often in their role as consumers, enter them by choice and tacitly agree to rules of conduct and behaviour.
- The decline in the use of public spaces and the increase in 'privatism' (Lasch 1980) and the retreat from public spaces (particularly in cities) to family and home life. Privatism is accompanied by increased 'fear of crime' (Lupton and Tulloch 1999). In effect, distance contributes to fear and tolerance is weakened (Hancock and Matthews 2001).

Tensions arising from the demands of managerialism

The rise of managerialism in the public sector and within criminal justice has been well documented (Raine and Wilson 1993), with increased attention to the three Es of economy, efficiency and effectiveness. This has been characterized as a move from 'social reasoning' in crime control to 'economic reasoning' and a response to the failure of 'penal modernism' (Garland 1985, 2001: 188-9). While seeking to replace hierarchical bureaucracy with more accountable management, accountability within and across partnerships has proved more problematic (Kemshall and Maguire 2001). The following have been presented as significant barriers to managerialism in partnerships:

- Accountability is dispersed across the partnership agencies and 'audit trails' of decision-making can be difficult to reconstruct in the event of performance failures.
- Managerialism works well within agencies and hierarchically (Crawford 2001) but does not operate so well horizontally across agencies.
- Responsibility can be weakened and agencies can displace their responsibilities (and their risk burdens) onto others.
- Establishing 'value for money' and using performance indicators suitable for partnership activities can be difficult. Partnership activities are often process and output based rather than outcome based, and activities can be peripheral to the core functions of the agency and therefore receive less attention, monitoring and evaluation.
- Partnerships are as prey to perverse incentives as any other aspect of public service, and may concentrate upon that which is most easily counted at the expense of that which really makes a difference.
- Partnerships often comprise agencies that are in competition for the same limited resources (for example police and probation).

(Peters 1986; Rhodes 1996; Crawford 2001; Kemshall and Maguire 2001; Maguire et al. 2001)

Thus the effectiveness of managerialism is challenged by partnership. One response to these difficulties has been the 'contractualisation of partnerships' (Crawford 1998: 182), comprising purchaser–provider relationships between public and private, and formal protocols between public agencies. In these arrangements contractual arrangements replace trust, and audit replaces traditional professional systems of accountability (Power 1999). However, a key ingredient in the effective operation of partnerships is trust, especially between different agencies with differing ideologies, values and objectives (Crawford 1998, 2001). Partnerships are also dependent upon trust in professional expertise. However, as Crawford (1999, 2001) points out, partnerships are a breeding ground of distrust due to conflicting ideological and value bases between partners and competition for resources, and where established it is eroded by managerial techniques such as audit and performance monitoring. For Crawford (1999; 60) such tensions and conflicts mean that the 'ethos and practice of "partnerships" embody deep structural antagonisms and unresolved tensions'.

Summary

The roots of crime prevention have been placed within New Right approaches to crime policy, given particular impetus by the rational choice development of crime control. Responsibilization within the broader 'risk society' has also been a key driver actively pursued under 'third way' governance. Crime prevention is underpinned by two key ideas: community and partnership. However, in practice both are problematic and contain the seeds of tension and conflict between experts and communities, and between criminal justice agencies.

Crime prevention in practice

Crime prevention has been subject to extensive prescription about its set-up and operation (see for example Bright 1997) and extensive evaluation (Tilley 2002) concerned with gaining feedback in order to improve the operation of crime prevention programmes. Such studies tend to focus on the relationship between inputs and outputs, and where possible the outcomes (for example crime reduction) (Gilling 1997). These have been complemented by studies concerned with the *processes* involved in crime prevention, and most usually the processes concerned with establishing and maintaining partnerships (Gilling 1997; Crawford 1998, 1999). In particular 'collaboration' and the subtle processes of partnership have posed a difficult investigative problem:

> Collaboration is a much neglected area in the evaluation of crime prevention initiatives, which invariably follows a quasi experimental pre-test/post-test design that neglects processes in favour of measurable outcomes of crime reduction. Consequently, it is difficult to know what effects collaborative problems have on these outcomes . . . but in so far as they may be manifested as implementational difficulties, one might anticipate that their effect may be considerable. Indeed, this may be one reason why attempts to replicate 'successful' crime projects are so often doomed to failure, as the mechanisms may be faithfully replicated, but the collaborative context may not.
>
> (Gilling 1997: 160)

As Gilling notes, terms like partnership and collaboration have different meanings and forms. Collaboration can mean mere communication at its lowest level, to shared problem definition and strategic deployment of shared resources to solve it at the highest (Liddle and Gelsthorpe 1994a, 1994b, 1994c). However, studies of crime prevention in its varied forms have identified key issues that hinder its effective delivery:

- Differential and conflictual power relations between criminal justice agencies, and between the statutory and voluntary sectors.
- Differing perspectives, values and ideological bases between agencies, for example police and probation.
- Partnership and collaborative arrangements can be hijacked by

powerful agencies for their own ends, for example, police may use such initiatives to gain local crime information. Arrangements are not always 'benevolent' although claims for 'conspiracy' may be over-stated.

- Collaboration itself may become the outcome, and little else is delivered: 'all talk and no action'.
- Initiatives can tend towards situational solutions only, too dependent upon a rational model of decision making that fails to account sufficiently for structural and political constraints.
- The emphasis upon a scientific mode of evaluation tends to prioritize 'what can be counted', and hence property crimes are prioritised. This again reinforces the situational approach.
- Audit and performance management can divert attention from a strategic approach.
- The decentralization of services and the emphasis upon the local can undermine a corporate approach and national consistency, resulting in ghettoization.

(from Hope and Murphy 1983; Blagg et al. 1988; Sampson et al. 1988; Pearson et al. 1992; Crawford and Jones 1995; Gilling 1997; Crawford 1998, 1999; Mills and Pearson 2000)

Hughes (1998) notes that evaluation studies have been largely pessimistic about the impact of multi-agency crime prevention and that crime prevention 'of a more ambitious "social" and genuinely "inter-agency" kind remains both marginal to the work of most agencies and unproven as a "successful" approach' (Hughes 1998: 86). This is in part due to the slippery nature of community and the causal link between community improvement and empowerment and crime reduction is notoriously difficult to examine and prove (Crawford 1999). Well-defined and limited situational crime prevention has been more successful. However, one well-documented unintended consequence of situational crime prevention is *displacement* (Pease 1997; Hughes 1998). This may involve displacing offending to another time or place, or alter the method or type of crime committed (Pease 1997). Displacement to other locales has been severely critiqued, not least where this displacement has been from affluent gated communities to those already impoverished and heavily victimized. This also suggests that community participation and empowerment are variable, with some communities both engaged and more powerful in the processes of crime prevention than others (Velez 2001).

Sutton and Cherney (2002) in a review of community-based crime prevention in Victoria, Australia since 1988 note that crime prevention and community safety are 'chameleon concepts' pragmatically co-opted and implemented by a range of political and administrative regimes. This local political experience they argue is central, as is the expressive function that such local initiatives fulfil. They conclude that evaluations must be concerned with such functions and processes as well as focus on the technical aspects of such schemes.

Extending the net of social control

Multi-agency crime prevention has also been critiqued on the grounds of *net-widening* (Cohen 1985), and for extending criminal justice surveillance techniques into all aspects of social life (Hughes 1998). In effect, the prison panopticon has become a community one, for example through the use of MAPPPs to manage high-risk sex offenders in the community after their release from prison, and the extension of such procedures to those who are cautioned, or through the extension of community policing to encompass incivilities rather than offences. However, as Hughes (1998) suggests, it is important to distinguish the rhetoric from the reality. For Hughes the sheer 'fluidity' and adaptability of key concepts and local arrangements in crime prevention mean that there is space for resistance against the more regressive trends of centralized law and order policies. While the panopticon has transferred to 'clearly defined, segregated institutional spaces' such as schools, factories and asylums (Fyfe and Bannister 1996), the model is less easily transferred to the ill-defined and fluid areas of communities. The state is extending its regulatory net not so much through an 'extended carceral net' (Pratt 1989) as through the strategy of responsibilization (O'Malley 1996) and the rise of an exclusionary society for those who fail to adequately risk manage or correct their risk-taking (Young 1999). This has become the key management technique of the risk society (van Swaaningen 1997; Hughes 2000). This results in a 'negative discourse of crime prevention' (Hughes 2000: 292) concerned with preventing risks (or excluding risk posers from communities) that outweighs the pursuit of 'social goods' such as justice or the equitable distribution of risk burdens. The spectre is of an affluent club of those able to avoid risks, with risk dumping on those less able to manage them. Hughes (2000: 288) asks whether those engaged in crime prevention work are 'likely to be risk assessors involved in the politics of sanitation rather than being promoters of justice and well-being?'

For Hughes, the key issue is whether the risk discourse and its potential negative consequences can be resisted by those 'on the ground', and whether there are any alternatives to risk-infused crime prevention.

Summary

Research investigations and evaluations of crime prevention have been largely negative, with emphasis upon their low impact, the difficulty in identifying outcomes, and issues around collaboration and partnership processes. Crime prevention has also been inscribed with a largely negative risk discourse that emphasizes exclusionary processes and the displacement of risk burdens.

Alternatives to risk: possible futures

The future is not already written, and it is important to recognize that there is more than one possible path. However, Hughes identifies three possible scenarios:

- the 'privatized fortress cities' model
- the 'authoritarian statist-communitarian' model
- the 'inclusive civic, safe cities' model

(Hughes 1998: 135)

The 'privatized fortress cities' model

The rise of 'defensive strategies' such as security technology, CCTV and gated communities, coupled with the increased polarization of rich and poor and the production of an urban 'underclass' is producing the spectre of fortress cities based upon exclusionary risk management (Davis 1990; Crawford 1998; Hughes 1998). Those with the option to pay can leave 'spoiled' inner-city areas, and purchase both geographic and technical security. Crawford has referred to this as 'ghettoization' based upon a 'defensive exclusivity' in which anxieties and fears about crime predominate (Crawford 1998: 264). Such developments are apparent in the USA (Davis 1990) with some '30 million US citizens – nearly 15% of the population' living in some kind of gated community (Crawford 1998: 265). The parallel in Britain is the flight to suburbia from decaying inner-city areas and an increasing preoccupation with safe spaces. A clear consequence of such a development is the increasing concentration of crime in impoverished locales coupled with a lack of individual, community and formal policing resources to manage it. The 'social' and the welfarist approach to shared risks is replaced by risk avoidance and its targeted management. Social policy is increasingly 'criminalized' (Rodger 2000), for example housing policy that manages disruptive and risky tenants through displacement to sink estates. Whilst 'fortress cities' may be an extreme example, there is evidence of increasing surveillance of both public and corporate spaces (such as shopping malls) through CCTV and private security guards and the restriction of access or displacement of those thought to present any kind of risk (Shearing and Stenning 1981; Norris et al. 1998) extending surveillance and control into the workplace and into the sphere of the consumer (Lyon 1994). This results in a very bleak view of the future, in which two forms of social control predominate: reward and a promise of safety for 'responsible' economically active and consumer citizens, and repression for those who are not (O'Malley 1992, 1995, 1997; Hughes 1998). Garland (2001: 204), while noting that the future is not inevitable, sees the present trends as indicative of an 'iron cage' of crime control in danger of self-perpetuation and carrying significant social costs such as a reduction in tolerance and a growth in authoritarianism.

The 'authoritarian statist-communitarian' model

This is the picture of the strong authoritarian state promoting cohesive communities as an antidote to the pluralism and individualism of late modern societies. This neo-statism advocates state control but towards market-oriented ends (Jessop 2000: 179). The Asian 'tiger economies' are seen as epitomizing this approach of strong state, mutual responsibility, high conformity and market. In such communities informal and formal social controls are strong, economic differentials are low, and security systems ever present. However, the market failure of the tiger economies at the close of the twentieth century may pose new difficulties for social order and such a model has not proven to have all the answers to the problems posed by post-modernity (Jessop 2000). The price for the apparent high trust of such societies is the acceptance of hierarchy and paternalism, and the minimization of individualism (Fukuyama 1996) raising the spectre of authoritarianism and the erosion of human rights.

The ' inclusive civic, safe cities' model

This is a positive (if not utopian) picture of the state replaced by empowered, participating and proactive local networks, based upon a premise of active and engaged citizenship (Stoker and Young 1993; Hughes 1998: 148). Citizenship and participation are seen as key mechanism for avoiding the polarization of risks and fortress cities. For Crawford (1998: 268) this means reintegrating 'the inner city islands of neglect into the larger social fabric'. However, this will not happen of its own accord. There is a key role for the state in promoting social inclusion as well as exclusion, and in returning to social policy and social justice agendas as well as crime management ones. While it is easy to espouse 'no rights without responsibilities' (Blair 1995), it must also be recognized that the acceptance and fulfilment of responsibilities requires resources. In the UK attention has focused on citizenship and inclusion as a means to combat the spectre of social exclusion (Social Exclusion Unit 2000). However, as Miller (2000) puts it:

> does tackling social exclusion mean that everyone should be included, and if so, what sort of a society are they being asked to join? Is it one that

values and encourages diverse life-styles and cultures, or one that requires uniformity? Also, is it an 'invitation' to be included, or a 'requirement'?

(Miller 2000: 11)

He identifies four types of societies:

- Exclusive diversity in which groups may live as they wish with minimal state regulation. This tends to work well for the 'haves' but there is minimal support for the 'have nots'.
- Voluntary inclusion in which there is a minimal state provision for all from which people may opt out if they so wish. Opting in, however, requires conformity to specific norms (for example working). Those who opt out give up their entitlement to state support.
- Required inclusion in which there is a mixture of basic and specialist services targeted at those deemed to be in special need. However, acceptance of assistance requires conformity and a requirement for minority groups to integrate.
- Inclusive diversity in which there is extensive and mixed state provision and acceptance does not carry any particular requirements. Diversity is not compromised. However, in a climate of scarce resources this will be hardest to deliver – groups may compete for resources and some lifestyles may be more supported than others.

(from Miller 2000: 11)

The current emphasis upon social responsibility from New Labour, and upon the creation of the 'neighbourly society' from the opposition (Letwin 2002) stresses conformity to 'virtuous habits' and positive relations in families and communities in order to combat the demise of traditional communities. The current concern with *social capital* (Putnam 1995) or the networks, norms and trust that underpin successful communities is in part a recognition that attention has to be paid to the social infrastructure in a climate of global change in order to preserve social cohesion (Frazer 1999). However, social capital can also be deployed as a blaming concept, blaming communities who lack it, and who fail to develop it as a response to their problems of disadvantage, risk and crime.

Promoting citizenship and participation is also beset with difficulties. In a society that has framed every aspect of life economically the altruism of citizenship has surely been undermined, and the increased participation of the 'haves' when some of the benefit is seen as for the morally stigmatized 'have nots' will be very difficult to achieve. Without clear state direction, it is difficult to see how the consumer society will accept the need to foster public good. At present, 'solidarity is not based on the positive feeling of connectedness but on the negative communality of fear' (Hughes 1998: 156–7). However, the emphasis upon inclusivity raises important questions about the value and desired outcomes of crime prevention and extends the debate from technical and evaluative questions to ethical and moral ones. Crime prevention discourse is, in part, ameliorated by a discourse of social justice, and Rose's (1996b) dead 'social' may thereby be resurrected.

Summary

The present features of crime prevention suggest that we have bleak futures before us as the price for risk avoidance and safety has to be paid. Two negative futures were presented from Hughes' (1998) overview based upon growing empirical evidence that these trends are developing in the USA and the UK. A third, more positive future has been posed, but this remains largely speculative and there are significant barriers to overcome if it is to be achieved.

Conclusion: is crime prevention a risky business?

Whilst Weatheritt (1986) reminds us that crime prevention does not take a significant proportion of the overall criminal justice budget, and is more honoured in the rhetoric than the reality it has assumed a growing importance. (One estimate is 2 per cent of the total criminal justice budget: Hughes 1998: 17.) This can be discerned in three areas: penal populism, displacing risk burdens from the state to locals, and in social control strategies of responsibilization. In penal populism, crime prevention initiatives can function as useful political devices for re-engaging waning popularity or being seen to act decisively on emerging crime problems (for example zero-tolerance policing). While it serves as a useful political sound bite, such initiatives can take different forms on the ground, and the police in particular may consider it little other than information gathering and public relations rolled into one. Crime prevention also functions as an acknowledgement that the state cannot solve crime and that management in place (or management by displacement) are legitimate policy objectives. Crime is thus reduced to an everyday normality, for which local communities in partnership with key agencies must accept responsibility. Responsibilization carries this state distancing into the heart of communities, making crime risk management both an individual and community responsibility. Within this scenario risk can be understood as an underpinning feature, and contributes to a 'refiguring of policing and prevention' (Loader and Sparks 2002: 87). It is the fuel of penal populism, a key driver in state displacement, and legitimizes responsibilization. To this extent crime prevention is a risk-based discourse.

Further reading

Crawford, A. (1998) *Crime Prevention and Community Safety: Politics, Policies and Practices*. London: Longman.

Crawford, A. (1999) *The Local Governance of Crime: Appeals to Community and Partnerships*. Oxford: Oxford University Press.

Hughes, G. (1998) *Understanding Crime Prevention: Social Control, Risk and Late Modernity*. Buckingham: Open University Press.

chapter seven

Concluding comments

Pulling the threads together
Risking the social

Pulling the threads together

This book has been about risk in contemporary criminal justice and the extent to which it can be discerned as a key feature of current policy and practice. Chapters 1 and 2 reviewed current academic debates about the penal shift from disciplinary to actuarial practices, and the subsequent chapters have examined the extent to which risk actuarialism is present in the 'material forms' of work in criminal justice. From this it is possible to discern key trends in crime control that are variably played out in practice settings. Of these the most significant are:

- an increasingly managed approach to crime control, including targeting, problem-oriented policing, crime profiling, risk profiling, the use of structured tools and so on
- accountability and performance management through audit, monitoring and quasi-scientific evaluations of 'what works'
- responsibilization of citizens for crime risks, both as victims and offenders
- displacement of risk burdens from the state centre to locales, although paradoxically this does not always empower local communities or agencies
- a mixed economy of crime provision including the private and statutory sectors
- experience of everyday life as risk-infused and 'anxiety production' fuelled by private security
- a rational approach to crime causation and control that results in a

moral blamism of those who fail to exercise the correct 'choice' and acceptable levels of responsibility

- exclusion of those who pose a risk and who fail to correct or manage it appropriately resulting in a penal policy of the 'Other'.

For Garland (2001) these are key features of crime control in 'high crime societies' in which the 'old fashioned sovereign state can deliver punishment but not security', but it is security that is increasingly demanded. These new methods of crime control offer security to 'core' economically active citizens, but without appearing to subsidize or reward the 'undeserving poor', the marginal and the outsiders (Garland 2001).

However, in *practice* these features are evidenced to varying degrees. In brief, the reasons for this are

- the interpretation and mediation of policies by operational managers required to balance and implement competing demands within limited resources
- the interpretation and mediation of policies by frontline workers operating within well-established working practices, ideologies and value bases
- circumvention of policy requirements in order to 'get the job done' in the face of the under-resourcing of policy change
- the fluid arrangements of partnership and the varying context of collaboration
- the nature of particular communities and locales within which crime control is delivered
- the specific relationship between the central state and local government in crime control delivery.

O'Malley has labelled such reasons as 'firewalls of resistance' and that 'disciplines are politically polyvalent and pragmatic' (O'Malley 2001b: 100). He contends that the transition to neo-liberal risk models is by no means automatic 'and government must be constantly vigilant against the breakdown or subversion of these techniques' (O'Malley 2001b: 97). Under New Labour there has been significant reaffirmation of neo-liberal risk models, most recently in the Halliday report and subsequent proposals for legislative change (Halliday 2001). The report *Making Punishments Work* recommends a new framework for punishment that 'should do more to support crime reduction and reparation, while meeting the needs of punishment' (Halliday 2001: 6). The report attempts to mesh concerns with punishment, public credibility and the broader agenda of crime reduction. Crime reduction is elevated to the status of a key objective alongside punishment, with the prevention of offending seen as a central outcome of the criminal justice system including sentencing. Halliday (2001) is infused with the managerialist enthusiasm for 'what works' and evidence-based evaluations reflecting New Labour's neo-liberal pragmatism towards policy-making. The subsequent White Paper: *Justice for All* (Home Office 2002b) continues the New Labour theme of 'tough on crime and tough on the causes of crime' by stating that:

Our goal is strong, safe communities. That means:

- tough action on anti-social behaviour, hard drugs and violent crime;
- rebalancing the criminal justice system in favour of the victim; and
- giving the police and prosecution the tools to bring more criminals to justice.

(Home Office 2002b: 1)

Tackling persistent offenders and dealing adequately with dangerous offenders are two key themes, as is the prioritization of victim rights and a more efficiently managed criminal justice system. This has been paralleled by the Criminal Justice and Police Act 2001, which provides increased police powers to investigate crime, and has a clear focus on crime and disorder, in particular 'alcohol-related disorder' (Home Office 2001c). Both of these legislative initiatives are taking place against a backdrop of overall stability in crime rates with the 'chances of being a victim of crime at around the lowest levels since the BCS [British Crime Survey] began in 1981' (Home Office 2002c: 1). Tough penal policy continues and we risk the twenty-first century becoming the century of 'mass imprisonment' (Hudson 2002: 250, 253).

Risking the social

The greatest challenge for post-Fordist societies is the effective management of diversity and individualism (Jessop 2000; Kemshall 2002a). Pluralism and heterogeneity are facts of postmodern life but they pose severe problems of control and regulation to any government (Rose 2000). The social is increasingly fragmented, and to some extent deliberately eroded by post-welfare social policies (Jordan 2000; Rodger 2000). Diversity management is increasingly located in the labour market (through membership of the economically active and consumer club: Jordan 2000), or through the imposed control and enforced homogeneity of crime control (Garland 2001). Hudson (2000, 2001, 2002) has expressed this as the justice system's failure to recognize and deal appropriately with difference. Rights and justice cannot necessarily be guaranteed where risk is concerned. Brutally, one is either in or out, and if out, then excluded to a residual underclass characterized by moral unworthiness, economic dependency and risk. Such policies themselves contain the seeds of risk: to social solidarity, social cohesion and social justice. In an era in which civil society and community mobilization has been retreating, and citizens have become detached from political activity and community life (Giddens 1990, 1991; Lash 1990; Crawford 1998) it is difficult to see how the 'social' can be protected from further erosion. This runs the risk of producing further fragmentation, isolation and individualism – a fertile ground for neo-liberal risk-based governance. It also means that the excluded Other is an almost permanently self-perpetuating group. In the future the most pressing problem may not be solving the 'problem of crime', but rather solving the 'problem of risk'.

Glossary

Advanced liberalism: a term used to describe a mode of governing most often associated with the emergence of globalization and postmodern societies. The key characteristic of advanced liberal societies is the displacement of the mechanisms of government from the state to the individual, and power is exercised through the 'regulated choices' of individuals and the communities in which they are located.

Discourse: a bounded body of knowledge that circumscribes our understanding of the world, both the natural world and social processes. Discourse defines 'problems' and our understanding and solutions to them. Discourse also delimits the possibilities of what can be known, and as such is about relations of power, particularly when institutionalized and embedded in social practices and organizational forms.

Governance: the mechanisms of governing, of achieving social control and order through the deployment of subtle techniques of power and institutionalized discursive practices rather than the use of overt state coercion. The major technique of governance in advanced liberal societies is self-regulation through a discourse of risk and prudentialism and the use of expert knowledge to guide the activities and choices of the 'prudential citizen'. Governance is therefore concerned with the deployment of those 'intentional techniques' used for the direction and guidance of conduct (Foucault 1982; Simon 1997).

Late modernity: most often associated with the work of Giddens and his analyses of social transformation at the close of the twentieth century. Globalization and the emergence of new and internally produced risks are key features of the late modernity thesis, with implications for the relationships of trust as traditional social bonds weaken.

Modernity: most commonly defined as the period of industrialization and capitalist expansion from the industrial revolution to the late 1970s in western societies. The period is characterized by capitalist expansion, imperialism, representative democracies and the formulation of the welfare state.

Normalization: a process that describes penal and welfare practices that are designed to 'normalize' the offender or deviant through specific interventions and treatments. The offender or deviant is thus 'corrected' towards pre-specified normative requirements that bring him or her into line with the normal citizen.

Post-fordism: the emerging mode of production and social regulation in late modern industrial societies. Post-Fordist states are characterized by flexible labour markets and production, technological innovation, economic regulation based upon flexibility and enterprise, and lean organizational forms and flexible supply.

Postmodernity: the period from the late 1970s onwards and the social transformations emerging at the start of the twenty-first century. Postmodernity is characterized by global risks, indeterminate and contingent knowledge about the probability of such risks, and uncertainty over future outcomes and impacts. The distinction between late and postmodernity is often expressed in terms of the impact of globalization, and the degree of uncertainty and pluralism detected in cultural forms.

Prudentialism: the citizen is required to adopt a calculating attitude towards almost all of his or her decisions. Thus the individual becomes the primary site of risk management, not society, and the 'good' citizen is the responsible, prudential one. Prudentialism is most often associated with mechanisms of governance in advanced liberal societies.

Reflexivity: a term most usually associated with the work of Giddens describing a key characteristic of life in post-traditional societies. The 'risk society' presents individuals with a myriad of risks, many of which are uncertain in nature. The individual therefore must constantly self-monitor risk decisions and risk choices.

Responsibilization: a term describing a form of governance dependent upon what Rose (2000) has described as 'responsibilisation', that is, individuals are made responsible for their own actions, including their own risks, and for their own effective self-management.

Risk society: most often associated with the work of Beck and Giddens and rooted in their analysis of late modern society and the social transformations impacting upon capitalist modes of production, modes of social regulation, and traditional social bonds. A key feature of such transformations is the internal production of risks, often globally located but individually experienced. The dominant culture is one of fearfulness and a precautionary principle based upon a desire for safety.

References

Adams, J. (1995) *Risk*. London: UCL Press.

Alaszewski, A. (1998) Risk in modern society, in A. Alaszewski, L. Harrison and G. Manthorpe (eds) *Risk, Health and Welfare*. Buckingham: Open University Press.

Alcock, P. (1996) Back to the future: Victorian values for the twenty-first century, in R. Lister (ed.) *Charles Murray and the Underclass: The Developing Debate*. London: Institute for Economic Affairs, Health and Welfare Unit.

Alderson, J. (1979) *Policing Freedom*. Plymouth: McDonald and Evans.

Alderson, J. (1982) Policing the eighties, *Marxism Today*, April: 9–14.

American Psychiatric Association (1994) *Diagnostic and Statistical Manual of Mental Disorders*. Washington DC: American Psychiatric Association.

Andrews, D.A. (1995) The psychology of criminal conduct and effective treatment, in J. McGuire (ed.) *What Works: Reducing Offending, Guidelines from Research and Practice*. Chichester: John Wiley.

Andrews, D.A. and Bonta, J. (1994) *The Psychology of Criminal Conduct* Cincinnati, OH: Anderson.

Andrews, D.A. and Bonta, J. (1995) *The Level of Supervision Inventory-Revised*. Toronto: Multi-Health Systems.

Andrews, D.A., Bonta, J. and Hoge, R.D. (1990) Classification for effective rehabilitation, *Criminal Justice and Behaviour*, 17: 19–51.

Ansell, J. and Wharton, F. (eds) (1992) *Risk: Analysis, Assessment and Management*. Chichester: John Wiley.

Association of Chief Officers of Probation (ACOP) (1994) *Guidance on the Management of Risk and Public Protection*. Wakefield: ACOP.

Association of Chief Officers of Probation (ACOP) (1995) *ACOP and Reconviction*. Wakefield: ACOP.

Association of Chief Police Officers (ACPO) (1999) *Sex Offenders: A Risk Assessment Model*. London: ACPO Working Party.

Aubrey, R. and Hough, M. (1997) *Assessing Offenders' Needs: Assessment Scales for the Probation Service*, a report for the Home Office Research and Statistics Directorate. London: Home Office.

Audit Commission (1993) *Helping with Enquiries: Tackling Crime Effectively.* London: Audit Commission.

Audit Commission (1996) *Streetwise: Effective Police Patrol.* London: Audit Commission.

Auerhahn, K. (1999) Selective incapacitation and the problem of prediction, *Criminology*, 37(4): 703–34.

Aye Maung, N. and Hammond, N. (2000) *Risk of Re-offending and Needs Assessment: The User's Perspective*, Home Office research study 216. London: Home Office.

Ayto, J. (1990) *Dictionary of Word Origins.* London: Bloomsbury.

Baird, J. (1981) Probation and parole classifications: the Wisconsin model, *Corrections Today*, 43: 36–41.

Banton, M. (1964) *The Policeman in the Community.* London: Tavistock.

Barr, R. and Pease, K. (1992) The problem of displacement, in D.J. Evans, N.R. Fyfe and D.T. Herbert (eds) *Crime, Policing and Place: Essays in Environmental Criminology.* London: Routledge and Kegan Paul.

Bartlett, P. (1997) *Closing the Asylum: The Mental Patient in Modern Society*, 2nd edn. Harmondsworth: Penguin.

Bauman, Z. (1997) *Postmodernity and its Discontents.* Cambridge: Polity Press.

Baxter, R. and Nuttall, C. (1975) Severe sentences: no deterrent to crime, *New Society*, 2 January.

Bayley, D.H. and Shearing, C.D. (1996) The future of policing, *Law and Society Review*, 30(3): 585–606.

Bean, P. (1976) *Rehabilitation and Deviance.* London: Routledge and Kegan Paul

Beaumont, B., Caddick, B. and Hare-Duke, H. (2001) *Meeting Offenders' Needs: A Summary Report on the Meeting Assessed Needs Evaluation*, a report for the National Probation Service. Nottinghamshire area. Nottingham: Home Office.

Beck, U. (1992a) *Risk Society: Towards a New Modernity.* London: Sage.

Beck, U. (1992b) From industrial society to the risk society: questions of survival, social structure and ecological enlightenment, *Theory, Culture and Society*, 1 (February): 97–123.

Beck, U. (1998) Politics of risk society, in J. Franklin (ed.) *The Politics of Risk Society.* Cambridge: Polity Press in association with the Institute for Public Policy Press.

Beck, U. (1999) *World Risk Society.* Cambridge: Polity Press.

Beetham, D. (1991) *The Legitimation of Power.* London: Macmillan.

Bennett, T. (1994) Recent developments in community policing, in M. Stephens and S. Becker (eds) *Police Force, Police Service.* London: Macmillan.

Bernstein, P.L. (1996) *Against the Gods: The Remarkable Story of Risk.* New York: John Wiley.

Beyer, L. (1991) The logic and possibilities of 'wholistic' community policing, in S. McKillop (ed.) *The Police and the Community.* Canberra: Australian Institute of Criminology.

Blackmore, J. and Welsh, J. (1983) Selective incapacitation: sentencing according to risk, *Crime and Delinquency*, October: 504–28.

Blagg, H., Pearson, G., Sampson, A., Smith, D. and Stubbs, P. (1988) Inter-agency co-ordination: rhetoric and reality, in T. Hope and M. Shaw (eds) *Communities and Crime Reduction.* London: HMSO.

Blair, T. (1993) *Interview January 1993, Today BBC Radio 4*, cited in P. Anderson and N. Mann (1997) *Safety First*. London: Granta.

Blair, T. (1995) The rights we enjoy reflect the duties we owe, *Spectator* Lecture, 22 March.

Blair, T. (1998) *The Third Way*. London: Fabian Society.

Blair, T. (2002) Rebalancing the CJS, *Criminal Justice Management*, September: 14–16.

Blakely, E. and Snyder, M.G. (1997) *Fortress America*. Washington, DC: Brookings Institution.

Bloor, M. (1995) *The Sociology of HIV Transmission*. London: Sage.

Blumstein, A., Cohen, J. and Nagin, D. (1977) The dynamics of a homeostatic punishment process, *Journal of Criminal Law and Criminology*, 67(3): 317–34.

Bonta, J. (1996) Risk-needs assessment and treatment, in A.T. Harland (ed.) *Choosing Correctional Options that Work*. Thousand Oaks, CA: Sage.

Bottoms, A. (1977) Reflections on the renaissance of dangerousness, *Howard Journal of Criminal Justice*, 16: 70–96.

Bottoms, A. (1990) Crime prevention facing the 1990s, *Policing and Society*, 1(1): 3–22.

Bottoms, A. (1995) The politics and philosophy of sentencing, in C. Clarkson and R. Morgan (eds) *The Politics of Sentencing*. Oxford: Clarendon Press.

Bottoms, A. and McWilliams, W. (1979) A non-treatment paradigm for probation practice, *British Journal of Social Work*, 9: 159–202.

Bottoms, A. and Wiles, P. (1996) Crime prevention and late modernity, in T. Bennett (ed.) *Crime Prevention: The Cropwood Papers*. Cambridge: Cropwood.

Bradbury, J. (1989) The policy implications of differing concepts of risk, *Science, Technology, and Human Values*, 14(4): 380–99.

Braithwaite, J. (1989) *Crime, Shame and Reintegration*. Cambridge: Cambridge University Press.

Bratton, W.J. (1997) Crime is down in New York City: blame the police, in N. Dennis (ed.) *Zero Tolerance: Policing a Free Society*. London: Health and Welfare Unit, Institute of Economic Affairs.

Bright, J. (1997) *Turning the Tide: Crime, Community and Prevention*. London: Demos.

Brown, M. (1996) Serious offending and the management of public risk in New Zealand, *British Journal of Criminology*, 36(1): 18–36.

Brown, M. (2000) Risk in contemporary penal practice, in M. Brown and J. Pratt (eds) *Dangerous Offenders: Punishment and Social Order*. London: Routledge.

Brown, M. and Pratt, J. (eds) (2000) *Dangerous Offenders: Punishment and Social Order*. London: Routledge.

Brown, S.L. and Forth, A.E. (1997) Psychopathy and sexual assault: static risk factors, emotional precursors, and rapist subtypes, *Journal of Consulting and Clinical Psychology*, 65: 848–57.

Burgess, E.W. (1928) Factors making for success of failure on parole, *Journal of Criminal Law and Criminology*, 19(2): 239–306.

Burgess, E.W. (1929) Is prediction feasible in social work?, *Social Forces*, 7: 533–45.

Burgess, E.W. (1936) Protecting the public by parole and parole prediction, *Journal of Criminal Law and Criminology*, 27: 491–502.

Butler-Schloss, E. (1988) *Report of the Commission of Inquiry into Child Sexual Abuse in Cleveland*. Presented to the Secretary of State for Social Services by the Right Honorable Lord Butler-Schloss, DBE, Cm 412. London: HMSO.

Campbell, B. (1993) *Goliath: Britain's Dangerous Places*. London: Methuen.

Canter, D. (1989) Offender profiles, *The Psychologist*, 2(1): 12–16.

Carlisle, Rt Hon. Lord of Bucklow (1988) *The Parole System in England and Wales: Report of the Review Committee*. London: HMSO.

Carson, D. (1996) Risking legal repercussions, in H. Kemshall and J. Pritchard (eds) *Good Practice in Risk Assessment and Risk Management*, vol. 1. London: Jessica Kingsley.

Castel, R. (1991) From dangerousness to risk, in G. Burchell, C. Gordon and P. Miller (eds) *The Foucault Effect: Studies in Governmentality*. Hemel Hempstead: Harvester Wheatsheaf.

Cavadino, M. and Dignan, J. (1997) *The Penal System: An Introduction*, 2nd edn. London: Sage.

Cavadino, M., Crow, I. and Dignan, J. (2000) *Criminal Justice 2000*. Winchester: Waterside Press.

Challinger, D. (1974) A predictive device for parolees in Victoria, *Australian and New Zealand Journal of Criminology*, 71: 102–6.

Christie, N. (1994) *Crime Control as Industry: Towards Gulags Western Style*. London: Routledge.

Clark, D. (2002) OASys – an explanation. Paper presented to Home Office 'Criminal Justice Conference: Using Risk Assessment in Effective Sentence Management', Pendley Manor Hotel, Tring, 14–15 March.

Clarke, J. and Newman, J. (1997) *The Managerial State*. London: Sage.

Clarke, J., Cochran, A. and McLaughlin, E. (eds) (1994) *Managing Social Policy*. London: Sage.

Clarke, R.V. (1981) *The Prospects for Controlling Crime*. Research Bulletin 12. London: Home Office.

Clarke, R.V. (1992) *Situational Crime Prevention: Successful Case Studies*. Albany, NY: Harrow and Heston.

Clarke, R.V. and Cornish, D. (1983) *Crime Control in Britain: A Review of Policy Research*. Albany, NY: State University of New York Press.

Clarke, R.V. and Mayhew, P. (eds) (1980) *Designing out Crime*. London: HMSO.

Clarkson, C. (1997) Beyond just deserts: sentencing violent and sexual offenders, *Howard Journal of Criminal Justice*, 36(3): 284–92.

Clements, C. (1986) *Offender Needs Assessment*. College Park, MD: American Corrections Association.

Cobley, C. (2000) *Sex Offenders: Law, Policy and Practice*. Bristol: Jordans.

Cohen, L.E. and Felson, M. (1979) Social change and crime rate trends: a routine activity approach, *American Sociological Review*, 44(4): 588–608.

Cohen, S. (1979) The punitive city: notes on the dispersal of social control, *Contemporary Crises*, 3: 339–63.

Cohen, S. (1985) *Visions of Social Control*. Cambridge: Polity Press.

Cohen, S. (1996) Crime and politics: spot the difference, *British Journal of Sociology*, 47: 1–23.

Cooke, D.J. (1991) Violence in prisons: the influence of regime factors, *Howard Journal of Criminal Justice*, 30: 95–100.

Cooke, D.J. (1998) Psychopathy across cultures, in D.J. Cooke, A.E. Forth, and R.D. Hare (eds) *Psychopathy: Theory, Research and Implications for society*. Dordrecht: Kluwer.

Cooke, D.J. (2000) Current risk assessment instruments. Annex 6 in the MacLean report, *A Report of the Committee on Serious Violent and Sexual Offenders*. Edinburgh: Scottish Executive.

Cooke, D.J. and Michie, C. (1999) Psychopathy across cultures: North America and Scotland compared, *Journal of Abnormal Psychology*, 108: 58–68.

Cooke, D.J., Michie, C. and Ryan, J. (2001) *Evaluating the Risk for Violence: A Preliminary Study of the HCR-20, PCL-R and VRAG in a Scottish Prison Sample*, occasional paper series 5/2001. Glasgow: Scottish Prison Service.

Copas, J. (1995) *Some Comments on Meta-Analysis*. Warwick: Department of Statistics, Warwick University.

Copas, J., Ditchfield, J. and Marshall, P. (1994) *Development of a New Reconviction Score*, research bulletin 36. London: HMSO.

Copas, J., Marshall, P. and Tarling, R. (1996) *Predicting Reoffending for Discretionary Conditional Release*, Home Office research study 150. London: HMSO.

Cornish, D. and Clarke, R. (1986) Situational crime prevention, displacement of crime and rational choice theory, in K. Heal and G. Laycock (eds) *Situational Crime Prevention: From Theory into Practice*. London: HMSO.

Cotswold District Council (1994) *Prison at the Crossroads: The House of Correction at Northleach*. Northleach, Gloucestershire: Cotswold District Council.

Cowburn, M. and Dominelli, L. (2001) Masking hegemonic masculinity: reconstructing the paedophile as the dangerous stranger, *British Journal of Social Work*, 31: 399–415.

Crackanthorpe, M. (1902) The Criminal Sentences Division up to date, *The Nineteenth Century*, November: 847–63.

Crawford, A. (1998) *Crime Prevention and Community Safety: Politics, Policies and Practices*. London: Longman.

Crawford, A. (1999) *The Local Governance of Crime: Appeals to Community and Partnerships*. Oxford: Oxford University Press.

Crawford, A. (2001) Joined-up but fragmented: contradiction, ambiguity and ambivalence at the heart of New Labour's 'Third Way', in R. Matthews and J. Pitts (eds) *Crime, Disorder and Community Safety: A New Agenda?* London: Routledge.

Crawford, A. and Jones, M. (1995) Inter-agency co-operation and community based crime prevention, *British Journal of Criminology*, 35(1): 17–33.

Craze, L. and Moynihan, P. (1994) Violence, meaning and the law: responses to Garry David, *Australian and New Zealand Journal of Criminology*, 27: 30–45.

Cruikshank, B. (1993) Revolutions within: self-government and self-esteem, *Economy and Society*, 22(3): 327–44.

Cruikshank, B. (1996) Revolutions within: self-government and self-esteem, in A. Barry, T. Osborne and N. Rose (eds) *Foucault and Political Reason: Liberalism, Neo-liberalism and Rationalities of Government*. London: UCL Press.

Dandeker, C. (1990) *Surveillance, Power and Modernity*. Cambridge: Polity Press.

Darwin, C. (1859) *On the Origin of Species by Means of Natural Selection*. London: Murray.

Daston, L. (1987) The domestication of risk: mathematical probability and insurance 1650–1830, in L. Kruger, L. Daston and M. Heidelberger (eds) *The Probabilistic Revolution*, Vol. 1, *Ideas in History*. Cambridge, MA: MIT Press.

Daston, L. (1988) *Classical Probability in the Enlightenment*. Princeton, NJ: Princeton University Press.

Davies, M. (1974) *Social Work in the Environment*. London: Heinemann.

Davies, M., Croall, H. and Tyner, J.C. (1995) *Criminal Justice: An Introduction to Criminal Justice in England and Wales*. London: Longman.

Davies, N. (1998) *Dark Heart*. London: Verso.

Davis, M. (1990) *City of Quartz: Excavating the Future of Los Angeles*. London: Verso.

Dean, M. (1995) Governing the unemployed self in an active society, *Economy and Society*, 24: 559–83.

Dean, M. (1999) *Governmentality: Power and Rule in Modern Society*. London: Sage.

Dennis, N. (1993) *Rising Crime and the Dismembered Family*. London: Institute of Economic Affairs.

Dennis, N. (1997) *The Invention of Permanent Poverty*. London: Institute of Economic Affairs.

Dennis, N. and Mallon, R. (1997) Confident policing in Hartlepool, in N. Dennis (ed.) *Zero Tolerance: Policing a Free Society*. London: Health and Welfare Unit, Institute of Economic Affairs.

Department of Health (1992) *The Health of the Nation: A Strategy for Health in England*. London: HMSO.

Dingwall, G. (1989) Some problems about predicting child abuse and neglect, in O. Stevenson (ed.) *Child Abuse: Public Policy and Professional Practice*. Hemel Hempstead: Harvester Wheatsheaf.

Dingwall, G. (1998) Selective incapacitation after the Criminal Justice Act 1991: a proportional response to protecting the public?, *Howard Journal of Criminal Justice*, 37(2): 177–87.

Ditchfield, J. (1991) *Control in Prison: A Review of the Literature*. London: HMSO.

Ditchfield, J. (1997) Actuarial prediction and risk assessment, *Prison Service Journal*, 113: 8–13.

Donzelot, J. (1980) *The Policing of Families*. London: Hutchinson.

Douglas, K.S., Ogloff, J.R.P., Grant, I. and Nicholls, T.L. (1999) Assessing risk for violence among psychiatric patients: the HCR-20 violence risk assessment scheme and the Psychopathy Checklist: screening version, *Journal of Consulting and Clinical Psychology*, 67(6): 917–30.

Douglas, M. (1986) *Risk Acceptability According to the Social Sciences*. London: Routledge and Kegan Paul.

Douglas, M. (1992) *Risk and Blame*. London: Routledge.

Douglas, M. and Wildavsky, A. (1982) How can we know the risks we face? Why risk selection is a social process, *Risk Analysis*, 2(2): 49–51.

Downes, D. (1998) Toughing it out: from Labour opposition to Labour Government, *Policy Studies*, 19(3, 4): 191–8.

Drakeford, M. and Vanstone, M. (2000) Social exclusion and the politics of criminal justice: a tale of two administrations, *Howard Journal of Criminal Justice*, 39(4): 369–81.

Dunbar, I. and Langdon, A. (1998) *Tough Justice Sentencing and Penal Policies in the 1990s*. London: Blackstone Press.

Dunsire, A. (1990) Holistic governance, *Public Policy and Administration*, 5(1): 4–19.

Ehrlich, S. (1998) The discursive reconstruction of sexual consent, *Discourse and Society*, 9(2): 149–71.

Ekblom, P. (1997) Gearing up against crime: a dynamic framework to help designers keep up with the adaptive criminal in a changing world, *International Journal of Risk, Security and Crime Prevention*, 214: 249–65.

Ekblom, P. (1999) Can we make crime prevention adaptive by learning from other evolutionary struggles?, *Studies on Crime and Crime Prevention*, 8/1: 27–51.

Ekblom, P. (2000) The conjunction of criminal opportunity: a tool for clear, 'joined-up' thinking about community safety and crime reduction, in S. Ballintyne, K. Pease and V. McLaren (eds) *Secure Foundations: Key Issues in Crime Prevention, Crime Reduction and Community Safety*. London: Institute of Public Policy Research.

Ekblom, P. (2001) Future imperfect: preparing for the crimes to come, *Criminal Justice Matters*, 46(winter): 38–40.

Elias, N. (1978) *The Civilizing Process*, Vol. 1, *The History of Manners*. Oxford: Basil Blackwell.

Elias, N. (1982) *The Civilizing Process*, Vol. 2, *State Formation and Civilization*. Oxford: Basil Blackwell.

Engel, U. and Strasser, H. (1998) Global risks and social inequality: critical remarks on the risk-society hypothesis, *Canadian Journal of Sociology*, 23: 91–103.

Ericson, R. (1994) The division of expert knowledge in policing and security, *British Journal of Sociology*, 45(2): 149–75.

Ericson, R. and Haggerty, K. (1997) *Policing the Risk Society*. Oxford: Clarendon Press.

Etter, B. and Palmer, M. (eds) (1995) *Police Leadership in Australia*. Sydney: Federation Press.

Etzioni, A. (1994) *The Spirit of Community: The Reinvention of American Society*. New York: Touchstone.

Etzioni, A. (1995) *The Spirit of Community*. London: Fontana.

Etzioni, A. (1997) *The New Golden Rule: Community and Morality in a Democratic Society*. London: Profile Books.

Faulkner, D. (1989) The future of the probation service: a view from government, in R. Shaw and K. Haines (eds) *The Criminal Justice System: A Central Role for the Probation Service*. Cambridge: Cambridge University Press.

Faulkner, D. (2001) *Crime, State and Citizen: A Field Full of Folk*. Winchester: Waterside Press.

Feeley, M. and Simon, J. (1992) The new penology: notes on the emerging strategy for corrections, *Criminology*, 30(4): 449–75.

Feeley, M. and Simon, J. (1994) Actuarial justice: the emerging new criminal law, in D. Nelken (ed.) *The Futures of Criminology*. London: Sage.

Felson, M. (1998) *Crime and Everyday Life*. London: Pine Forge Press.

Fielding, N. (1995) *Community Policing*. Oxford: Clarendon Press.

Fielding, N. (2002) Theorizing community policing, *British Journal of Criminology*, 42: 147–63.

Fischoff, B., Slovic, P., Lichenstein, S., Read, S. and Combs, B. (1978) How safe is safe enough? A psychometric study of the attitudes towards technological risks and benefits, *Policy Studies*, 9: 127–52.

Fletcher, H. (1995) New reconviction scale, *NAPO News*, 72: 1.

Flynn, E.E. (1978) Classification for risk and supervision: a peliminary conceptualization, in J.C. Freeman (ed.) *Prisons Past and Future*. London: Heinemann.

Folkard, M.S., Smith, D.E. and Smith, D.D. (1976) *IMPACT Vol. II: The Results of the Experiment*. London: HMSO.

Foucault, M. (1965) *Madness and Civilization: The History of Insanity in the Age of Reason*. New York: Pantheon.

Foucault, M. (1973) *The Birth of the Clinic: An Archaeology of Medical Perception*. London: Tavistock.

Foucault, M. (1977) *Discipline and Punish: The Birth of the Prison*. London: Allen Lane.

Foucault, M. (1978) About the concept of the 'dangerous individual' in 19th century legal psychiatry, *International Journal of Law and Psychiatry*, 1: 1–18.

Foucault, M. (1979) *The History of Sexuality*, Vol. 1. London: Allen Lane.

Foucault, M. (1982) The subject and power, in H.L. Dreyfus and P. Rabinow (eds) *Michel Foucault: Beyond Structuralism and Hermeneutics*. Chicago: University of Chicago Press.

Foucault, M. (1989) *The Archaeology of Knowledge*. London: Routledge.

Foucault, M. (1991) Governmentality, in G. Burchell, C. Gordon and P. Miller (eds) *The Foucault Effect: Studies in Governmentality*. London: Harvester Wheatsheaf.

Frazer, H. (1999) Capital common sense, *SCOPE*, September: 12–13.

Freiberg, A. (2000) Guerillas in our midst? Judicial responses to governing the dangerous, in M. Brown and J. Pratt (eds) *Dangerous Offenders: Punishment and Social Order*. London: Routledge.

Freiberg, A. (2001) Affective versus effective justice: instrumentalism and emotionalism in criminal justice, *Punishment and Society*, 3(2): 265–78.

Freudenberg, W.R. (1988) Perceived risk, real risk: social science and the art of probabilistic risk assessment, *Science*, 242 (October): 44–49.

Freudenberg, W.R. (1993) Risk and recreancy: Weber, the division of labour, and the rationality of risk perception, *Social Forces*, 71: 909–32.

Fukuyama, F. (1996) *Trust*. Harmondsworth: Penguin.

Furedi, F. (1997) *Culture of Fear: Risk-taking and the Morality of Low Expectation*. London: Cassell.

Furlong, A. and Cartmel, F. (1997) *Young People and Social Change: Individualisation and Risk in Late Modernity*. Buckingham: Open University Press.

Fyfe, N. and Bannister, J. (1996) City watching: closed circuit television surveillance in public spaces, *Area*, 28(1): 37–46.

Gamble, A. (1979) The free economy and the strong state, in R. Miliband and J. Saville (eds) *The Socialist Register*. London: Merlin Press.

Gamble, A. (1986) The political economy of freedom, in R. Levitas (ed.) *The Ideology of the New Right*. Cambridge: Polity.

Gamble, A. (1988) *The Free Economy and the Strong State*. London: Macmillan.

Garland, D. (1985) *Punishment and Welfare: A History of Penal Strategies*. Aldershot: Gower.

Garland, D. (1990) *Punishment and Modern Society: A Study in Social Theory*. Oxford: Clarendon Press.

Garland, D. (1995) Penal modernism and postmodernism, in T. Blomberg and S. Cohen (eds) *Punishment and Social Control: Essays in Honor of Sheldon Messinger*. New York: Aldine de Gruyter.

Garland, D. (1996) The limits of the sovereign state: strategies of crime control in contemporary society, *British Journal of Criminology*, 36(4): 445–71.

Garland, D. (1997a) The social and political context, in R. Burnett (ed.) *The Probation Service: Responding to Change. Proceedings of the Probation Studies Unit First Annual Colloquium*, Probation Studies Unit, Oxford, December 1996.

Garland, D. (1997b) 'Governmentality' and the problem of crime: Foucault, criminology and sociology, *Theoretical Criminology*, 1(2): 173–214.

Garland, D. (1999) The commonplace and the catastrophic: interpretations of crime in late modernity, *Theoretical Criminology*, 3(3): 353–64.

Garland, D. (2000) The culture of high crime societies, *British Journal of Criminology*, 40: 347–75.

Garland, D. (2001) *The Culture of Crime Control: Crime and Social Order in Contemporary Society*. Oxford: Oxford University Press.

Garland, D. and Sparks, R. (2000) Criminology and social theory and the challenge of our times, *British Journal of Criminology*, 40: 189–204.

Geason, S. and Wilson, P. (1989) *Crime Prevention: Theory and Practice*. Canberra: Australian Institute of Criminology.

Gendreau, P. and Andrews, D. (1990) Tertiary prevention: what the meta-analysis of the offender treatment literature tells us about 'what works', *Canadian Journal of Criminology*, 32: 173–84.

Gerbner, G. (1987) Charting the mainstream: television's contributions to political orientations, in D. Lazere (ed.) *American Media and Mass Culture: Left Perspectives*. Berkeley, CA: University of California Press.

Gibbs, J.C., Basinger, K.C., and Fuller, D. (1992) *Moral Maturity: Measuring the Development of Sociomoral Reflection*. Hillsdale, NJ: Erlbaum.

Giddens, A. (1990) *Consequences of Modernity*. Cambridge: Polity Press.

Giddens, A. (1991) *Modernity and Self-Identity*. Oxford: Polity Press with Blackwell.

Giddens, A. (1998a) Risk society: the context of British politics, in J. Franklin (ed.) *The Politics of Risk Society*. Oxford: Polity Press in association with Institute for Public Policy Research.

Giddens, A. (1998b) *The Third Way: The Renewal of Social Democracy*. Oxford: Polity Press.

Giddens, A. (1999) *BBC 1999 Reith Lectures*. BBC Radio Four. Also published as *Runaway World: How Globalisation is Reshaping our Lives*. London: Profile Books.

Gilling, D. (1997) *Crime Prevention: Theory, Policy and Politics*. London: UCL Press.

Glaser, D. (1955) The efficacy of alternative approaches to parole prediction, *American Sociological Review*, 20: 283–7.

Glaser, D. (1962) Prediction tables as accounting devices for judges and parole boards, *Crime and Delinquency*, 8(3): 239–58.

Glaser, D. (1975) *Routinizing Evaluation*. Rockville, MD: National Institute of Mental Health.

Gocke, B. (1995) Working with people who have committed sex offences. In: B. Williams (ed.) *Probation Values*. Birmingham: Venture Press.

Gordon, C. (1991) Governmental rationality: an introduction, in G. Burchell, C. Gordon and P. Miller (eds) *The Foucault Effect: Studies in Governmentality*. Chicago: University of Chicago Press.

Gordon, P. (1984) Community policing: towards the local police state, *Critical Social Policy*, 10(summer): 39–58.

Gordon, P. (1987) Community policing towards the local police state?, in P. Scraton (ed.) *Law, Order and the Authoritarian State*. Milton Keynes: Open University Press.

Gottfredson, S.D. and Gottfredson, D.M. (1985) Screening for risk among parolees: policy, practice and research, in D.P. Farrington and R. Tarling (eds) *Predicting Crime and Delinquency*. Albany, NY: Suny Press.

Gottfredson, S.D. and Gottfredson, D.M. (1993) The long-term predictive utility of the base expectancy score, *Howard Journal of Criminal Justice*, 32(4): 276–90.

Greco, M. (1993) Psychosomatic subjects and the 'duty to be well': personal agency within medical rationality, *Economy and Society*, 22(3): 357–72.

Green, J. (1997) *Risk and Misfortune*. London: UCL Press.

Greengrass, M. (1996) English Projectors and Contingency Planning in the Later Seventeenth Century. Paper presented to 'Publicists and Projectors in Seventeenth Century Europe Conference', Herzog August Bibliothek, Wolfenbuttel, 8–10 February.

Greenwood, P. and Abrahamse, A. (1982) *Selective Incapacitation*. Santa Monica, CA: RAND Corporation.

Greenwood, P. and Turner, S. (1987) *Selective Incapacitation: Why the High Rate Offenders are Hard to Predict*. Santa Monica, CA: RAND Corporation.

Greenwood, P., Rydell, C., Abrahamse, A., Caulkins, J., Chiesa, J., Model, K. and Klein, S. (1996) Estimated benefits and costs of California's new mandatory sentencing law, in D. Shichor and D. Sechrest (eds) *Three Strikes and You're Out: Vengeance as Public Policy*. Thousand Oaks, CA: Sage.

Grimshaw, R. and Jefferson, T. (1987) *Interpreting Policework*. London: Unwin.

Grinyer, A. (1995) Risk, the real world and naïve sociology, in J. Gabe (ed.) *Medicine, Health and Risk: Sociological Approaches*. Oxford: Blackwell.

Grubin, D. (1998) *Sex Offending against Children: Understanding the Risk*, Police research series 99. London: Home Office.

Grubin, D. (2000) Risk Matrix 2000. Paper presented to Risk Assessment and Management Police Conference, Moat House Hotel, Cheltenham, 19–20 October.

Grubin, D. and Wingate, S. (1996) Sexual offence recidivism: prediction versus understanding, *Criminal Behaviour and Mental Health*, 6: 349–59.

Hacking, I. (1975) *The Emergence of Probability*. Cambridge: Cambridge University Press.

Hacking, I. (1986) Making up people, in T. Heller, M. Sosna and D. Wellbery (eds) *Reconstructing Individualism*. Stanford, CA: Stanford University Press.

Hacking, I. (1987) Was there a probabilistic revolution 1800–1930?, in L. Kruger, L. Daston and M. Heidelberger (eds) *The Probabilistic Revolution*, Vol. 1, *Ideas in History*. Cambridge, MA: MIT Press.

Hacking, I. (1990) *The Taming of Chance*. Cambridge: Cambridge University Press.

Hagell, A. (1998) *Dangerous Care: Reviewing the Risk to Children from their Carers*. London: Policy Studies Institute and the Bridge Child Care Trust.

Hall, S. (1979) *Drifting into a Law and Order Society*. London: Cobden Trust.

Halliday, J. (2001) *Making Punishments Work: Report of a Review of the Sentencing Framework for England and Wales*. London: Home Office.

Hancock, L. and Matthews, R. (2001) Crime, community safety and toleration, in R. Matthews and J. Pitts (eds) *Crime, Disorder and Community Safety*. London: Routledge.

Hannah-Moffat, K. (1999) Moral agent or actuarial subject: risk and Canadian women's imprisonment, *Theoretical Criminology*, 3(1): 71–94.

Hannah-Moffat, K. and Shaw, M. (1999) Women and risk: a genealogy of classification. Paper presented to the British Criminology Conference, Liverpool, July.

Hanson, R.K. (1997) *The Development of a Brief Actuarial Risk Scale for Sexual Offence Recidivism*, user report 1997–04. Ottawa: Department General of Solicitor General of Canada.

Hanson, R.K. and Bussiere, M.T. (1998) Predicting relapse: a meta-analysis of sexual offender recidivism studies, *Journal of Consulting Clinical Psychology*, 66(2): 348–62.

Hanson, R.K. and Thornton, D.M. (1999) *Static 99: Improving Actuarial Risk Assessments for Sex Offenders*. Ottawa: Public Works and Government Services, Canada.

Hanson, R.K. and Thornton, D.M. (2000) Improving risk assessments for sex offenders: a comparison of three actuarial scales, *Law and Human Behaviour*, 24(1): 119–36.

Hardiker, P. (1977) Social work ideologies in the Probation Service, *British Journal of Social Work*, 7(2): 131–54.

Hare, R.D. (1991) *The Hare Psychopathy Check-list Revised*. Toronto: Multi-Health Systems.

Hare, R.D. (1998) *Without Conscience: The Disturbing World of Psychopaths among Us*. New York: Pocket Books.

Hare, R.D. (2000) Presentation to 'Risk Assessment and Risk Management: Implications for the Prevention of Violence' Conference, Vancouver, 17–19 November. Reproduced in Annex 4 of the MacLean Report, *A Report for the Committee on Serious Violent and Sexual Offenders*. Edinburgh: Scottish Executive.

Hare, R.D. and Hart, S.D. (1993) Psychopathy, mental disorder, and crime, in S. Hodgins (ed.) *Mental Disorder and Crime*. Newbury Park, CA: Sage.

Harris, G.T., Rice, M.E. and Quinsey, V.L. (1993) Violent recidivism of mentally disordered offenders: the development of a statistical prediction instrument, *Criminal Justice and Behaviour*, 20: 387–97.

Harris, P. (1994) Client management classification and prediction of probation outcomes, *Crime and Delinquency*, 40(2): 154–74.

Harris, P. (1999) Public welfare and liberal governance, in A. Petersen, I. Barns, J. Dudley and P. Harris (eds) *Poststructuralism, Citizenship and Social Policy*. London: Routledge.

Hart, G. and Boulton, M. (1995) Sexual behaviour in gay men: towards a sociology of risk, in P. Aggleton, P. Davies and G. Hart (eds) *AIDS: Safety, Sexuality and Risk*. London: Taylor & Francis.

Hart, H. (1923) Predicting parole success, *Journal of Criminal Law and Criminology*, 14: 405–13.

Hart, S.D. (1999) Assessing violence risk: thoughts and second thoughts. Violent offenders: appraising and managing risk, *Contemporary Psychology*, 44: 6–8.

Hart, S.D., Hare, R.D. and Forth, A.E. (1994) Psychopathy as a risk marker for violence: development and validation of a screening version of the revised psychopathy checklist, in J. Monahan and H. Steadman (eds) *Violence and Mental Disorder: Developments in Risk Assessment*. Chicago: University of Chicago Press.

Hebenton, B. and Thomas, T. (1995) *Policing Europe: Co-operation, Conflict and Control*. London: Macmillan.

Hebenton, B. and Thomas, T. (1996) Tracking sex offenders, *Howard Journal of Criminal Justice*, 35(2): 97–112.

Hebenton, B. and Thomas, T. (1997) *Keeping Track? Observations on Sex Offender Registers in the U.S.*, Police Research Group Crime Detection and Prevention paper 83. London: Home Office.

Her Majesty's Inspectorate of Probation (HMIP) (1995) *Dealing with Dangerous People: The Probation Service and Public Protection. Report of a Thematic Inspection*. London: Home Office.

Her Majesty's Inspectorate of Probation (HMIP) (1998) *Exercising Constant Vigilance: The Role of the Probation Service in Protecting the Public from Sex Offenders. Report of a Thematic Inspection*. London: Home Office.

Her Majesty's Inspectorate of Probation (HMIP) (2000) *Serious Incidents. Probation Services' Compliance with the Notification Requirements of Probation Circular 71/1998*. London: Home Office.

Heydebrand, W. and Seron, C. (1990) *Rationalizing Justice: The Political Economy of Federal District Courts*. Albany, NY: State University of New York Press.

Higgs, H. (ed.) (1931) *Richard Cantillon: Essay on the Nature of Commerce in General*. London: Royal Economics Society.

Home Office (1984a) *Probation Service in England and Wales: Statement of National Objectives and Priorities*. London: Home Office.

Home Office (1984b) *Crime Prevention*, Home Office circular 8/84. London: Home Office.

Home Office (1988) *Home Office Letter to Chief Probation Officers, July 1988: The Registration and Review of Serious Offenders*. London: Home Office.

Home Office (1990) *Crime, Justice and Protecting the Public: The Government's Proposals for Legislation*, Cm 965. London: HMSO.

Home Office (1991) *Safer Communities: The Local Delivery of Crime Prevention through the Partnership Approach*. London: Home Office.

Home Office (1994a) *The Police and Magistrates Court Act*. London: Home Office.

Home Office (1994b) *Review of the Police Core and Ancillary Tasks: Interim Report*. London: HMSO.

Home Office (1995a) *National Standards for the Supervision of Offenders in the Community*. London: Home Office.

Home Office (1995b) *Review of the Police Core and Ancillary Tasks: Final Report*. London: HMSO.

Home Office (1996a) *Three Year Plan for the Probation Service 1996–1999*. London: HMSO.

Home Office (1996b) *Protecting the Public: The Government's Strategy on Crime in England and Wales*. London: HMSO.

Home Office (1998) *Joining Forces to Protect the Public: Joint Prisons–Probation Review*. London: Home Office.

Home Office (1999) *Managing Dangerous People with Severe Personality Disorder*. London: Home Office.

Home Office (2000a) Government proposals to better protect children from sex and violent offenders, Home Office news release, 15 September.

Home Office (2000b) *Recorded Crime Statistics, England and Wales, October 1998–September 1999*, Statistical Bulletin 1/00. London: Home Office.

Home Office (2001a) *The Offender Assessment System: OASys*. London: Home Office.

Home Office (2001b) *Initial Guidance to the Police and Probation Services on Sections 67 and 68 of the Criminal Justice and Court Services Act 2000*. London: Home Office.

Home Office (2001c) *Criminal Justice and Police Act 2001*. London: Home Office.

Home Office (2002a) *Further Guidance to the Police and Probation Services on the Criminal Justice and Court Services Act 2000, Sections 67 and 68*. London: Home Office.

Home Office (2002b) *Justice for All*, Criminal Justice White Paper. London: Home Office.

Home Office (2002c) Home secretary welcomes stable crime figures, news and press release, 12 July. http: www.Homeoffice.gov.uk

Home Office and Association of Chief Officers of Probation (ACOP) (1997) *The Management and Assessment of Risk*. London: Home Office and ACOP.

Home Office, Northern Ireland Office and Scottish Office (1993) *Inquiry into Police Responsibilities and Rewards* (Sheehy report); Cm 2280. London: HMSO.

Home Office Special Conference Unit (1997) *Inter-agency Work with Dangerous Offenders: Sharing Information to Manage Risk*. London: Home Office.

Hood, C. (1991) A public management for all seasons?, *Public Administration*, 69(1): 3–19.

Hood, C. (1996) Where extremes meet sprat: sprat versus shark in public risk management, in C. Hood and D.K.C. Jones (eds) *Accident and Design: Contemporary Debates in Risk Management*. London: UCL Press.

Hood, C. and Jones, D.K.C. (eds) (1996) *Accident and Design: Contemporary Debates in Risk Management*. London: UCL Press.

Hood, C., Jones, D., Pidgeon, N., Turner, B. and Gibson, R. (1992) Risk management, in The Royal Society, *Risk: Analysis, Perception and Management*, report of a Royal Society Study Group. London: Royal Society.

Hood, R. and Shute, S. (2000a) *Parole Decision-Making: Weighing the Risk to the Public*, research findings 114. London: Home Office Research, Development and Statistics Directorate.

Hood, R. and Shute, S. (2000b) *The Parole System at Work: A Study of Risk Based Decision Making*, Home Office research study 202. London: Home Office.

Hope, T. (1996) Community crime prevention, in M. Tonry and D. Farrington (eds) *Building a Safer Society: Strategic Approaches to Crime Prevention*. Chicago: University of Chicago Press.

Hope, T. and Murphy, D.J. (1983) Problems of implementing crime prevention: the experience of a demonstration project, *Howard Journal of Criminal Justice*, 22(1): 38–50.

Hope, T. and Shaw, M. (eds) (1988) *Communities and Crime Reduction*. London: HMSO.

Hope, T. and Sparks, R. (eds) (2000) *Crime, Risk and Insecurity*. London: Routledge.

Hopton, J. (1998) Risk assessment using psychological profiling techniques: an evaluation of possibilities, *British Journal of Social Work*, 28: 247–61.

Horlick-Jones, T. (1998) Meaning and contextualisation in risk assessment, *Reliability Engineering and System Safety*, 5: 79–89.

Hough, M. and Tilley, N. (1998) *Auditing Crime and Disorder: Guidance for Local Partnerships*, Crime Detection and Prevention series 91. London: HMSO.

Hudson, B. (1987) *Justice through Punishment*. London: Macmillan.

Hudson, B. (1993) *Penal Policy and Social Justice*. London: Macmillan.

Hudson, B. (1996) *Understanding Justice*. Buckingham: Open University Press.

Hudson, B. (1998) Punishment and governance, *Social and Legal Studies*, 7(4): 581–7.

Hudson, B. (2000) Balancing risks and rights: dilemmas of justice and difference. Paper presented at the Colloquium on Risk and Criminal Justice, Cardiff University, 18–19 May.

Hudson, B. (2001) Crime, risk and justice, in K. Stenson and R. Sullivan (eds) *Crime, Risk and Justice: The Politics of Crime Control in Liberal Democracies*. Cullompton, Devon: Willan.

Hudson, B. (2002) Punishment and control, in M. Maguire, R. Morgan and R. Reiner (eds) *The Oxford Handbook of Criminology*. Oxford: Oxford University Press.

Hughes, G. (1998) *Understanding Crime Prevention: Social Control, Risk and Late Modernity*. Buckingham: Open University Press.

Hughes, G. (2000) Community safety in the age of risk society, in S. Ballintyne, K. Pease and V. McLaren (eds) *Secure Foundations: Key Issues in Crime Prevention, Crime Reduction and Community Safety*. London: Institute for Public Policy Research.

Humphrey, C., Carter, P. and Pease, K. (1992) A reconviction predictor for probationers, *British Journal of Social Work*, 22: 33–46.

Irwin, A. and Wynne, B. (1996) *Misunderstanding Science? The Public Reconstruction of Science and Technology*. Cambridge: Cambridge University Press.

Jackson, S. and Scott, S. (1999) Risk anxiety and the social construction of childhood, in D. Lupton (ed.) *Risk and Sociocultural Theory: New Directions and Perspectives*. Cambridge: Cambridge University Press.

James, A. and Jenks, C. (1996) Public perceptions of childhood criminality, *British Journal of Sociology*, 47(2): 315–31.

James, A. and Raine, J. (1998) *The New Politics of Criminal Justice*. London: Longman.

Jasanoff, S. (1993) Bridging the two cultures of risk analysis, *Risk Analysis*, 13(2): 123–9.

Jessop, B. (1993) Towards a Schumpeterian welfare state? Preliminary remarks on post-Fordist political economy, *Studies in Political Economy*, 40: 7–39.

Jessop, B. (1994) The transition to a Post-Fordist and Schumpeterian Welfare State, in R. Burrows and B. Loader (eds) *Towards a Post-Fordist Welfare State?* London: Routledge.

Jessop, B. (2000) From the KWNS to the SWPR, in G. Lewis, S. Gerwitz and J. Clarke (eds) *Rethinking Social Policy*. London: Sage and Open University.

Johnston, L. (1987) Controlling policework: problems of organisational reform in large public bureaucracies, *Work, Employment and Society*, 2: 1.

Johnston, L. (1992) *The Rebirth of Private Policing*. London: Routledge.

Johnston, L. (1994) Policing plutonium: issues in the provision of policing services and security systems at nuclear facilities and for related materials in transit, *Policing and Society*, 4: 53–72.

Johnston, L. (1997) Policing communities of risk, in P. Francis, P. Davies and V. Jupp (eds) *Policing Futures. The Police, Law Enforcement and the Twenty-First Century*. London: Macmillan.

Johnston, L. (2000) *Policing Britain: Risk, Security and Governance*. London: Longman.

Jones, P.R. (1996) Risk prediction in criminal justice, in A.T. Harland (ed.) *Choosing Correctional Options that Work*. Thousand Oaks, CA: Sage.

Jones, T. and Newburn, T. (1994) *How Big is the Private Security Industry?* London: Policy Studies Institute.

Jones, T. and Newburn, T. (1997) *Policing after the Act*. London: Policy Studies Institute.

Jones, T. and Newburn, T. (1998) *Private Security and Public Policing*. Oxford: Oxford University Press.

Jones, T. and Newburn, T. (2002) The transformation of policing? Understanding current trends in policing systems, *British Journal of Criminology*, 4(1): 129–46.

Jones, T., Newburn, T. and Smith, D. (1994) *Democracy and Policing*. London: Policy Studies Institute.

Jordan, B. (1992) Basic income and common good, in P. van Parijs (ed.) *Arguing for Basic Income*. London: Verso.

Jordan, B. (1996) *A Theory of Poverty and Social Exclusion*. Cambridge: Polity Press.

Jordan, B. (1998) *The New Politics of Welfare*. London: Sage.

Jordan, B. (2000) *Social Work and the Third Way: Tough Love as Social Policy*. London: Sage.

Kanka, M. (2000) How Megan's death changed us all: the personal story of a mother and anti-crime advocate. The Megan Nicole Kanka Foundation: http://www.apbnews.com/safetycenter/family/kanka/sooo/03/28/kanka0328_ol.htm (accessed 28 March 2002).

Karmen, A. (1990) *Crime and Victims: An Introduction to Victimology*. Pacific Grove, CA: Brooks Cole.

Keat, R. (1991) Introduction: starship Britain or universal enterprise?, in R. Keat and N. Abercrombie (eds) *Enterprise Culture*. London: Routledge.

Kellner, D. (1999) Theorizing the present moments: debates between modern and postmodern theory, *Theory and Society*, 28: 639–56.

Kemshall, H. (1993) Are we all accountants now? Financial management in the Probation Service, *Probation Journal*, 41: 2–8.

Kemshall, H. (1995) Risk in probation practice: the hazards and dangers of supervision, *Probation Journal*, 42(2): 67–72.

Kemshall, H. (1996) *Reviewing Risk: A Review of Research on the Assessment and Management of Risk and Dangerousness: Implications for Policy and Practice in the Probation Service*, report for the Home Office Research and Statistics Directorate. London: Home Office.

Kemshall, H. (1997a) Risk in probation practice training issues, in Home Office and Association of Chief Officers of Probation (ACOP) *Management and Assessment of Risk in the Probation Service, Part 3*. London: Home Office and ACOP.

Kemshall, H. (1997b) Training materials for risk assessment and risk management, in Home Office and Association of Chief Officers of Probation (ACOP) *Management and Assessment of Risk in the Probation Service, Part 2*. London: Home Office ACOP.

Kemshall, H. (1998) *Risk in Probation Practice*. Aldershot: Ashgate.

Kemshall, H. (2000) Conflicting knowledges of risk: the case of risk knowledge in the probation service, *Health, Risk and Society*, 2(2): 143–58.

Kemshall, H. (2001) *Risk Assessment and Management of Known Sexual and Violent Offenders: A Review of Current Issues*, Police Research series 140. London: Home Office.

Kemshall, H. (2002a) *Risk, Social Policy and Welfare*. Buckingham: Open University Press.

Kemshall, H. (2002b) Effective probation practice: an example of 'advanced liberal' responsibilisation?, *Howard Journal of Criminal Justice*, 41(1): 41–58.

Kemshall, H. and Maguire, M. (2001) Public protection, partnership and risk penality: the multi-agency risk management of sexual and violent offenders, *Punishment and Society*, 3(2): 237–64.

Kemshall, H. and Maguire, M. (2002) Community justice, risk management and Multi-Agency Public Protection Panels, *Community Justice*, 1(1): 11–27.

Kemshall, H., Parton, N., Walsh, M. and Waterson, J. (1997) Concepts of risk in relation to organisational structure and functioning within the Personal Social Services and Probation, *Social Policy and Administration*, 31(3): 213–32.

Kemshall, H., Holt, P., Boswell, G. and Bailey, R. (2002) *The Implementation of Effective Practice in the Northwest Probation Region*, report for the Northwest Probation Region. Leicester: DeMontfort University.

Kitzinger, J. (1999a) Researching risk and the media, *Health, Risk and Society*, 1(1): 55–70.

Kitzinger, J. (1999b) The ultimate neighbour from hell: media framing of paedophiles, in B. Franklin (ed.) *Social Policy, Media and Misrepresentation*. London: Routledge.

Kitzinger, J. and Skidmore, P. (1995) Playing safe: media coverage of child sexual abuse prevention strategies, *Child Abuse Review*, 4: 47–56.

Klassen, C. (1999) Predicting aggression in psychiatric in-patients using 10 historical factors: validating the 'H' of the HCR-20. Unpublished PhD thesis, Simon Fraser University, Vancouver.

Knock, K. and Thomas, N. (2002) Issuing orders, *Police Review*, 2 August: 22–3.

Labour Party (1997) *New Labour Because Britain Deserves Better (1997 General Election Manifesto)*. London: Labour Party.

Langan, M. (1998) *Welfare: Needs, Rights and Risks*. London: Open University and Routledge.

Lasch, C. (1980) *The Culture of Narcissism*. London: Sphere.

Lash, S. (1990) *The Sociology of Postmodernism*. London: Routledge.

Lawrie, C. (1996) Dealing with dangerous people: the Probation Service and public protection. Paper presented to the Public Protection Conference, Her Majesty's Inspectorate of Probation, Daventry, 27–29 March.

Lawrie, C. (1997) Risk: the role and responsibilities of middle managers, in H. Kemshall and J. Pritchard (eds) *Good Practice in Risk Assessment and Risk Management: Protection, Rights and Responsibilities*. Vol. 2. London: Jessica Kingsley.

Laycock, G. and Heal, K. (1989) Crime prevention: the British experience, in D.J. Evans and D.T. Herbert (eds) *The Geography of Crime*. London: Routledge.

Leishman, F., Cope, S. and Starie, P. (1996) Reinventing and restructuring: towards a 'new policing order', in F. Leishman, B. Loveday and S. Savage (eds) *Core Issues in Policing*. London: Longman.

Leiss, W. and Chociolko, C. (1994) *Risk and Responsibility*. Toronto: McGill-Queen's University Press.

Leonard, P. (1997) *Postmodern Welfare*. London: Sage.

Letwin, O. (2002) *Beyond the Causes of Crime*, Sixth Keith Joseph Memorial Lecture. London: Centre for Policy Studies.

Lianos, M. with Douglas, M. (2000) Dangerization and the end of deviance, *British Journal of Criminology*, 40: 261–78.

Liddle, M. and Gelsthorpe, L. (1994a) *Crime Prevention and Inter-agency Cooperation*, Crime Prevention Unit paper 52. London: HMSO.

Liddle, M. and Gelsthorpe, L. (1994b) *Inter-agency Crime Prevention: Organising Local Delivery*, Crime Prevention Unit paper 53. London: HMSO.

Liddle, M. and Gelsthorpe, L. (1994c) *Inter-agency Crime Prevention: Further Issues*, Supplementary Paper to Crime Prevention Unit papers 52, 53. London: HMSO.

Lister, R. (ed.) (1996) *Charles Murray and the Underclass: The Developing Debate*. London: Health and Welfare Unit, Institute of Economic Affairs.

Lloyd, C., Mair, G. and Hough, M. (1994) *Explaining Reconviction Rates: A Critical Analysis*, Home Office research study 136. London: HMSO.

Loader, I. (1996) *Youth, Policing and Democracy*. London: Macmillan.

Loader, I. (1997a) Private security and the demand for protection in contemporary Britain, *Policing and Society*, 7: 143–62.

Loader, I. (1997b) Thinking normatively about private security, *Journal of Law and Society*, 24(3): 377–94.

Loader, I. (1999) Consumer culture and the commodification of policing and security, *Sociology*, 33(2): 373–92.

Loader, I. and Sparks, R. (2002) Contemporary landscapes of crime, order and control: governance, risk and globalisation, in M. Maguire, R. Morgan and R. Reiner (eds) *The Oxford Handbook of Criminology*. Oxford: Oxford University Press.

Losel, E. (1995) The efficacy of correctional treatment: a review and synthesis of meta-evaluation, in J. McGuire (ed.) *What Works: Reducing Reoffending. Guidelines from Research and Practice*. Chichester: John Wiley.

Loveday, B. (1991) The new police authorities, *Policing and Society*, 1(3): 193–212.

Loveday, B. (1994) The Police and Magistrates Court Act, *Policing*, 10(4): 221–33.

Loveday, B. (1995) Reforming the police: from local service to state police?, *Political Quarterly*, 66(2): 141–56.

Loveday, B. (1996) Contemporary challenges to police management in England and Wales: developing for effective service delivery, *Policing and Society*, 5(4): 281–302.

Lupton, D. (1993) Risk as a moral danger: the social and political functions of risk discourse in public health, *International Journal of Health Services*, 23: 425–35.

Lupton, D. (1995) *The Imperative of Health: Public Health and the Regulated Body*. London: Sage.

Lupton, D. (1999a) *Risk*. London: Routledge.

Lupton, D. (1999b) Dangerous places and the unpredictable stranger: constructions of fear of crime, *Australian and New Zealand Journal of Criminology*, 32(1): 1–15.

Lupton, D. (2000) Part of living in the late twentieth century: notions of risk and fear in relation to crime, *Australian and New Zealand Journal of Criminology*, 33(1): 21–36.

Lupton, D. and Tulloch, J. (1999) Theorizing fear of crime: beyond the rational/ irrational opposition, *British Journal of Sociology*, 50(3): 507–23.

Lynch, M. (1998) Waste managers? The new penology, crime fighting and the parole agent identity, *Law and Society Review*, 32(4): 839–69.

Lynch, M. (2000) Rehabilitation and rhetoric: the ideal of reformation in contemporary parole discourse and practices, *Punishment and Society*, 2(1): 40–65.

Lynch, W. (1996) Method in the early Royal Society of London. PhD thesis, Cornell University (cited in Rigakos and Hadden 2001).

Lyon, D. (1994) *The Electronic Eye: The Rise of Surveillance Society*. Cambridge: Polity Press.

Lyon, D. (2001) *Surveillance Society: Monitoring Everyday Life*. Buckingham: Open University Press.

McConville, M. and Shepherd, D. (1992) *Watching Police, Watching Communities*. London: Routledge.

McEwan, S. and Sullivan, J. (1996) Sex offender risk assessment, in H. Kemshall and J. Pritchard (eds) *Good Practice in Risk Assessment and Risk Management*, Vol. 1. London: Jessica Kingsley.

McGuire, J. (ed.) (1995) *What Works: Reducing Reoffending: Guidelines from Research and Practice*. Chichester: John Wiley.

McGuire, J. (ed.) (1997) A short introduction to meta-analysis, *VISTA*, 3(3): 163–76.

McGuire, J. and Priestley, P. (1995) Reviewing 'what works': past, present and future, in J. McGuire (ed.) *What Works: Reducing Reoffending: Guidelines from Research and Practice.* Chichester: John Wiley.

McIvor, G. (1997) Evaluative research in probation: progress and prospects, in G. Mair (ed.) *Evaluating the Effectiveness of Community Penalties.* Aldershot: Avebury.

McIvor, G., Moodie, K. with Perrott, S. and Spencer, F. (2001) *The Relative Effectiveness of Risk Assessment Instruments,* Social Work research findings No. 40. Edinburgh: Scottish Executive Central Research Unit.

Mackenzie, G. (1996) Danger, necessity and tribulation: a theme for reason. Paper presented to the Public Protection Conference, Her Majesty's Inspectorate of Probation, Daventry, 27–29 March.

McLaughlin, E. (1991) Police accountability and black people: into the 1990s, in E. Cashmore and E. McLaughlin (eds) *Out of Order? Policing Black People.* London: Routledge.

McLaughlin, E. (1994) *Community Policing and Accountability: The Politics of Policing in Manchester in the 1980s.* Aldershot: Avebury.

McLaughlin, E. (1996) Political violence, terrorism and crimes of the State, in J. Muncies and E. McLaughlin (eds) *The Problem of Crime.* London: Sage.

McLaughlin, E. and Muncie, J. (1996) *Controlling Crime.* London: Sage.

McLaughlin, E. and Murji, K. (1993) The end of public policing. Paper presented to British Criminology Conference, Cardiff, July.

McMullan, J.L. (1987) Policing the criminal underworld: state power and decentralised social control in London 1550–1700, in J. Lowman, J. Menzies and T.S. Palys (eds) *Transcarceration: Essays in the Sociology of Social Control.* Aldershot: Gower.

McMullan, J.L. (1998) Social surveillance and the rise of the 'police machine', *Theoretical Criminology,* 2(1): 93–117.

McNeill, W.H. (1977) *Plagues and People.* Oxford: Basil Blackwell.

MacPherson, W. (1999) *The Stephen Lawrence Inquiry.* London: HMSO.

McWilliams, W. (1987) Probation, pragmatism and policy, *Howard Journal of Criminal Justice,* 25: 97–121.

McWilliams, W. (1992a) Statement of purpose for the Probation Service: a criticism, *NAPO News,* 39: 8–9.

McWilliams, W. (1992b) The rise and development of management thought, in R. Statham and P. Whitehead (eds) *Managing the Probation Service.* London: Longman.

McWilliams, W. and Pease, K. (1990) Probation practice and the end to punishment, *Howard Journal of Criminal Justice,* 29: 14–24.

Maguire, M. (1998) POP, ILP and partnership, *Criminal Justice Matters,* 32: 21–2.

Maguire, M. (2000) Policing by risks and targets: some dimensions and implications of intelligence-led crime control, *Policing and Society,* 9: 315–36.

Maguire, M. and John, T. (1995) *Intelligence, Surveillance and Informants: Integrated Approaches,* Crime Detection and Prevention series 64. London: Home Office.

Maguire, M., Kemshall, H., Noaks, L. and Wincup, E. (2001) *Risk management of sexual and violent offenders: The work of Public Protection Panels,* Police Research series 139. London: Home Office.

Mair, G. (1996) Intensive probation, in G. McIvor (ed.) *Working with Offenders*. London: Jessica Kingsley.

Mair, G. (ed.) (1997) *Evaluating the Effectiveness of Community Penalties*. Aldershot: Avebury.

Martinson, R. (1974) What works? Questions and answers about prison reform, *The Public Interest*, 10: 22–54.

Mastrofski, S.D. (1991) Community policing as reform: a cautionary tale, in C.B. Klockars and S.D. Mastrofski (eds) *Thinking about Policing*. New York: McGraw-Hill.

Matthews, R. and Pitts, J. (eds) (2001) *Crime, Disorder and Community Safety: A New Agenda?* London: Routledge.

Maupin, J.R. (1993) Risk classification systems and the provision of juvenile aftercare, *Crime and Delinquency*, 39: 90–105.

May, C. (1999) *Explaining Reconviction Following a Community Sentence: The Role of Social Factors*, Home Office research study 192. London: Home Office.

Maynard-Moody, S., Musheno, M. and Palumbo, D. (1990) Street-wise social policy: resolving the dilemma of street-level influence and successful implementation, *Western Political Quarterly*, 43: 831–48.

Meek, J. (1995) The revival of preventive detention in New Zealand 1986–1993, *Australian and New Zealand Journal of Criminology*, 28(3): 225–57.

Menzies, R., Webster, C.D., McMain, S., Stanley, S. and Scaglione, R. (1994) The dimensions of dangerousness revisited, *Law and Human Behaviour*, 18(1): 1–20.

Millar, M. and Buchanan, J. (1995) Probation: a crisis of identity and purpose, *Probation Journal*, 42(4): 195–8.

Miller, C. (2000) Citizenship and inclusion, *Openmind*, 105(Sept./Oct): 10–11.

Miller, P. and Rose, N. (1988) The Tavistock programme: the government of subjectivity and social life, *Sociology*, 22(2): 171–92.

Miller, P. and Rose, N. (1992) Political power beyond the state: problematics of government, *British Journal of Sociology*, 43(2): 173–205.

Mills, A. and Pearson, S. (2000) From audit to strategy: a practice view, in S. Ballintyne, K. Pease and V. McLaren (eds) *Secure Foundations: Key Issues in Crime Prevention, Crime Reduction and Community Safety*. London: Institute for Public Policy Research.

Moir, P. and Eijkman, H. (eds) (1992) *Policing Australia*. Sydney: Macmillan.

Moir, P. and Moir, M. (1992) Community based policing and the role of community consultation, in P. Moir and H. Eijkman (eds) *Policing Australia*. Sydney: Macmillan.

Monahan, J. (1981) *The Clinical Prediction of Violence*. Beverly Hills, CA: Sage.

Monahan, J., Steadman, H., Appelbaum, P. et al. (2000) Developing a clinically useful actuarial tool for assessing violence risk, *British Journal of Psychiatry*, 176: 312–19.

Moore, B. (1996) *Risk Assessment: A Practitioner's Guide to Predicting Harmful Behaviour*. London: Whiting Birch.

Morgan, J. (1991) *Safer Communities: The Local Delivery of Crime Prevention through the Partnership Approach*, Standing Conference on Crime Prevention (Morgan report). London: Home Office.

Morris, L. (1994) *Dangerous Classes, the Underclass and Social Citizenship*. London: Routledge.

Morris, A. and Giller, H. (1987) *Understanding Juvenile Justice*. London: Croom Helm.

Moss, P., Dillon, J. and Statham, J. (2000) The 'child in need' and 'the rich child': discourses, constructions of practice, *Critical Social Policy*, 20(2): 233–54.

Mossman, D. (1994) Assessing prediction of violence: being accurate about accuracy, *Journal of Consulting and Clinical Psychology*, 62(4): 783–92.

Mudd, J. (1984) *Neighbourhood Services*. New Haven, CT: Yale University Press.

Muncie, J. (1999) Exorcising demons: media, politics and criminal justice, in B. Franklin (ed.) *Social Policy, the Media and Misrepresentation*. London: Routledge.

Muncie, J., Coventry, G. and Walters, R. (1994) Politics of youth crime prevention: developments in Australia and England and Wales, in L. Noaks, M. Leive and M. Maguire (eds) *Contemporary Issues in Criminology*. Cardiff: University of Wales Press.

Murray, C. (1990) *The Emerging British Underclass*. London: Health and Welfare Unit, Institute for Economic Affairs.

Murray, C. (1994) *The Underclass: The Crisis Deepens*. London: Institute for Economic Affairs.

Murray, C. (1996) The underclass, in J. Muncie and E. McLaughlin (eds) *Criminological Perspectives*. London: Sage.

Murray, C. (1997) *Does Prison Work?* Choice in welfare 38. London: Institute for Economic Affairs.

Mykannen, J. (1994) To methodize and regulate them: William Petty's governmental science of statistics, *History of the Human Sciences*, 7: 65–88.

Nash, M. (1999) *Police, Probation and Protecting the Public*. London: Blackstone Press.

Nash, M. (2000) Deconstructing the Probation Service: The Trojan Horse of public protection, *International Journal of the Sociology of Law*, 28: 201–13.

National Association of Probation Officers (NAPO) (1977) *Risk*. London: NAPO.

National Probation Service (2001) *A New Choreography: An Integrated Strategy for the National Probation Service for England and Wales. Strategic Framework 2001–2004*. London: Home Office.

Nellis, M. (1995) Probation values for the 1990s, *Howard Journal of Criminal Justice*, 34(1): 19–44.

Nellis, M. (1999) Towards the field of corrections: modernizing the Probation Service in the late 1990s, *Social Policy and Administration*, 33: 302–23.

Newburn, T. (1992) *Permissiveness and Regulation*. London: Routledge.

Newman, O. (1972) *Defensible Space: People and Design in the Violent City*. London: Architectural Press.

Noaks, L. (2000) Private cops on the block: a review of private security in residential communities, *Policing and Society*, 10: 143–61.

Norris, C., Moran, J. and Armstrong, G. (eds) (1998) *Surveillance, Closed Circuit Television and Social Control*. Aldershot: Ashgate.

Nuffield, J. (1982) *Parole Decision-making in Canada*. Ottawa: Solicitor General of Canada.

Nuttall, C. with Barnard, E.E., Fowles, A.J., Frost, A. et al. (1977) *Parole in England and Wales*. London: Her Majesty's Stationery Office.

Ohlin, L. (1951) *Selection for Parole*. New York: Russell Sage.

O'Malley, P. (1992) Risk, power and crime prevention, *Economy and Society*, 21(3): 252–75.

O'Malley, P. (1994) Responsibility and crime prevention: a response to Adam Sutton, *Australian and New Zealand Journal of Criminology*, 21(4): special edition.

O'Malley, P. (1995) Neo-liberal crime control: political agendas and the future of crime prevention in Australia, in D. Chappell and P. Wilson (eds) *The Australian Criminal Justice System: The Mid-1990s*. Adelaide: Butterworth.

O'Malley, P. (1996) Post-social criminologies. Some implications of current political trends for criminological theory and practice, *Current Issues in Criminal Justice*, 8(1): 26–39.

O'Malley, P. (1997) The politics of crime prevention, in P. O'Malley and A. Sutton (eds) *Crime Prevention in Australia: Issues in Policy and Research*. Sydney: Federation Press.

O'Malley, P. (1999a) Volatile and contradictory punishment, *Theoretical Criminology*, 3(2): 175–96.

O'Malley, P. (1999b) Imagining insurance: risk, thrift and industrial life in Britain, *Connecticut Insurance Law Journal*, 5(2): 675–705.

O'Malley, P. (2000) Risk societies and the government of crime, in M. Brown and J. Pratt (eds) *Dangerous Offenders: Punishment and Social Order*. London: Routledge.

O'Malley, P. (2001a) Discontinuity, government and risk, *Theoretical Criminology*, 5(1): 85–92.

O'Malley, P. (2001b) Risk, crime and prudentialism revisited, in K. Stenson and R. Sullivan (eds) *Crime, Risk and Justice: The Politics of Crime Control in Liberal Democracies*. Cullompton, Devon: Willan.

O'Malley, P. and Palmer, D. (1996) Post-Keynesian policing, *Economy and Society*, 25(2): 137–55.

O'Malley, P., Weir, L. and Shearing, C. (1997) Governmentality, criticism and politics, *Economy and Society*, 26(4): 501–17.

Osborne, D. and Gaebler, T. (1993) *Reinventing Government*. New York: Plume.

Osborne, T. (1993) On liberalism, neo-liberalism and the 'liberal profession' of medicine, *Economy and Society*, 22: 345–56.

Otway, H.J. and Thomas, K. (1982) Reflections on risk perception and policy, *Risk Analysis*, 2: 69–82.

Oxford English Dictionary (1989) *The Oxford English Dictionary*, 2nd edn. Prepared by J.A. Simpson and E.S.C. Weiner, Oxford: Clarendon Press.

Parker, H. (1982) *The Moral Hazard of Social Insurance*, research monograph 37. London: Institute of Economic Affairs.

Parton, N., Thorpe, D. and Wattam, C. (1997) *Child Protection and the Moral Order*. London: Macmillan.

Pearson, G., Blagg, H., Smith, D., Sampson, A. and Stubbs, P. (1992) Crime, community and conflict, in D. Downes (ed.) *Unravelling Criminal Justice*. London: Routledge.

Pease, K. (1997) Crime prevention, in M. Maguire, R. Morgan and R. Reiner (eds) *Oxford Handbook of Criminology*, 2nd edn. Oxford: Clarendon Press.

Peters, A.G. (1986) Main currents in criminal law theory, in J. van Dijk (ed.) *Criminal Law in Action: An Overview of Current Issues in Western Societies.* Arnhem: Gowda Quint.

Petersen, A. (1997) Risk, government and the new public health, in A. Petersen and R. Bunton (eds) *Foucault, Health and Medicine.* London: Routledge.

Petersen, A. and Lupton, D. (1996) *The New Public Health: Health and Self in the Age of Risk.* London: Sage.

Petrunik, M.G. (2002) Managing unacceptable risk: sex offenders, community response, and social policy in the United States and Canada, *International Journal of Offender Therapy and Comparative Criminology*, 46(4): 483–511.

Phillips (Lord) (2000) *The BSE Inquiry – Main Volume: Vol. 1, Findings and Conclusions.* London: The Stationery Office.

Pitts, J. (1992) The end of an era, *Howard Journal of Criminal Justice*, 31: 133–49.

Plotnikoff, J. and Woolfson, R. (2000) *Where are They Now? An Evaluation of Sex Offender Registration in England and Wales.* London: Home Office.

Police Foundation and Policy Studies Institute (PSI) (1994) *Independent Committee of Inquiry into the Role and Responsibilities of the Police.* London: PSI.

Pollard, C. (1997) Zero tolerance: short-term fix, long-term liability?, in N. Dennis (ed.) *Zero Tolerance: Policing a Free Society.* London: Health and Welfare Unit, Institute of Economic Affairs.

Pollock, N., McBain, I. and Webster, C.D. (1989) Clinical decision making and the assessment of dangerousness, in K. Howells and C.R. Hollin (eds) *Clinical Approaches to Violence.* Chichester: John Wiley.

Polvi, N. and Pease, K. (1991) Parole and its problems: a Canadian–English comparison, *Howard Journal of Criminal Justice*, 30(3): 218–30.

Posner, R.A. (1985) An economic theory of the criminal law, *Columbia Law Review*, 85: 1193–231.

Power, H. (1998) The Crime and Disorder Act 1998: sex Offenders, privacy and the police, *Criminal Law Review*, 3–16.

Power, M. (1999) *The Audit Society: Pitfalls of Verification.* Oxford: Oxford University Press.

Pratt, J. (1989) Corporatism: the third model of juvenile justice, *British Journal of Criminology*, 29(3): 236–54.

Pratt, J. (1995) Dangerousness, risk and technologies of power, *Australian and New Zealand Journal of Criminology*, 28(1): 3–31.

Pratt, J. (1996) Governing the dangerous: an historical overview of dangerous offender legislation, *Social and Legal Studies*, 5(1): 21–36.

Pratt, J. (1997) *Governing the Dangerous.* Sydney: Federation Press.

Pratt, J. (2000a) The return of the wheelbarrow men: or, the arrival of postmodern penality?, *British Journal of Criminology*, 40: 127–45.

Pratt, J. (2000b) Emotive and ostentatious punishment: its decline and resurgence in modern society, *Punishment and Society*, 2(4): 417–39.

Pratt, J. (2000c) Dangerousness and modern society, in M. Brown and J. Pratt (eds) *Dangerous Offenders: Punishment and Social Order.* London: Routledge.

Pratt, J. (2000d) Civilization and punishment, *Australian and New Zealand Journal of Criminology*, 33(2): 183–201.

Prentky, A. (1996) Community notification and constructive risk reduction, *Journal of Interpersonal Violence*, 11(2): 295–8.

Probation Services Division (1994) *Risk Assessment for Temporary Release of Prisoners*, Probation Circular PC96/1994. London: Probation Services Division, Home Office.

Probation Services Division (1996) *Guidance to the Probation Service on the Offender Group Reconviction Scale (OGRS)*, Probation Circular PC63/1996. London: Probation Services Division, Home Office.

Probation Services Division (1997) *Serious Incident Reports: Analysis*, Probation Circular PC36/1997. London: Probation Services Division, Home Office.

Probation Services Division (1999) *Early Warning Mechanism for the Release or Discharge of Potentially Dangerous Offenders*, Probation Circular PC15/1999. London: Probation Services Divisions, Home Office.

Putnam, R.D. (1995) Bowling alone: America's declining social capital, *Journal of Democracy*, 6(1): 65–78.

Quinsey, V.L., Rice, M.E. and Harris, G.T. (1995) Actuarial prediction of sexual recidivism, *Journal of Interpersonal Violence*, 10: 85–103.

Quinsey, V.L., Harris, G., Rice, M. and Cornier, C. (1998) *Violent Offenders: Appraising and Managing the Risk*. Washington, DC: American Psychological Association.

Radzinowicz, L. (1999) *Adventures in Criminology*. London: Routledge.

Radzinowicz, L. and Hood, R. (1986) *A History of the Criminal Law and its Administration from 1750*, Vol. V, *The Emergence of Penal Policy*. London: Stevens.

Raine, J. and Wilson, M. (1993) *Managing Criminal Justice*. London: Harvester Wheatsheaf.

Rayner, S. (1986) Management of radiation hazards in hospitals: plural rationalities in a single institution, *Social Studies of Science*, 16: 573–91.

Rayner, S. (1992) Cultural theory and risk analysis, in S. Krimsky and D. Golding (eds) *Social Theories of Risk*. Westport CT: Praeger.

Raynor, P. (1980) Is there any sense in social inquiry reports?, *Probation Journal*, 27(3): 78–84.

Raynor, P. (1997a) *Implementing the 'Level of Service Inventory-Revised' (LSI-R) in Britain: Initial Results from Five Probation Areas*. Swansea: Cognitive Centre Foundation.

Raynor, P. (1997b) Some observations on rehabilitation and justice, *Howard Journal of Criminal Justice*, 36(3): 248–62.

Raynor, P. (1999) Risk, needs and effective practice: the impact and potential of new assessment methods in probation. Paper presented to the British Criminology Conference, Liverpool, July.

Raynor, P. (2002) Community penalties: probation, punishment and 'what works', in M. Maguire, R. Morgan and R. Reiner (eds) *The Oxford Handbook of Criminology*. Oxford: Oxford University Press.

Raynor, P. and Vanstone, M. (1994) Probation practice, effectiveness and the non-treatment paradigm, *Howard Journal of Criminal Justice*, 36: 248–62.

Raynor, P., Kynch, J., Roberts, C. and Merrington, S. (2000) *Risk and Need Assessment in Probation Services: An Evaluation*, Home Office research study 211. London: Home Office.

Reason, J. (1990) *Human Error*. Cambridge: Cambridge University Press.

Reddy, S. (1996) Claims to expert knowledge and the subversion of democracy: the triumph of risk over uncertainty, *Economy and Society*, 25(2): 222–54.

Reichman, N. (1986) Managing crime risks: towards an insurance based model of social control, *Research in Law and Social Control*, 8: 151–72.

Reiner, R. (1992) Policing a postmodern society, *Modern Law Review*, 55(6): 761–81.

Reiner, R. (1993) Race, crime and justice: models of interpretation, in L. Gelsthorpe and W. McWilliams (eds) *Minority Ethnic Groups and the Criminal Justice System*. Cambridge: Institute of Criminology, University of Cambridge.

Reiner, R. (1997a) *Policing and the Police*, in M. Maguire, R. Morgan and R. Reiner (eds) *The Oxford Handbook of Criminology*, 2nd edn. Oxford: Oxford University Press

Reiner, R. (1997b) Media made criminality, in M. Maguire, R. Morgan and R. Reiner (eds) *The Oxford Handbook of Criminology*, 2nd edn. Oxford: Oxford University Press.

Reiner, R. (2000) *The Politics of the Police*, 3rd edn. Oxford: Oxford University Press.

Reiner, R. and Cross, M. (eds) (1991) *Beyond Law and Order: Criminal Justice and Politics into the 1990s*. London: Macmillan.

Rhodes, R. (1996) The new governance: governing without government, *Political Studies*, 44: 652–67.

Rhodes, T. (1997) Risk theory in epidemic times: sex, drugs and the social organisation of 'risk behaviour', *Sociology of Health and Illness*, 19(2): 208–27.

Rice, M.E. and Harris, G.T. (1995) Violent recidivism: assessing predictive validity, *Journal of Consulting and Clinical Psychology*, 63: 737–48.

Rigakos, G. (1999) Risk society and actuarial criminology: prospects for a critical discourse, *Canadian Journal of Criminology*, 41: 137–50.

Rigakos, G. and Hadden, R.W. (2001) Crime, capitalism and the 'risk society': towards the same olde modernity?, *Theoretical Criminology*, 5(1): 61–84.

Roberts, C. and Robinson, G. (1997) *A Comparative Study of Assessment Tools to Aid the Preparation of Pre-Sentence Reports: A Summary Report for the Greater Manchester Probation Service*. Oxford: Centre for Criminological Research.

Robertson, A. (2000) Embodying risk, embodying political rationality: women's accounts of risks for breast cancer, *Health, Risk and Society*, 2(2): 219–36.

Robertson, K. (1994) Practical police co-operation in Europe: the intelligence dimension, in M. Anderson and M. Den Boer (eds) *Policing across National Boundaries*. London: Pinter.

Robinson, G. (1999) Risk management and rehabilitation in the Probation Service: collision and collusion, *Howard Journal of Criminal Justice*, 38(4): 421–33.

Robinson, G. (2001) Power, knowledge and 'what works' in Probation, *Howard Journal of Criminal Justice*, 40(3): 235–54.

Robinson, G. (2002) A rationality of risk in the Probation Service: its evolution and contemporary profile, *Punishment and Society*, 4(1): 5–25.

Rodger, J. (2000) *From a Welfare State to a Welfare Society: The Changing Context of Social Policy in a Postmodern Era*. London: Macmillan.

Rose, N. (1993) Government, authority and expertise in advanced liberalism, *Economy and Society*, 22(3): 283–99.

Rose, N. (1996a) Governing 'advanced' liberal democracies, in A. Barry, T. Osborne and N. Rose (eds.) *Foucault and Political Reason: Liberalism, Neo-liberalism and Rationalities of Government*. London: UCL Press.

Rose, N. (1996b) The death of the social? Re-figuring the territory of government, *Economy and Society*, 25(3): 327–56.

Rose, N. (2000) Government and control, *British Journal of Criminology*, 40: 321–39.

Rosenbaum, D.P. (1988) Community crime prevention: a review and synthesis of the literature, *Justice Quarterly*, 5(3): 323–93.

Rosenbaum, D.P. (1994) *The Challenge of Community Policing: Testing the Promises*. London: Sage.

Rotman, E. (1990) *Beyond Punishment: A New View of the Rehabilitation of Offenders*. Westport, CT Greenwood Press.

Rowe, M.D. (1977) *An Anatomy of Risk*. Chichester: John Wiley.

Royal Society Study Group (1983) *Risk: Analysis, Perception and Management*. London: Royal Society.

Rudin, J. (1996) Megan's Law: can it stop sexual predators – and at what cost to constitutional rights? *Criminal Justice*, 11(3): 2–10, 60–3.

Ryan, T. (1996) Risk management and people with mental health problems, in H. Kemshall and J. Pritchard (eds) *Good Practice in Risk Assessment and Risk Management*, Vol. 1. London: Jessica Kingsley.

Sampson, A., Stubbs, P., Smith, D., Blagg, H. and Pearson, G. (1988) Crime, localities and the multi-agency approach, *British Journal of Criminology*, 28: 478–93.

Sanders, C.R. and Lyon, E. (1995) Repetitive retribution: media images and the cultural construction of criminal justice, in J. Ferrell and C. Sanders (eds) *Cultural Criminology*. Boston, MA: Northeastern University Press.

Satayamurti, C. (1981) *Occupational Survival*. Oxford: Blackwell.

Scarman, L. (1981) *The Brixton Disorders: 10–12 April 1981*, Cmnd 8427. London: HMSO.

Schram, D. and Milloy, C. (1995) *Community Notification: A Study of Offender Characteristics and Recidivism*. Seattle, WA: Urban Policy Research.

Shaw, R. (1991) Supervising the dangerous offender: communication, the vital but often missing factor, *NASPO News*, 10: 4.

Shaw, R. (1996) Supervising the dangerous in the community, in N. Walker (ed.) *Dangerous People*. Oxford: Blackstone Press.

Shearing, C. (1992) The relation between public and private policing, in M. Tonry and N. Morris (eds) *Modern Policing: Crime and Justice: A Review of Research*, Vol. 15. Chicago: University of Chicago Press.

Shearing, C. (2001) Punishment and the changing face of governance, *Punishment and Society*, 3(2): 203–20.

Shearing, C. and Stenning, P.C. (1981) Private security: its growth and implications, in M. Tonry and N. Morris (eds.) *Crime and Justice: An Annual Review of Research*. Chicago: University of Chicago Press.

Shearing, C. and Stenning, P.C. (eds) (1987) *Private Policing*. Newbury Park, CA: Sage.

Sheehy, P. (1993) *Report of the Inquiry into Police Responsibilities and Rewards*, Cm 2280. London: HMSO (see also Home Office, Northern Ireland Office and Scottish Office 1993).

Sheppard, D. (1996) *Learning the Lessons: Mental Health Inquiry Reports Published in England and Wales between 1969–1996 and their Recommendations for Improving Practice*. London: Zito Trust.

Sheptycki, J. (1995) Transnational policing and the makings of a modern state, *British Journal of Criminology*, 35(4): 613–35.

Sheptycki, J. (1997) Transnationalism, crime control and the European state system: a review of the literature, *International Criminal Justice Review*, 7.

Simon, J. (1987) The emergence of a risk society: insurance, law and the state, *Socialist Review*, 95: 61–89.

Simon, J. (1988) The ideological affects of actuarial practices, *Law and Society Review*, 22(4): 772–800.

Simon, J. (1993) *Poor Discipline: Parole and the Social Control of the Underclass*. Chicago: University of Chicago Press.

Simon, J. (1997) Governing through crime, in M. Lawrence Friedman and G. Fisher (eds) *The Crime Connection: Essays in Criminal Justice*. Boulder, CO: Westview Press.

Simon, J. (1998) Managing the monstrous: sex offenders and the new penology, *Psychology, Public Policy and Law*, 4(1–2): 452–67.

Slovic, P. (1987) Perceptions of risk, *Science*, 236: 280–5.

Slovic, P. (1992) Perceptions of risk: reflections on the psychometric paradigm, in S. Krimsky and D. Golding (eds) *Social Theories of Risk*. Westport, CT: Praeger.

Slovic, P., Fischoff, B. and Lichtenstein, S. (1980) Facts and fears: understanding perceived risk, in R.C. Schwing and W.A. Albers (eds) *Societal Risk Assessment: How Safe is Safe Enough?* New York: Plenum Press.

Slovic, P., Fischoff, B. and Lichtenstein, S. (1985) Regulation of risk: a psychological perspective, in R.G. Noll (ed.) *Regulatory Policy and the Social Sciences*. Berkeley, CA: University of California Press.

Smith, D. (1996) Developments in Probation in England and Wales 1984–1993, in G. McIvor (ed.) *Working with Offenders*. London: Jessica Kingsley.

Smith, G. (1996) Dealing with dangerous people: the Probation Service and public Protection. Paper presented to the Public Protection Conference, Her Majesty's Inspectorate of Probation, Daventry, 27–29 March.

Smith, K. (1992) *Environmental Hazards: Assessing Risk and Reducing Disaster*. London: Routledge.

Smith, R. (2002) Foucault's Law: The Crime and Disorder Act 1988, *Youth Justice*, 1(2): 17–29.

Social Exclusion Unit (SEU) (2000) *National Strategy for Neighbourhood Renewal*. London: SEU.

Solly, H. (1887) Our vagrant and leisure classes, *The Leisure Hour*, 36: 763–7.

Soothill, K. and Francis, B. (1997a) Sexual reconvictions and the Sex Offenders Act 1997 (part one), *New Law Journal*, 5 September: 1285–6.

Soothill, K. and Francis, B. (1997b) Sexual reconvictions and the Sex Offenders Act 1997 (part two), *New Law Journal*, 12 September: 1324–5.

Soothill, K. and Soothill, D. (1993) Prosecuting the victim? A study of the reporting barristers' comments in rape cases, *Howard Journal of Criminal Justice*, 32: 12–24.

Soothill, K. and Walby, S. (1991) *Sex Crime in the News*. London: Routledge.

Soothill, K., Francis, B. and Ackerley, E. (1998) Paedophilia and paedophiles, *New Law Journal*, 12 June: 882–3.

Sparks, R. (1992) *Television and the Drama of Crime*. Buckingham: Open University Press.

Sparks, R. (1997) Recent social theory and the study of crime and punishment, in M. Maguire, R. Morgan and R. Reiner (eds) *The Oxford Handbook of Criminology*, 2nd edn. Oxford: Oxford University Press.

Sparks, R. (2000) Risk and blame in criminal justice controversies: British press coverage and official discourse on prison security (1993–6), in M. Brown and J. Pratt (eds) *Dangerous Offenders: Punishment and Social Order*. London: Routledge

Sparks, R. (2001a) 'Bringin' it all back home': populism, media coverage and the dynamics of locality and globality in the politics of crime control, in K. Stenson and R.R. Sullivan (eds) *Crime, Risk and Justice: The Politics of Crime Control in Liberal Democracies*. Cullompton. Devon: Willan.

Sparks, R. (2001b) Degrees of enstrangement: the cultural theory of risk and comparative penology, *Theoretical Criminology*, 5(2): 159–76.

Spitzer, S. (1987) Security and the secret thereof, in J. Lowman, R.J. Menzies and T.S. Palys (eds) *Transcarceration: Essays in the Sociology of Social Control*. Aldershot: Gower.

Spitzer, S. and Scull, A. (1977) Privatisation and capitalist development: the case of the private police, *Social Problems*, 25(1): 18–29.

Stenson, K. (1993) Community policing as a government technology, *Economy and Society*, 22: 373–89.

Stenson, K. (1999) Crime control, governmentality and sovereignty, in R. Smandych (ed.) *Governable Places: Readings in Governmentality and Crime Control*. Aldershot: Dartmouth.

Stenson, K. (2000a) Crime control, social policy and liberalism, in G. Lewis, S. Gerwitz and J. Clarke (eds) *Rethinking Social Policy*. London: Sage.

Stenson, K. (2000b) Someday our prince will come: zero tolerance policing in Britain, in T. Hope and R. Sparks (eds) *Crime, Risk and Insecurity*. London: Routledge.

Stenson, K. (2001) The new politics of crime control, in K. Stenson and R.R. Sullivan (eds) *Crime, Risk and Justice: The Politics of Crime Control in Liberal Democracies*. Cullompton, Devon: Willan.

Stenson, K. and Edwards, A. (2001) Crime control and liberal government: the 'third way' and the return to the local, in K. Stenson and R.R. Sullivan (eds) *Crime, Risk and Justice: The Politics of Crime Control in Liberal Democracies*. Cullompton, Devon: Willan.

Stenson, K. and Sullivan, R.R. (eds) (2001) *Crime, Risk and Justice: The Politics of Crime Control in Liberal Democracies*. Cullompton, Devon: Willan.

Stenson, K. and Watt, P. (1999) Crime, risk and governance in a Southern English village, in G. Dingwall and S. Moody (eds) *Crime and Conflict in the Country-side*. Cardiff: University of Wales Press.

Steuer, M. (1998) A little too risky, *London School of Economics Magazine*, 10: 15–16.

Stockdale, J.E., Whitehead, C.M.E. and Gresham, P.J. (1999) *Applying Economic Evaluation to Policing Activity*, Police research series 103. London: The Stationery Office.

Stoker, G. and Young, P. (1993) *Cities in the 1990s*. London: Longman.

Strand, S., Belfrage, H., Fransson, G. and Levander, S. (1999) Clinical and risk management factors in risk prediction of mentally disordered offenders – more important than historical data, *Legal and Criminological Psychology*, 4(1): 67–76.

Sullivan, R.R. (2001) The schizophrenic state: neo-liberal criminal justice, in K. Stenson and R.R. Sullivan (eds) *Crime, Risk and Justice: The Politics of Crime Control in Liberal Democracies*. Cullompton, Devon: Willan.

Sutton, A. (1994) Crime prevention: promise or threat? *Australian and New Zealand Journal of Criminology*, 27: 5–20.

Sutton, A. and Cherney, A. (2002) Prevention and politics? The cyclical progress of crime prevention in an Australian state, *Criminal Justice*, 2(3): 325–44.

Teggin, V. (1998) Crime (Sentences) Act 1997, *Legal Action*, June: 18–20.

Tewksbury, R. (2002) Validity and utility of the Kentucky Sex Offender Registry, *Federal Probation*, June: 21–6.

Thomas, T. (2001) Sex offenders, the Home Office and the Sunday papers, *Journal of Social Welfare and Family Law*, 23(1): 103–4.

Thompson, K. (1998) *Moral Panics*. London: Routledge.

Thompson, M. and Wildavsky, A. (1982) A proposal to create a cultural theory of risk, in H.C. Kunreuther and E.V. Ley (eds) *The Risk Analysis Controversy: An Institutional Perspective*. New York: Springer-Verlag.

Thornton, D. and Travers, R. (1991) *A Longitudinal Study of the Criminal Behaviour of Convicted Sex Offenders: Proceedings of the Prison Psychologists' Conference*. London: HM Prison Service.

Thorpe, D.H., Smith, D., Green, C.J. and Paley, J.G. (1980) *Out of Care: The Community Support of Juvenile Offenders*. London: George Allen and Unwin.

Tilley, N. (2001) Evaluation and evidence-led crime reduction policy and practice, in R. Matthews and J. Pitts (eds) *Crime, Disorder and Community Safety: A New Agenda?* London: Routledge.

Tilley, N. (2002) *Evaluation for Crime Prevention*. New York: Criminal Justice Press.

Tonry, M. (1999) Rethinking unthinkable punishment policies in America. *UCLA Law Review*, 46: 1751.

Turner, B.S. (2001) Risks, rights and regulation: an overview, *Health, Risk and Society*, 3(1): 9–18.

Tutt, N. and Giller, H. (1984) *Social Inquiry Reports*. Lancaster: Audiotape Lancaster Information Systems.

Uglow, S. (1995) *Criminal Justice*. London: Sweet and Maxwell.

Van Reenen, P. (1989) Policing Europe after 1992: co-operation and competition, *European Affairs*, 3(2): 45–53.

Vanstone, M. (2000) Cognitive-behavioural work with offenders in the UK: a history of an influential endeavour, *Howard Journal of Criminal Justice*, 39(2): 171–83.

Van Swaaningen, R. (1997) *Critical Criminology: Visitors from Europe*. London: Sage.

Van Swaaningen, R. (2000) Dutch crime prevention politics and the possibilities of a replacement discourse. Paper delivered to the symposium on 'Rethinking Crime Prevention and Community Safety', The Open University, Milton Keynes, 29 June.

Velez, M.B. (2001) The role of public social control in urban neighbourhoods: a multi-level analysis of victimization risk, *Criminology*, 39(4): 837–64.

Vennard, J. (1996) Evaluating the effectiveness of community programmes with offenders, *VISTA*, 2(1): 15–27.

Visser, K. (1991) First reaction, *Shell World: The International Business Magazine of Royal Dutch Shell*, February.

Von Hirsch, A. and Ashworth, A. (1996) Protective sentencing under section 2 (2) b: the criteria for dangerousness, *Criminal Law Review*, 175–83.

Waddington, P. (1999) *Policing Citizens*. London: UCL Press.

Walker, N. (1996) *Dangerous People*. London: Blackstone Press.

Walklate, S. (1996) Community and crime prevention, in E. McLaughlin and J. Muncie (eds) *Controlling Crime*. London: Sage.

Walklate, S. (1997) Risk and criminal victimisation, *British Journal of Criminology*, 37(1): 35–45.

Walklate, S. (1998) *Understanding Criminology: Current Theoretical Debates*. Buckingham: Open University Press.

Walklate, S. (2000) Trust and the problem of community in the inner city, in T. Hope and R. Sparks (eds) *Crime, Risk and Insecurity*. London: Routledge.

Walklate, S. and Evans, K. (1999) *Zero Tolerance or Community Tolerance?* Aldershot: Ashgate.

Wallis, E. (1997) A new choreography: breaking away from the elaborate corporate dance, in R. Burnett (ed.) *The Probation Service: Responding to Change*. Oxford: Probation Studies Unit, Oxford University.

Walters, A. (2001) *Acid Row*. London: Macmillan.

Wasik, M. and Taylor, R.D. (1991) *Blackstone's Guide to the Criminal Justice Act 1991*. Oxford: Blackstone Press.

Weatheritt, M. (1983) Community policing: does it work and how do we know?, in T. Bennett (ed.) *The Future of Policing*, Cropwood Conference Series 15. Cambridge: Institute of Criminology.

Weatheritt, M. (1986) *Innovations in Policing*. London: Croom Helm.

Weatheritt, M. (1987) Community policing now, in P. Wilmott (ed.) *Policing and the Community*. London: Policy Studies Institute.

Weatheritt, M. (1988) Community policing: rhetoric or reality?, in J.R. Greene and S.D. Mastrofski (eds) *Community Policing Rhetoric or Reality?* New York: Praeger.

Weatheritt, M. (2002) Risk assessment in parole decisions. Paper presented to Home Office 'Criminal Justice Conference: Using Risk Assessment in Effective Sentence Management', Pendley Manor Hotel, Tring, 14–15 March.

Weber, M. (1949) *The Methodology of the Social Sciences*, translated and edited by E.A. Shils and H.A. Finch. Glencoe, IL: The Free Press.

Webster, C.D., Harris, G.T., Rice, M.E., Cormier, C. and Quinsey, V.L. (1994) *The Violence Prediction Scheme: Assessing Dangerousness in High Risk Men*. Toronto: Centre for Criminology, University of Toronto.

Webster, C.D., Eaves, D., Douglas, K. and Wintrup, A. (1995) *The HCR-20 Scheme: The Assessment of Dangerousness and Risk*. Vancouver: Simon Fraser University.

Webster, C.D., Douglas, K.S., Eaves, D. and Hart, S.D. (1997) *HCR-20 Assessing Risk for Violence: Version 2*. Vancouver: Simon Fraser University.

Welch, M., Fenwick, M. and Roberts, M. (1997) Primary definitions of crime and moral panic: a content analysis of experts' quotes in feature newspaper articles on crime, *Journal of Research on Crime and Delinquency*, 34: 474–94.

Wilczynski, A. and Sinclair, K. (1999) Moral tales: representations of child abuse in the quality and tabloid media, *Australian and New Zealand Journal of Criminology*, 32(3): 262–83.

Wildavsky, A. (1985) *Trial without Error: Anticipation versus Resilience as Strategies for Risk Reduction*. Sydney: Centre for Independent Studies.

Wildavsky, A. (1988) *Searching for Safety*. New Brunswick, NJ: Transaction Books.

Wilson, J.Q. and Kelling, G.L. (1982) Broken windows, *Atlantic Monthly*, March: 29–38.

Wilson, J.Q. and Kelling, G.L. (1989) Making neighbourhoods safe, *Atlantic Monthly*, February: 46–52.

Wintrup, A. (1996) *Assessing Risk of Violence in the Mentally Disordered with the HCR-20*. Vancouver: Simon Fraser University.

Wood, D. (1988) Dangerous offenders and the morality of protective sentencing, *Criminal Law Review*, 424–33.

Worrall, A. (1997) *Punishment in the Community: The Future of Criminal Justice*. London: Longman.

Wright Mills, C. (1970) *The Sociological Imagination*. New York: Oxford University Press.

www.foresight.gov.uk *Turning the Corner*. London: Home Office.

Wynne, B. (1982) *Rationality and Ritual: The Windscale Inquiry and Nuclear Decisions in Britain*. Chalfont St Giles: The British Society for the History of Science.

Wynne, B. (1988) Unruly technology, *Social Studies of Science*, 18: 155.

Wynne, B. (1989) Sheepfarming after Chernobyl, *Environment*, 31(11–115): 33–9.

Wynne, B. (1992) Risk and social learning: reification to engagement, in S. Krimsky and D. Golding (eds) *Social Theories of Risk*. Westport, CT: Praeger.

Wynne, B. (1996) May the sheep safely graze? A reflexive view of the expert–lay knowledge divide, in S. Lash, B. Szerszynski and B. Wynne (eds) *Risk, Environment and Modernity*. London: Sage.

Wyre, R. (1997) Marked for life, *Community Care*, 26–7, February: 20–6.

Young, A. (1996) *Imagining Crime: Textual Outlaws and Criminal Conversations*. London: Sage.

Young, J. (1986) The failure of criminology: the need for a radical realism, in R. Matthews and J. Young (eds) *Confronting Crime*. London: Sage.

Young, J. (1992) Ten points of realism, in J. Young and R. Matthews (eds) *Rethinking Criminology: The Realist Debate*. London: Sage.

Young, J. (1994) Incessant chatter: recent paradigms in criminology, in M. Maguire, R. Morgan and R. Reiner (eds) *Oxford Handbook in Criminology*, 1st edn. Oxford: Clarendon Press.

Young, J. (1997) Charles Murray and the American prison experiment: the dilemmas of a libertarian, in C. Murray (ed.), *Does Prison Work?* London: Health and Welfare Unit, Institute of Economic Affairs.

Young, J. (1998) From inclusive to exclusive society: nightmares in the European dream, in V. Ruggiero, N. South and I. Taylor (eds) *The New European Criminology: Crime and Social Order in Europe*. London: Routledge.

Young, J. (1999) *The Exclusive Society*. London: Sage.

Zevitz, R. and Farkas, M. (2000a) Sex offender community notification: managing high risk criminals or exacting further vengeance?, *Behavioural Sciences and the Law*, 18(2/3): 375–91.

Zevitz, R. and Farkas, M. (2000b) Sex Offender community notification: examining the importance of neighbourhood meetings, *Behavioural Sciences and the Law*, 18(2/3): 393–408.

Index

UNDERSTANDING JUSTICE
AN INTRODUCTION TO IDEAS, PERSPECTIVES AND CONTROVERSIES IN MODERN PENAL THEORY

Barbara Hudson

- Why should offenders be punished – what should punishments be designed to achieve?
- Why has imprisonment become the *normal* punishment for crime in modern industrial societies?
- What is the relationship between theories of punishment and the actual penalties inflicted on offenders?

This revised and updated edition of a highly successful text provides a comprehensive account of the ideas and controversies that have arisen within law, philosophy, sociology and criminology about the punishment of criminals. Written in a clear, accessible style, it summarises major philosophical ideas – retribution, rehabilitation, incapacitation – and discusses their strengths and weaknesses. This new edition has been updated throughout including, for example, a new section on recent cultural studies of punishment and on the phenomenon of mass imprisonment that has emerged in the United States. This second edition includes a new chapter on restorative justice, which has developed considerably in theory and in practice since the publication of the first edition.

The sociological perspectives of Durkheim, the Marxists, Foucault and their contemporary followers are analysed and assessed. A section on the criminological perspective on punishment looks at the influence of theory on penal policy, and at the impact of penal ideologies on those on whom punishment is inflicted. The contributions of feminist theorists, and the challenges they pose to masculinist accounts of punishment, are included. The concluding chapter presents critiques of the very idea of punishment, and looks at contemporary proposals which could make society's response to crime less dependent on punishment than at present.

Understanding Justice has been designed for students from a range of disciplines and is suitable for a variety of crime-related courses in sociology, social policy, law and social work. It will also be useful to professionals in criminal justice agencies and to all those interested in understanding the issues behind public and political debates on punishment.

Contents
Series foreword – Acknowledgements – Perspectives on punishment – Part one: The goals of punishment: the juridical perspective – Utilitarian approaches – Retribution – Hybrids, compromises and syntheses – Restorative justice: diversion, compromise or replacement discourse – Part two: Punishment and modernity: the sociological perspective – Punishment and progress: the Durkheimian tradition – The political economy of punishment: Marxist approaches – The disciplined society: Foucault and the analysis of penalty – Understanding contemporary penalty – Part three: Towards justice? – The struggle for justice: critical criminology and critical legal studies – Postscript: beyond modernity: the fate of justice – Glossary – Further reading – References – Index.

232pp   0 335 21036 8 (Paperback)   0 335 21037 6 (Hardback)

UNDERSTANDING CRIMINOLOGY
CURRENT THEORETICAL DEBATES

Sandra Walklate

- What does contemporary criminological theory look like?
- What impact does it have on policy?
- What might its future be?

This substantially revised and updated text provides the student with an accessible under-standing of the current nature of criminological theory. Its main focus is on development in criminological theorising over the past twenty-five years paying particular attention to 'right realism', 'left realism' and developments arising from the influence of theorising around gender. The relationship of criminological theory and knowledge to current policy agendas is given particular attention in this second edition, and a key concern of the text is to paint a picture for the student of the complex interplay between criminology, criminal justice, social justice and politics. The author concludes by offering an insight into some of the theoretical concerns that might better inform the future development of criminological theory. In all, this represents an ideal theoretical text for students of criminology and trainees in criminal justice, including clear summaries, an expanded glossary and suggestions for further reading.

Contents
Series foreword – Preface – Introduction: some key problems in criminology – Perspectives in crimino-logical theory – Understanding 'right realism' – Understanding 'left realism' – Gendering the criminal – Crime, politics and welfare – Criminal victimisation, politics and welfare – Conclusion: new directions for criminology? – Glossary – Bibliography – Index.

192pp   0 335 20951 3 (Paperback)   0 335 20952 1 (Hardback)

UNDERSTANDING PSYCHOLOGY AND CRIME
PERSPECTIVES ON THEORY AND ACTION

James McGuire

- What contributions can psychology make to the understanding of crime?
- How can theories of crime that focus on the individual be integrated in a wider social perspective?
- How can psychological models and research be applied in crime prevention and the reduction of repeat offending?

This book bridges the gap between criminology and psychological perspectives and ideas concerning crime. It sets this in historical context and provides an outline of the contributions that psychological approaches can make understanding crime and how to respond to it. It is argued that some objections to the use of psychology within criminology are based on out-dated or erroneous conceptions about psychology itself.

Throughout the book there is an emphasis on the close relationships between theory, research and practice, and a central part of this is to demonstrate how a methodical approach to the study of criminal behaviour can generate both systematic findings and practical solutions to problems. This authoritative and stimulating text provides essential reading for courses in criminology and psychology alike, moving from theory and research to how such ideas can be applied in crime prevention and reduction, and concluding with discussion of the ethical and political implications.

Contents
Series editor's foreword – Why psychology? – Explaining crime – Psychological processes in crime – Individual factors in crime – Crime and punishment: a psychological view – Preventing and reducing crime – Values in criminology and psychology – Glossary – Index.

192pp   0 335 21119 4 (Paperback)   0 335 21120 8 (Hardback)